'Written in her off-the-cuff, witty style, *Mama Mia* magnifies the world of women's magazines, the conflicts she faced and fought (diets and unrealistic body image), and her experiences of motherhood.' *Sun Herald*

'Freedman writes with a sense of intimacy, as if she has set out to tell the truth and not hold back, no matter how painful it's retelling. The result inspires empathy, interest, curiosity and laughter, but never boredom.' *Courier Mail*

'Even when she experiences her lowest times – both personally and professionally – Freedman manages to see the humorous side and also realises that it is during these sad, intense and stressful times that we truly learn about ourselves and ultimately become more fulfilled.'
Good Reading

Also by Mia Freedman

The New Black

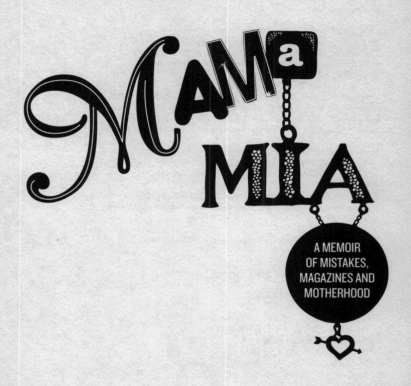

MIA FREEDMAN

HarperCollins*Publishers*

HarperCollins*Publishers*

First published in Australia in 2009
This edition published in 2011
by HarperCollins*Publishers* Australia Pty Limited
ABN 36 009 913 517
harpercollins.com.au

HarperCollins*Publishers*
25 Ryde Road, Pymble, Sydney, NSW 2073, Australia
31 View Road, Glenfield, Auckland 0627, New Zealand
A 53, Sector 57 Noida, UP, India
77–85 Fulham Palace Road, London, W6 8JB, United Kingdom
2 Bloor Street East, 20th floor, Toronto, Ontario M4W 1A8, Canada
10 East 53rd Street, New York NY 10022, USA

National Library of Australia Cataloguing-in-Publication data:

Freedman, Mia.
    Mama Mia: a memoir / Mia Freedman.
    2nd ed.
    ISBN: 978 0 7322 9238 6 (pbk.)
    Freedman, Mia.
    Working mothers – Australia – Biography.
    Periodical editors – Australia – Biography.
    Women – Australia – Identity.
    Parenting – Australia – Social aspects.
    Motherhood – Australia – Psychological aspects.
    Motherhood in popular culture – Australia.
306.8743092

Cover design and illustration by Natalie Winter
Internal design by Natalie Winter
Author photograph by Jason Ireace
Typeset in Bembo by Kirby Jones
Printed and bound in Australia by Griffin Press
50gsm Bulky News used by HarperCollins*Publishers* is a natural, recyclable product made
from wood grown in sustainable plantation forests. The manufacturing processes
conform to the environmental regulations in the country of origin, New Zealand.

5 4 3 2 1   11 12 13 14

To my mum and dad,
with endless love and gratitude

CONTENTS

AUTHOR'S NOTE

This memoir is a personal account of my life with all its quirks, imperfections and mistakes as I've interpreted them. Some names and identifying details have been changed to protect the privacy of others.

PROLOGUE

It's 4 pm on a hot Thursday afternoon in December and I'm preparing to go on stage to perform with Kylie Minogue. Except it's not really a stage; it's the internal staircase of a restaurant. And it's not really Kylie Minogue; it's a drag queen impersonator.

Along with *Cosmo*'s deputy editor, fashion editor, beauty editor, sub-editor and drag-Kylie (a beautiful, fine-boned, twenty-two-year-old gay boy), I'm crammed into a makeshift dressing area the size of a toilet cubicle having glittery stage make-up applied. Heavily.

After my hair is teased and tortured into submission, I will wriggle into the costume sourced by the *Cosmo* fashion department: sky-high, diamante-studded prostitute shoes made of Perspex, and a Lycra frock. Very Kylie. Not very me. Mercifully, the frock is neither tight nor revealing, but it is fuchsia and extremely cheap-looking.

Once we're frocked up, the *Cosmo* girls and I will perform with drag-Kylie to real Kylie's song 'Can't Get You Out Of My Head'. The occasion is *Cosmopolitan*'s annual Christmas event, but because our budget hasn't stretched to a stage, we'll be dancing on the staircase in the middle of the restaurant, with the audience below us, hopefully not able to peer up our cheap skirts.

I am thirty-three years old. I'm a wife and a mother. And I'm about to stand in front of an assembled crowd of media, advertising clients, celebrities, industry colleagues, my boss and my staff to perform a badly choreographed dance routine with a drag queen on some steps.

How did this happen?

Even as I asked the question, I knew I had no one to blame but myself. It had been my idea. All of it. For the past five years, I'd orchestrated an annual *Cosmo* Christmas event designed specifically to create maximum media buzz.

From the outside, like all the *Cosmo* events I'd hosted, this one looked like extraordinary fun. Yes, compared to working in a supermarket — which I'd done seventeen years earlier — it was. But it was also work. And as an editor, parties were one of my least favourite parts of the job.

Magazine events always have a dual purpose. The primary aim is to create positive PR for your title via splashy media coverage. You might pull some TV crews if you're lucky, but mostly it's about getting photos of your glamorous guests in the newspaper. Celebrities are crucial. Associated gossip helps. A pop star pashing a model. A pretty socialite hooking up with a female fashion designer. Anything that will make your brand look hip and newsworthy by association. Anything that creates buzz.

Less interesting — but equally important — are the advertisers and media buyers who book their ads. They will not create buzz but they will have a few champagnes, brush up against some celebrities and feel warm and fuzzy towards your magazine. Hopefully, this will prompt them to buy more ad pages in future issues.

Against this background, it had somehow seemed logical for me to theme this year's party with celebrity drag queens. As well as drag-Kylie, we had drag-Madonna, or Mogadonna as she called herself. At least we were in a nice restaurant. The previous year, I'd pushed the envelope perilously close to the edge of good taste by holding the party in a strip club. With pole dancers. A couple of uptight advertisers had tut-tutted and refused to attend but there was an unexpectedly robust turnout from senior male management to fill any gaps in the crowd.

Since I didn't want to venture any further in that direction and throw this year's party in, say, a brothel, I'd decided we should do a U-turn and go somewhere posh. But since an upmarket, sophisticated event didn't have much media cut-through and wasn't in keeping with *Cosmo*'s reputation for controversial Christmas parties, I'd thrown in the celebrity drag queens to sex things up.

The idea of me and a few staff acting as back-up dancers had sprung from my fond memories of dancing for an audience at ballet concerts when I was eight years old. And did I mention my tendency to show off?

We wobble our way nervously down the stairs and launch into our routine to the surprised whoops and cheers of the audience. Drag-Kylie camps her way expertly through the song and leaves us to lose all dignity as her very average back-up dancers. We giggle, we execute our moves and we are hugely grateful when the song ends without any of us falling down the stairs or flashing our knickers to the crowd below.

This is my last event as *Cosmopolitan*'s editor and there is no doubt in my mind that it is time to go. After more than seven years and one hundred issues, the struggle to reconcile my work life with my real life has become overwhelming. I need a change.

Publicly, I'm the face of a magazine aimed predominantly at young, single girls. Girls who liked to party. Girls who read sealed sections. Girls in their teens and early twenties. Girls revelling in their Me-Years.

Privately, my Me-Years are a dim memory. I haven't been that type of carefree single girl for more than a decade. I am managing a staff of thirty, a budget of several million dollars and I'm responsible for steering the Australian arm of an iconic international magazine brand with fifty-eight editions around the world.

I've kept my two lives apart for seven years but it's becoming more difficult, more of a strain. I don't want to have to hide the fact I'm married or a mother from my readers any more, and I don't want to be in the media defending stories about oral sex tips.

As I stand making my speech after the performance, I can't shake the creeping sense of fraudulence that has grown stronger over the past year or two. I feel inappropriate. I'm not the *Cosmo* girl any more — perhaps I never was.

I am proud of what I've achieved at *Cosmo* but now I am more than ready to make way for someone else. I've never wanted to stay too long at the party, to be one of those editors working on a magazine that is years (or even decades) removed from their day-to-day life experience. It happens. You get comfortable. Your job and the associated profile come to define you until stepping away feels too scary.

But I'm not scared at all. I am ready.

Balancing on my stupid shoes, I thank our advertisers for their support and my staff for their hard work. I pay tribute to my boss for her faith in me and finally I introduce *Cosmo*'s new editor, a great girl I've hand-picked to replace me.

I won't be leaving the magazine entirely. My new role will see me as Editor-in-Chief of *Cosmopolitan*, *Cleo* and *Dolly* magazines. But next time *Cosmo* has an event, I'll be a background player, an elder stateswoman. I will no longer be the face and voice of *Cosmo* and at this prospect I feel only relief.

After finishing my speech, I slip away to change into my real outfit for the evening, a chiffon no-name frock with bell sleeves that I found at a vintage store near the office for a hundred dollars. I had it altered from floor-length caftan to just above the knee and have paired it with some beautiful pink, feathery mules, which have languished in the back of my cupboard for years along with all the other inappropriate shoes I almost never have occasion to wear.

I grab the nearest cocktail — a *Cosmopolitan* naturally — and work the room. I am saturated with that familiar mix of adrenaline, tension and the urge to run away from everyone. I have always dreaded *Cosmo* events because while I know I'm capable of being the bright and bubbly hostess the situation requires, I find it to be a strain. And even though I invariably get into it and enjoy myself, riding the buzz, it is always an enormous drain on my energy.

As editor, it is my responsibility to make the advertisers and media buyers feel special, important and acknowledged. They are invited to a million magazine events like this and it is vital for me to subtly convey that the thousands of bucks they spend on ad pages in *Cosmo* are a sound investment. Then I have to schmooze the media. The aim is for them to leave the event with the impression that *Cosmo* is hot, happening and worthy of ample positive coverage. The celebrities need some TLC as well because they are the ones pulling the media coverage; also we might need them editorially some time in the future. It is a lot of plates to keep spinning at once.

As things wind up, a group of *Cosmo* staff and assorted guests make plans to keep partying at a nearby bar. It is still only 8.30 pm and they are just getting started. They are mostly single, mostly under twenty-five. I'm not quite ready to go home either, but I need time off from my role as party-girl hostess. My social energy is sapped.

I catch my husband's eye across the room and we make our way towards each other. My anchor. 'Let's grab a pizza somewhere,' I whisper. 'I'm done.'

Having made sure my boss and our important clients have already left and that most guests are starting to drift away, we slip away from the fray and into a pizza place a few doors down the road.

One slice in and my phone rings. It's the babysitter. Luca is sick. We grab the bill, ask for our pizza to be boxed up to go and are home by 9.15 pm. Less than an hour after being photographed for the social pages in my pretty new frock, I am on my hands and knees with my party dress tucked into my undies, scrubbing vomit out of the carpet in my son's bedroom.

While the *Cosmo* girls party into the night, drinking, dancing and flirting, I am in mum-mode, tag-teaming with my husband as we clean up vomit, change sheets and administer Panadol.

Far from feeling bitter or disappointed at the way my glamorous night has ended, I feel oddly happy. Grounded. This is my real life. And it feels a whole lot more natural and appropriate than dancing with Kylie in sparkly shoes.

I am thoroughly ready for the next phase in my career, one where I don't have to pretend any more.

THE MIDGET MODEL AGENCY

Answering machine message:

'Hello, Mia. This is Susan Manfred calling; I'm Lisa Wilkinson's personal assistant. Lisa would like you to come in to meet her next week on Wednesday at 12.45. Can you please call me back to confirm that's okay? Thanks.'

'Are you here for the casting?' asked the woman with long blonde hair who I immediately recognised as *Cleo*'s fashion editor.

I was already overcome by the glamour of my immediate surroundings: five grey plastic chairs shoved against a wall opposite a door to the ladies toilets. But truthfully, I'd barely noticed the décor. I'd been too distracted by the tall, pretty girls traipsing in and out of the office with their modelling portfolios tucked under skinny arms. Models. Actual editorial models. My eyes were on stalks and I hadn't even made it past reception.

I had come to the fourth floor of the ACP building for an interview with Lisa Wilkinson, *Cleo*'s editor and my idol. Now *Cleo*'s fashion editor had just mistaken me for a model. Hot damn, could this day possibly get any better?

I'd first become aware of models at the same time as I became aware of Lisa, when I picked up my first copy of *Dolly* aged twelve. After a few months, I knew the regular *Dolly* models by name even though it would be years before models of any kind became super and commanded mainstream celebrity status. These were editorial girls who were only famous to magazine groupies like me.

Alison Brahe, Sonia Klein, Renée Simonsen, Toneya Bird, Anne-Louise Gould and Sarah Nursey were the stars of *Dolly* and I plastered their photos on my bedroom walls and schoolbooks. Thrillingly, Sarah Nursey went to my school and I had the opportunity to observe her up close. She was several years older than me so we were never going to be friends, but I'd often find myself sitting a few metres from her in the library or a classroom during a study period. I stared at her intently. Staring is a habit I still can't shake. When someone captures my attention, I blatantly fix my gaze on them, until they become uncomfortable or the person I'm with elbows me and hisses, 'Mia, STOP STARING.'

Sarah was a huge star in the Australian modelling industry during the 1980s, appearing on the cover of *Dolly* every few months and starring in fashion shoots almost every issue. She did TV commercials too and I couldn't quite believe such a famous person was also part of my daily world. She was a tall, strapping Aussie beach girl: athletic with wild blonde corkscrew curls and a tan.

I was the opposite of this: small and nondescript with mousy brown hair and no hope of becoming a model. Ever. And yet still I hoped. Twice, in fact, I more than hoped. I actually tried. Both times it was a disaster. It would be fair to say my attempts to crack the modelling industry collapsed unspectacularly before ever leaving the starting gate.

At sixteen, I was unexpectedly talent-scouted by a booker from a reputable modelling agency while watching a friend's deportment-school graduation parade. The scout, a chic woman in her early twenties, suggested I come into the agency the following week for a chat. 'We have open calls on Wednesdays after 3 pm,' she told me as I tried to look nonchalant at the prospect of my schoolgirl fantasies coming true. 'Bring some snapshots so we can see how you photograph.'

That weekend, after I'd covered my pimples and teased my fringe, my mum took a couple of rolls of black-and-white shots of me leaning in a doorway and sitting in a lounge chair, wearing a white T-shirt and 501s. I was the epitome of eighties style. In my mind.

The following Wednesday, I arrived at the agency with a carefully chosen handful of shots and waited expectantly for my new life as a model to begin. 'I never expected to make a career out of modelling,' I imagined telling a reporter while on the set of some fabulous fashion shoot in the south of France. 'It just kind of happened.'

It never happened.

My chat with the booker lasted all of one minute. After passing a practised eye over my height (less than average), body (average) and snapshots (awful), she killed my dreams in a sentence. 'You're not right for editorial or for Chadwicks but you could try an agency that does commercials.' Oh. 'You might have better luck there.' And I was out the door. Brushed off like dandruff from the shoulder of a black jacket.

Three years later I gave it another shot. After I finished school I was looking for cash and glamour and nothing involving actual hard work. So I signed up with a midget model agency. Well, not technically for midgets. For short models. Or rather, girls-who-really-wanted-to-be-models-but-had-not-a-chance-in-France. It was called something stupid and patronising like 'Low Profiles'.

The premise was patently ridiculous because no fashion editor has ever declared, 'You know what type of girl I want for this denim shoot? A short one!' No fashion designer has ever called a model agency and said, 'My vision for this season is vertically challenged. Please can you send me some shrimps?'

Not understanding this, I forked out $1000 for some 'professional' photos which were ghastly and involved a bored photographer and several different looks including a fedora and a swimsuit — worn at the same time. I also paid an extra $250 for one hundred composite cards which featured the agency logo, two photos (one face and one full-length) and my measurements. I was a size ten and this was a problem.

'You need to lose some weight and clear up your skin,' instructed the agency's owner and only visible employee, a sleazy guy called Guy. And then he asked me out for a drink. Pretending I hadn't heard the drink bit, I mumbled my agreement about the weight and the skin but I wasn't able to do either. Optimistically, I still went along to a handful of dodgy castings for low-budget commercials and never landed a single modelling job.

After a couple of months, I realised it wasn't going to happen for me. Elle Macpherson didn't have to sleep with one eye open. I couldn't be bothered to lose weight, I didn't know how to clear up my skin and I discovered modelling was equal parts boring, intimidating and humiliating — and that was just the go-sees. I didn't want to spend my days at castings, waiting in stairwells with tall, beautiful girls for no money.

Reluctantly, I stashed my sad little portfolio in the back of a cupboard and retired. Being briefly mistaken for a model by *Cleo*'s fashion editor was the pinnacle of my non-existent modelling career.

Just to be sure she was talking to me, I looked over my shoulder. The other grey plastic chairs were empty. Excellent. 'Oh, no, I'm just, um, waiting to see Lisa Wilkinson,' I stammered, failing to hide the brag in my voice. You see, my goals had changed. I no longer wanted to be a model. I wanted to be a journalist. More specifically, I wanted to work on a magazine. Even more specifically, that magazine had to be *Cleo*. It just HAD to be.

CLEO NERD

Answering machine message to my mum from me:

'Oh my God, Mum, guess what? Lisa Wilkinson wants to see me!
I have an interview with her next week. I'm so excited! Can
I borrow the car?'

The only thing better than waiting to see *Cleo*'s fashion editor was waiting to see *Cleo*'s editor. But if the fashion editor was deeply impressed that I had an interview with Lisa, she hid it well. With a polite smile and a flick of her long blonde ponytail, she vanished back into the office.

Her name was Diana and I knew this with certainty because I'd spent years studying the staff list that appears in the front of every magazine. I'd eagerly matched those names with the captions on staff snapshots which sometimes appeared on the editor's page. I was a *Cleo* nerd.

For years, I'd idolised the women who worked on the magazines I loved. How could it be possible to have a better job, I wondered, even though the concept of having a job was still a very vague one. Like having a baby.

★

As a teenager, my favourite part of *Dolly* had always been the editor's letter and I pored over every detail about what was happening in the office and what the staff were doing.

As with any magazine, the queen of *Dolly* was its editor; back then it was Lisa, although she never came across as a queen. With waist-length straight brown hair, a radiant, open face and a friendly smile, she seemed just like a grown-up version of me or any other girl. Real. Approachable. That was Lisa's skill and appeal, inside and out — and still is today.

It would be decades until the head shots on editors' pages would become as glamorous, stylised and air-brushed as the fashion pages. In the 1980s, Lisa had the same small and unglamorous picture on her page every month. Occasionally she'd update it, maybe once a year. In her editor's photo, she'd usually be sitting at her desk, not wearing much make-up, in no tricky outfit. Just her big smile and her long hair. Sometimes, glasses. Maybe a jumper. Her image was that of a regular Aussie girl. Who just happened to have a job beyond my wildest dreams.

I'd first begun to buy magazines as a schoolgirl, looking for photos and headlines to paste into my school diary and onto my folders. It was instant love.

My fascination with magazines was so extreme that my monthly *Dolly* fix soon wasn't enough. Even though I was twelve, I began to buy magazines aimed at my mother (who never showed any interest in reading them) like *Woman's Day*, the *Australian Women's Weekly* and *New Idea*. With their breezy gossip and lifestyle content, they appealed to me over *Cosmo* and *Cleo*, which felt too raunchy and sophisticated. Sometimes I bought them anyway, but *Dolly* was my favourite — the mag with which I identified most passionately.

One hot summer day when I was about fourteen, I was slathered in baby oil, sunbaking in the garden with my brand-new copy of *Dolly*. With that familiar rush of excitement and anticipation, I turned automatically to the editor's page. One paragraph in and I was traumatised. Lisa was leaving. It was her last issue as *Dolly*'s editor. She wrote about how much she'd miss the staff and the readers and how much she was looking forward to her new challenge: editing *Cleo*.

This was devastating news. I wasn't ready to move to *Cleo* with her. I wasn't ready to grow up and leave *Dolly* behind. I felt bereft and abandoned in that dramatic, self-absorbed way teenage girls have of placing themselves in the centre of any given event.

In time, I healed. I stayed loyal to *Dolly* for another year or two but I never bonded with the editors who followed Lisa. No one could take her place or strike the same self-deprecating yet aspirational tone of her editor's letters.

Eventually, at about sixteen, I was ready to graduate to *Cleo*. I quickly found myself a new love. *Cleo* had the Aussie familiarity of *Dolly* but with an irreverent cheekiness and intelligent tone that appealed to women all the way into their thirties.

Dolly, *Cleo* and *Cosmo* were each aimed at a far older audience in the seventies, eighties and even nineties than they are today. Mostly because there were far fewer magazines to choose from. The typical progression for an Aussie girl was to buy *Dolly* when you were a teenager, then *Cleo* or *Cosmo* during your twenties and thirties, and, finally, when you got married and had kids, you bought the *Women's Weekly*, where you stayed till you died. As the adage went, '*Dolly* teaches you what the word orgasm means, *Cleo* teaches you how to have an orgasm and the *Women's Weekly* teaches you how to knit one.'

Being the teenage magazine junkie I was, I bought *Cosmo* as well, but for me it was always a poor relation. *Cleo* was my true love. My perfect magazine match.

In a stroke of luck, after leaving school I met a girl whose father worked for the Packer family, who owned Australian Consolidated Press. He wasn't with the magazine division but he worked in the same building. I jumped at the chance to write this poor man a very formal letter BEGGING for the chance to work in magazines and mentioning my particular devotion to *Cleo* and to Lisa.

I hand-delivered my letter to his secretary, taking the bus into the city and walking awestruck into the building that housed all my favourite magazines. At the time, ACP published *Dolly*, *Cleo*, *Cosmo*, the *Australian Women's Weekly*, *Harper's Bazaar*, *Woman's Day*, *House & Garden*, *Elle*, *Mode*, *Wheels* and dozens of other titles.

Many people don't realise — I didn't — that even though many of these magazines compete with each other, they all share an owner and publisher. And building. The same one I'd soon be walking into every day for the next fifteen years.

I will forever be grateful that my schoolgirlish letter and woefully inadequate CV was passed on to Lisa. When you're an editor, you receive dozens and dozens of similar unsolicited letters every week and, unfortunately, most go ignored. There's just no time and no space to accommodate every girl who dreams of a magazine career.

I've always remembered the kindness that was shown to me and the invaluable chance I was given, at nineteen, to prove myself to Lisa. It was the elusive foot in the door.

In six years' time, I'd be an editor myself and count Lisa among my close friends. We would have babies in the same week — her third, my first. Six years after that, I'd be responsible for *Cleo*, *Cosmo*, *Dolly* and several other magazines in the building. But at that moment, as a precocious, pimply teenager waiting on a grey plastic chair to meet her for the first time, I was absolutely terrified.

★

'Sorry to keep you waiting; she's ready to see you now.' Susan, Lisa's assistant, showed me into her office, and while walking the three metres from reception, I nearly tripped on some loose carpet being held down with masking tape. Nice.

Lisa greeted me with a smile and gestured for me to sit in one of the dilapidated chairs opposite her desk. Later, I would learn the history of this infamous chair. Once, when Kerry Packer walked into Lisa's office for a meeting, he'd sat in it and promptly tipped over backwards onto the floor. Me, I just perched carefully and tried to process my surroundings. I kept getting stuck at the part where I was actually sitting in front of Lisa Wilkinson. In her office. While she sat behind her desk casting a polite eye over my unimpressive CV.

Highlights included part-time jobs as a checkout chick at Woolies and a sales assistant at fashion chain Cherry Lane during high school. I'd loved those jobs. My parents had instilled a strong work ethic in me early. My older brother had worked at David Jones when he was at high school, and more than anything I wanted to be like him. I applied to be a checkout chick as soon as I hit Woolworths' minimum age requirement for casuals: fifteen. This was before scanning, mind you. When you had to find a price tag on every item and punch the number into the cash register. By hand. I did one or two shifts per week through much of Year Eleven and the money came in handy for going out on weekends.

After leaving school, I'd decided to defer university for a year and live in Italy for six months with three girlfriends. To fund my trip, I worked as a waitress in a posh restaurant serving salads to Ladies Who Lunched. It was unspeakably tedious. By the end of it, I hated people, food and utensils, but I'd saved my airfare and some spending money. My parents generously kicked in some extra.

The idea had been to study Italian in Florence but we spent much more time in bars, nightclubs and cafés than we did attending classes. I came back with conversational Italian and ten extra kilos.

I then spent the next nine months at university, studying Arts–Communications and majoring in journalism. I was living at home and working part time as a promotions girl at car shows as well as waitressing again to make some cash.

University was not going well. I was bored, frustrated and impatient. After the firm boundaries and strict school rules that had helped me do well in the HSC, I lacked the discipline for university. Uninspired by the process of learning, I was plagiarising my journalism assignments from a local gay newspaper, which was particularly brainless given that my lecturer was gay. I began to skip lectures and I was struggling to stay focused. (Thoughtfully, I'd left those last few points off my CV.)

After skimming what was in front of her, Lisa glanced up at me, smiled wryly and said, 'So, Mia. You went to a private girls school. You just spent six months in Florence and you live in the eastern suburbs. Why shouldn't I hate you?'

Her tone was not unkind but there was an unspoken challenge in what she said: are you a precious princess? This was classic Lisa. In an instant, she'd extracted the pertinent details from my patchy CV and made a valid point veiled with humour.

I can't remember how I replied, probably by saying something inspired like 'Cleo is my favourite magazine!', but I do recall her launching into the 'Magazines are not glamorous' speech. This was one I would come to recite dozens of times myself to hopeful, naïve girls sitting on the other side of my own (future) desk.

After listening patiently to me babble about how much I loved writing and how my favourite subject at school was English and blah blah blah, Lisa suggested I come and do work experience for a fortnight, assisting the features editor. I couldn't

11

say yes fast enough, although a small, arrogant voice in my head grumbled with disappointment at not having been offered a full-time, paying job on the spot. Because that's what I wanted.

As Lisa walked me to the door of her office, she said something I'd never forget. 'You know, Mia, magazines aren't for everyone. You might be better suited to a different form of journalism like newspapers or TV. Or radio. Magazines are either in your blood or they're not.'

She was absolutely right about that. For the next fifteen years, I would live for magazines. In my blood? You bet.

WOULD YOU LIKE 8000 FREE LIPSTICKS WITH THAT?

Answering machine message to Lisa's PA from me:

'Um, hi Susan, it's Mia calling again. I know we spoke yesterday but just wondering if Lisa had made a decision about the beauty editor position yet because, you know, well, I'm pretty keen to find out. Sorry to hassle. Gosh, I don't mean to be a stalker or anything and I know you're probably flat out and — "beeeeeeeep"'

It's no accident that so many editors begin their magazine careers as beauty editors. *Cleo*, *Vogue*, the *Australian Women's Weekly*, *Elle*, *Harper's Bazaar*, *Shop Til You Drop*, *Dolly*, *Girlfriend*, *InStyle*, *Yen*, *House & Garden*, *Cosmo* and *Madison* have all had editors who started that way.

To be a proficient beauty editor, you need three key skills, all of them — plus more — required by good editors. First, you need to be an outstanding ambassador for your magazine. A personification of the brand. This is because you spend a large chunk of your time outside the office at functions, representing the magazine to advertisers and the media. You're the staff member most likely to appear in the social pages because the editor and everyone else are back at the office, writing, designing, shooting, sub-editing. Meanwhile, you are on the frontline. It's like Afghanistan … with mascara and gift bags. So it's vital to look the part.

You must be well groomed and well behaved. You must know how to make small talk and subtly sell your magazine to advertisers who are persistently trying to flog their products to your readers via you. Bedhead and a hangover won't cut it. Neither will shyness. Or too much free champagne.

The endless daily churn of product launches and lunches may seem superficial because … oh wait, it is. But the champagne and canapés belie your true mission: to suck up to the advertisers.

This is the second way in which a beauty editor is a lot like an editor. In both jobs, you straddle the two different worlds of magazines, editorial (the pages created by the magazine's staff) and advertising (paid pages created by advertisers). A smart beauty editor can lubricate the passage of advertising dollars from the client into the magazine. She understands both the implicit and explicit connections between advertising and editorial. She knows how to keep clients happy without compromising her editorial integrity. Well, no more than she has to, anyway.

It's an open secret that big advertisers are looked after on the editorial pages of virtually every magazine in which their ads appear. There is so much competition for a limited pool of advertising dollars that ethical lines are often blurred. The basic equation is simple: we'll give you positive editorial mentions for as long as you give us advertising dollars.

The specifics of this relationship depend upon the type of magazine and its circulation. On some titles, 'looking after' may mean a guaranteed number of editorial mentions or just a mutual understanding that the client's products will be featured positively and frequently on the editorial pages. But it's not quite as simple as cash-for-comment. Not always. If an advertiser pays tens of thousands of dollars to buy a dozen ad pages in your magazine, it will only be because their products are targeted directly to your readers' demographic. Chanel won't buy pages in *Dolly*, they'll advertise in *Vogue*. So it's not exactly a stretch for *Vogue* to write about Chanel lipstick. That's where the skill of the beauty editor comes into play. If you know you have to suck up to a particular advertiser, it's your job to find a way to do it without openly lying to your readers. First you find a product you genuinely like and then you find a genuine reason to write about it.

Sometimes, though, it's plainly dodgy. Smaller, lower circulating titles have to bend over much further to secure ad dollars, often publishing entire suck-up stories about the launch of, say, a new perfume or eye cream under the guise of editorial. Fashion magazines are particularly prone to running these kinds of 'stories'.

These are not to be confused with 'advertorials', which are paid advertising pages created to look like editorial. Advertorials are often conceived, written and designed by the editorial staff, who do this on their own time for freelance rates. The idea of an advertorial is to integrate the advertiser's product into the editorial look and tone of the magazine. This is also known as trying-to-trick-the-reader.

Clients love advertorials because they blur the line between advertising and editorial. Editors hate advertorials because they blur the line between advertising and editorial — even though they have to run with a line at the top of the page saying 'promotion' or something similar. Editors think advertorials look ugly and compromise the quality of the surrounding editorial. Editors do not like to trick the reader because readers do not like to be tricked. It makes readers angry and cynical, and it erodes their loyalty. But the more advertising pages your sales team can book, the more editorial pages you can run. So you shut up and you say thank you to your advertisers for their lovely advertorials.

Until I worked in magazines, like many readers, I had a common complaint. 'Why are there so many damn ads?' I'd whinge, flicking crankily past glossy advertisements for lip gloss and sports bras. The answer is a purely economic one: the advertising pages pay for the editorial ones. All magazines work on a strict advertising to editorial page ratio. This ratio depends on the business model of the magazine, but at *Cosmo* a typical issue was about sixty per cent editorial, forty per cent advertising.

Most magazines sold on news-stands (as opposed to the ones that come free in a newspaper) have two revenue streams. The first comes from the cover price and the second is from advertising pages. But not all work that way. Some magazines are purely circulation models, like *Take 5* and *That's Life* which sell hundreds of thousands of copies but don't carry much advertising. Others are advertising models — typically, prestige magazines that sell, say, fifty thousand copies but whose wealthy readers are very attractive to advertisers. That's why magazines like *Belle*, *Gourmet Traveller* and *Vogue* have so many advertising pages.

The publishing industry uses ad count as one way to measure the health of a magazine. Generally, a mag full of ad pages is more likely to be profitable and successful than one with only a few.

Beauty editors know all of this. The clever ones do, anyway. They have to because the bulk of advertising in a glossy mag like *Cleo* or *Cosmo* comes from beauty companies. As the only person apart from the editor who has regular contact with the advertiser, they develop an intrinsic understanding of the delicate balance between editorial integrity and the crucial revenue that ad dollars provide.

There's one key benefit that comes with all this sucking up. By attending all the advertisers' functions and presenting at pitch meetings with the magazine's advertising sales reps, beauty editors quickly develop a high profile among advertisers. And, when publishers are appointing editors, this matters. Publishers prefer their new editors to be familiar to the magazine's advertisers so as not to spook the horses and risk precious advertising dollars leaking elsewhere.

The third way a beauty editor is a mini-me editor is a journalistic one. Ah yes, journalism. Sadly, this is not the biggest part of a beauty editor's job but it's important nonetheless. And deceptively difficult. Beauty pages are always a mix of words and pictures: pictures of products of different hair and make-up looks. Features writers work exclusively with words; fashion editors and graphic artists work exclusively with pictures. Only the editor and the beauty editor must always consider both and use them to tell their story.

I knew none of this when I was offered the role of beauty writer at *Cleo*. I was just beside myself to have a paying job. Of course, I'd already decided I wanted to be the editor. I'd even given myself a deadline: before I turned twenty-five.

Who knows where I pulled this age from, but since I was nineteen at the time, twenty-five felt sufficiently far away to be possible but near enough to be impressive. The fact Lisa had chosen the beauty door through which to shove me on to my career path was, I believe, entirely coincidental. Did she think I had editor potential? Unlikely. I was young and a total novice.

Anyway, all I knew was that I'd just been appointed *Cleo*'s beauty writer by my hero and it felt like Christmas on steroids.

It had taken me months to get this gig. At the end of my initial fortnight of work experience, I'd persuaded Lisa to extend it and let me come in one day every week. For free, obviously. I was still living at home and making a token appearance at university while I waited for my proper life to start. I didn't have many expenses and my casual jobs covered me for incidentals.

Excited halfway out of my pants to be in the *Cleo* office and in such close proximity to Lisa, I was delighted by every work-experience task thrown my way, no matter how menial. From fetching Lisa's morning cappuccino to photocopying references, from foreign magazines to making half a dozen trips down to the mailroom each day, from returning clothes from the fashion department to typing bought stories into the computer, opening mail and filing correspondence, I was in heaven.

Gradually, I started turning up on extra days, praying that no one would ask what the hell I was doing or send me home. They didn't. They were too busy working. For money. Within a month, I was coming in two days a week and then three. Then four. There was always plenty to do and my goal was to make myself as indispensable as possible, to create a Mia-shaped hole that would gape inconveniently when I wasn't there. Then Lisa would have to give me a full-time job, wouldn't she?

As part of my work experience, *Cleo*'s then deputy editor, Deborah Thomas, had thrown me a few bits to write for the beauty pages. *Cleo* was between beauty editors at the time and Deborah wasn't happy with the work she'd received from a freelancer who was filling the gap. She had nothing to lose by tossing it my way to see if I could do better. I was young and green but I was also free, eager and sitting right there.

To test me, she'd give me a press release for a beauty product, say a new Revlon mascara, and a rough word count — usually about one hundred to two hundred words. My brief was to write an entertaining, informative paragraph or two to go on the beauty pages.

Knowing nothing technical about beauty, I wrote these bits very much as a regular nineteen-year-old. A consumer. An outsider. I liked make-up as much as the next girl but I'd certainly never been a beauty junkie or a label queen when it came to skincare and cosmetics. My skin was pretty lousy and I used any old thing from the supermarket to try and scrub it into submission. As for make-up, it never occurred to me to consider brands. I was hopeless at putting it on, and as a result didn't wear too much. The cosmetics I did use usually came from Woolworths and were super cheap. Department-store cosmetics counters intimidated me. They still do.

While my utter lack of professional beauty knowledge was in some ways a liability that would frequently land me in trouble, it was also an asset because I wrote in language the reader could understand. It was trial and error at first. Everything I wrote needed work but still I couldn't quite believe it when a version of something I'd written appeared in the magazine. Deborah was encouraging without being effusive. I didn't know beauty-speak so I couldn't write it. Later, this would stand me in good stead for writing and editing for the reader instead of myself.

This was Lisa's greatest skill as an editor, her ability to slip into the skin of the *Cleo* reader. She literally viewed the magazine through their eyes. She didn't edit *Cleo* for herself or her friends or her staff or other people in the industry. She always took an external perspective, putting aside all her inside knowledge and personal preferences.

I was hugely lucky that Lisa was my first editor because this skill is not innate. Writing or editing or shooting for your peers is a common trap and it's always to the detriment of your product. People who work on magazines are not typical of those who read them.

To this day, I automatically slip into the mindset of a reader when I'm assessing something in a magazine. 'I don't understand what this story is about,' I'll say when looking at a layout. Obviously I do know what the story is about because chances are I commissioned it and chose the pictures with the art department, but I'm not speaking as *me*, I'm speaking as *the reader*. It's probably disconcerting for people who aren't used to working with me but I can't help it. And generally, that external perspective is crucial.

Beauty writer was an unusual title. My colleagues at other magazines were called beauty editors. Beauty writer was created especially for me to reflect the fact I was a kid and barely knew one end of a mascara wand from the other.

Giving me a junior title was a smart move by Lisa because the other beauty editors were almost all a decade or two older than me and infinitely more experienced. To have given me the same title would have been insulting to them and made *Cleo* look foolish.

Calling me beauty writer also gave me room to grow, and something to aspire to. In time, I could be promoted to beauty editor. When Lisa believed I was ready. When I deserved it.

Frankly, I couldn't have cared if I was called beauty dunce — which would have been entirely fair and accurate. I had a job at *Cleo*. I had a desk and a computer on it. A phone with my own extension. A business card. My name was in the front of the magazine. Lisa Wilkinson was my boss and I actually got to talk to her every day. And that was even before the perks began.

Deborah Thomas was my direct boss, the person in charge of teaching me about beauty and making sure I didn't stuff up and embarrass the magazine in person or print. She, too, had been a *Cleo* beauty editor and this made her an ideal teacher. She was very patient.

She needed to be. My first public outing as beauty writer was a private meet-and-greet with the PR person for Clinique, an important *Cleo* advertiser and part of the even more important Estée Lauder group. Naturally, I didn't know this. Just as many magazines are owned and published by the same company, so it is with many cosmetics brands. Who knew?

Hell, I was nineteen, I knew nothing. Certainly not that Estée Lauder owned Clinique and Prescriptives. Today, the company also owns M.A.C, Bobbi Brown, Origins and Aveda, among many other brands. Similarly, L'Oréal owns Garnier, Biotherm, Maybelline and Lancôme, to name just a few. Not that the average consumer would realise this. You're not meant to. The idea is that every brand has a distinct and separate identity, helping the mother company cast as wide a net as possible over consumer demographics to maximise sales and profits.

As a beauty editor, however, it's crucial to know who owns who because having a big company as a parent allows smaller brands to punch above their editorial weight. This means more editorial love — and mentions — in the pages of your magazine. No one dares piss off L'Oréal or Estée Lauder.

'Is there a family tree that explains it all?' I asked Deborah hopefully in the cab on the way to Clinique as she quickly mentioned the Estée Lauder connection.

She gave a small laugh. 'No, I'm afraid not. Ha, ha.'

Except I wasn't joking.

We met with Jenny, Clinique's head of public relations, whom Deborah had known for years. After introductions were made, we sat down for tea and biscuits while Jenny talked us through Clinique's next big launch. I tried to keep my mouth shut so my ignorance wouldn't fall out.

Regrettably, I failed. I've never been very good at shutting up. Sometimes it's as if I have Tourette syndrome. During the meeting I was dimly aware that I might have been saying some dumb things but I couldn't quite put my finger on what it was I shouldn't be saying — which made it difficult to stop talking.

In the cab on the way back to the office, Deborah pointed out where I'd gone wrong. 'Look, Mia, it was totally inappropriate for you to say, "Wow! My mum uses Clinique!"'

Oh. Sorry.

'It was irrelevant to what we were discussing and it made you look young and silly.'

Oh. Sorry. Cringe.

As she continued with the mortifying feedback, I kept glancing furtively at the bag of products Jenny had thrust into my hands as we left. 'Um, what do I do with these?' I now asked.

'Write about them, have them photographed for your pages and then you can keep them.'

Seriously? Keep them? For myself? To use? Dear Lord, was there a better job on earth? For the next two years, there was not.

Noting my wide eyes and slack jaw, Deborah cautioned me. 'Mia, you always need to remember this about working in a magazine: all the products and the invitations and the presents the PRs send you? They're not sending them to you; they're sending them to your job. Don't ever confuse the two.'

These were the wisest words I heard about the industry and I've repeated them to every beauty editor I ever hired. As easy as it is to mistake the PRs' endless solicitations for genuine kindness and become entranced with your own power and influence, you have to stay a little cynical. As long as you can help them by writing nice things about their products, they love you. But as soon as you can't? Bye-bye. There would be one or two exceptions to this rule, but generally it rings true.

There would be several points in my future career when I'd watch the contact from PRs evaporate instantly. Until I was appointed to another position of power where I could help them out, and the pretend love would come back overnight. You can't take it personally.

Thanks to Deborah's sage advice, I never let those gifts and perks turn my head. Yes, they were nice — who's going to bin a free Chanel perfume or a CD player sent by a cosmetics company along with some new lip glosses? But I never deluded myself into thinking those perks had anything to do with me.

When you work in editorial, you are a job, not a person. And to PRs, your worth is measured in the exposure you can deliver.

As a journalist, I'd like to think I was a quick learner. It certainly helped that each time I submitted my copy, Deborah made me pull up a chair next to her desk so I could watch while she rewrote it and explained her changes word by word. This was invaluable and slightly humiliating at the same time. She always made what I'd written sound better. It was months before I found my voice and my words made it onto the page without extensive surgery.

Writing beauty copy is part science, part politics and part bullshit with a sprinkling of journalism on top. There is a language of beauty writing steeped heavily in cheesy cliché that's best avoided if you want to succeed. Nowhere but in magazines is hair called 'locks' or 'tresses' or a 'mane'. Only in mag-speak are legs called 'pins' or lips referred to as 'your pout'. I've always hated that language. As a reader then a writer then an editor. But it's easy to slip into, especially at first when I didn't have a clue what I was doing.

My first published feature with my name on it was a story about nails, titled imaginatively: The Nail File. This caused much hilarity among my friends and family because I was a chronic nail biter to the point where my cuticles would sometimes bleed. Not a good look for a beauty journalist. Must try harder …

★

My first public function as a beauty writer was daunting. Deborah wasn't there to hold my hand. I was nervous to the point of mild nausea.

It was the launch of a new perfume and a cocktail party for about forty journalists was held at a fancy five-star hotel in the city. I arrived shortly after the start time, took a quick look around at the dozen or so assembled women and — recognising no one — headed straight for the plush bathrooms. I put the toilet lid down and sat quietly in a cubicle for the next forty minutes, too shy to venture out and introduce myself to anyone, too fearful of saying something stupid to make conversation. Out of my depth in every way.

When all was quiet and I was sure the formalities had started, I emerged from the loo and slunk into a chair in the back row ready for the presentation. As soon as it was over, I bolted, collecting my gift bag — containing a full-size bottle of the perfume and a press release — on the way out.

Even though it was an awkward experience, I was still awed by my job, wide-eyed about everything. Especially my beauty cabinet at home, which had spilled over into drawers and cupboards within weeks.

However, like working in a chocolate factory, the perks soon lost their perkiness. There were only so many posh restaurants you could be wined and dined at. Only so many lipsticks and mascaras and nail polishes and perfumes you could wear. Or give to friends. Or stash in cupboards for future use. Only so many glasses of champagne you could sip while discussing the relative merits of free radicals as a skincare ingredient. It was a dream job in so many ways. But I had a different dream. And it had nothing to do with mascara.

MISPLACING MY SELF-ESTEEM

Voicemail to Charlie from me:

'Hi. Don't worry about picking me up after work today. I'm going to a L'Oréal launch and then I thought I might have dinner with Karen. I'll be home early, I promise! Bye!'

Less than two years after becoming a beauty writer, things were going swimmingly at work. I was being given lots of stories to write and shoot, which meant lots of by-lines and a growing profile in the industry.

After a year of full-time uni before I'd started at *Cleo*, I'd limped along part time for another nine months before abandoning it, confident in my belief that future jobs would come from the one I had, not a degree. My parents thought I'd deferred, but I had no intention of going back to uni. My career was too intoxicating.

I was becoming more self-assured in my writing, more comfortable at functions and more capable dealing with PRs and advertisers. Lisa had promoted me to beauty editor, which meant no real change in my job description or salary but it was public acknowledgement that I was on my way up the ladder.

On the home front though? Miserable. A mess. In a pattern that would repeat itself several times over the next few years, my work life was on an upwards trajectory while my personal life was heading rapidly in the other direction.

I was living with a guy called Charlie. It was the first time I'd lived with a boyfriend, and it was a disaster.

We'd met at 2 am in a nightclub, which, I find, is always a terrific way to start. I'd been at *Cleo* for a few months and I was having a ball, going out constantly for work and play. Life was fun. I wasn't looking for a boyfriend.

Charlie was in a struggling band that had recently moved to Sydney from Brisbane to do some gigs and hopefully get signed to a record label. He played bass. I'd seen him around a few times and we'd had a few amusing chats. He was a good flirt. I picked up straight away that he fancied me but I didn't pay much attention because I wasn't attracted to him.

His personality was a big one, though, and he did a stellar job of dismantling my defences. Pretty soon, we were seeing each other although I was determined to keep it casual.

I truly meant this. No bluff. No attempt at reverse psychology. It was obvious that Charlie wouldn't be an ideal boyfriend and, anyway, I was Just Not That Into Him. Nonetheless, he was entertaining to be around and the idea of dating someone without wanting a solid commitment seemed novel. Modern! Empowered! Just like a guy! Woo!

I braced myself for the conversation — the one where he'd tell me he wanted a proper relationship. I practised my speech where I'd let him down gently.

As it turned out, I never delivered that speech because we never had the conversation. He seemed as keen as me to keep it casual. No strings.

And that's when my empowerment began to falter. It was one

thing to have decided I didn't want commitment but it was slightly less empowering when I realised he didn't either. What was the point of telling someone not to pursue you when they weren't actually pursuing you, dammit?

This is when a confusing change in the balance of power began to occur. It was subtle but potent. The less he chased me for a relationship, the more I wanted one. I have no idea why or how this happened or when exactly my brain clicked from independent to needy. Was my pride hurt? Was it ego? Was it that pesky brain chemistry that made me confuse sex with love?

The idea of one person pulling away and the other person scampering after them was hardly original but I'd never experienced it. This push—pull dynamic would precipitate an insidious downward spiral of my self-esteem until I finally felt so worthless, I barely had the strength to walk away.

The snapshots I have in my mind from the two years I spent with Charlie still baffle me. I was smart, educated and confident. I had a job I loved, a nice apartment I rented on my own, a car and financial independence. I was surrounded by supportive family and friends. I knew a thing or two about a thing or two.

When we met, Charlie was living with his bandmates in a rundown house on the other side of the city. The band wasn't earning much from their sporadic gigs so he did the occasional shift as a waiter to earn extra cash. From the start, he never offered to pay for anything but that was okay. I'd dated broke guys my whole life and I was always happy to pay my own way.

The share house was grungy and Charlie slept on a mattress on the floor so staying there wasn't an option for me. Within a few months, I suggested he move into the apartment I was renting. He already spent a few nights a week there and in my haste to move the relationship forward, I thought living together was an obvious decision. He was reticent at first, which made me push harder. I knew cash was a problem so I told him not to worry about rent, I'd cover it. He didn't argue.

From the moment he moved in, it began. The gradual ebbing away of my confidence and the imperceptible shift from me being in the driver's seat of my life and my relationship, to him decisively taking the wheel. Of both.

One night as we were getting ready to go out, I put on a bright blue satin shirt. It was new and a Gucci rip-off and I loved it.

'What are you wearing that for?' he sneered.

'What do you mean?' I replied, surprised. 'What's wrong with it?'

'Look at yourself in the mirror! It's so bright. Are you trying to get attention? Trying to flirt with all the boys? Hoping they'll notice you?' His tone was now mocking, his face contorted into a scowl.

'What are you talking about?' I was crestfallen and genuinely confused. 'It's a shirt not a midriff top. It's not even tight.'

'Yeah but it's all … bright and that's because you want guys to look at you, don't you, Mia? You know you do. Don't deny it. That's what you're like. A flirt.'

Crushed, I took off the shirt and put on something black and shapeless. I wore black a lot during that relationship. It was appropriate, really. My wardrobe was in mourning for my self-esteem.

The clothes I wore were one of a million different ways in which I apparently tried to attract men. The more outlandish Charlie's accusations, the more desperately I tried to prove otherwise until I stopped talking to any guys when we went out, even my male friends and his. Especially my male friends and his.

Eventually, it was easier to just stay home rather than have to defend myself and justify every action. My increasing isolation gave him more power and me less. And so the cycle continued.

Infuriatingly, the same rules never applied to him. He'd flirt openly. Even though his band was pretty awful, there were always girls who came to gigs and tried to pick him up afterwards. One night in a pub, he humiliated me by pulling a pissed girl over to sit on his lap and sharing his drink with her. When I hesitantly complained about it later at the bar, he exploded. 'Stop being an unreasonable bitch, Mia! Nothing was going on and if you can't see that, you have a fucking mental problem.' I left in tears. He stayed out partying until 4 am. There was no apology and when I tried to discuss it the next day, he simply shouted at me. 'Maybe we should just break up! Maybe you should get another boyfriend, if I'm such a loser!'

Somehow, he always managed to turn every argument around and cast himself as the victim. I never understood how he did this but it worked every time. I was repeatedly left feeling powerless, mute, needy and backed into a corner.

I had no name for his behaviour at the time. I'd never heard of emotional abuse. It's easy to mistake control for passion and possessiveness for love and I did. If he was so jealous and fiery, he must really love me, right?

Emotional abuse is very different to the now famous 'he's just not that into you' syndrome. With emotional abuse, he's into you big time. So into you that he seeks to control you, to ensure you won't leave him. When I first met Charlie, I had all the cards and he knew it. The only way to capture my attention and keep it was to systematically dismantle my confidence and isolate me from my support network.

To this day, I don't know if he did it consciously. I hope not. I don't think he was an evil person, just one with very mixed-up ideas about relationships.

Emotionally abusive men are often extremely charismatic. Charlie certainly was. Charming, amusing and great fun to be around. When it was good it was great, or so I thought. But when it was bad, it was paralysing.

One day Charlie was yelling abuse at me so aggressively, I found myself thinking, 'Please just hit me.' The thought shocked me but I knew physical violence was a very clear line in the sand for me. A tangible reason for ending the relationship and never looking back. I wanted that tangible reason because when you're being shouted at and taunted and belittled and criticised every day, the line between a volatile relationship and an abusive one becomes strangely blurred. You lose sight of what's normal. Even so, I thought my situation was unique. I felt trapped and ashamed by the way Charlie treated me. Had I read an article about emotional abuse, it would have changed my life. But in the early 1990s it was not yet a mainstream issue and it wasn't a subject I ever saw featured in magazines. When I became an editor, I would change that.

My situation wasn't something I could discuss with my friends or family. I'd gradually distanced myself from them during this relationship. It seemed easier to keep my life with Charlie quarantined from the people who knew me best. He didn't like my friends and because he was very possessive of my time — which at first I found endearing — I began seeing them less and then barely at all.

I knew if they spent time around me and saw our relationship up close, they'd immediately see how damaging it was. Despite my unhappiness, I wasn't yet ready to hear the truth or to have a mirror held up in front of me.

Often when Charlie's band had gigs, I went and hung out in whatever small pub they were playing at. I became quite friendly with some of the other girlfriends and one night when Charlie was doing a rare income-producing shift as a waiter, some of them asked me along to a party. We met up with Charlie after he finished work and he was ominously quiet. I could sense an explosion brewing.

That night when we got home he used some tiny excuse to erupt. 'And what do you think you're doing hanging out with my friends, anyway?' he shouted. 'They're not your friends, they don't even like you.'

I felt like I'd been slapped. Again. I knew it wasn't true; well, I hoped it wasn't true. Was it true? Maybe it was true. It must be true.

That's how my mind had begun to work. My self-esteem was so low, my insecurity so overwhelming that I quickly believed what Charlie said. Clearly, I'd done the wrong thing by going out with them on my own. I wouldn't make that mistake again. Next time I'd stay home alone.

The following weekend one of his friends pulled me aside to say, 'You know I was so pissed off with Charlie for saying we weren't your friends. That's bullshit. He's just being an idiot.'

Yes, he was. So why didn't I just say, 'Fuck off and get out of my house?' I truly don't know. Not then and not now.

I knew I was miserable and that I was living with a man who didn't respect me and treated me like shit. But somehow, I was stuck. The idea of being alone was too scary. So I backed down. Every time.

The other major feature of my dysfunctional relationship with Charlie was dope. I'd hear that first 'tap tap tap' of the bong cone being banged on the coffee table about 10 am on weekends and it would continue every few hours until he crashed out at midnight. I assumed the same thing happened while I was at work.

I grew to loathe that sound. It meant glazed eyes, toxic lethargy, an inability to make decisions or conversation, extreme paranoia and inertia. It also meant he'd eat every piece of food in the house while playing Nintendo for hours.

Charlie didn't have a car and since I left for work each day at 8 am and didn't come home until seven in the evening, this was a problem. For Charlie, and so for me. I didn't want him to be unhappy because it would make my life more difficult. So I was forever trying to find ways to smooth his path and clear roadblocks, even when they had been carelessly strewn there by Charlie himself.

Somehow, I came up with the genius idea of catching a cab to work each morning so Charlie could have my car during the day. The reason he couldn't drop me at *Cleo* was because he had an urgent meeting with his pillow, after a late night. Pulling bongs and playing Nintendo.

I never complained. I didn't dare. Charlie's temper was something I'd quickly learned to fear. Worse, was the unspoken threat that if it all got too hard, he'd leave. Mysteriously, I still didn't want him to and redoubled my efforts to make him happy.

If he felt like it, Charlie might agree to pick me up from work. As the end of my day loomed, I'd grow increasingly tense. I worked in a small room with three other women, one of whom was my direct boss. She always worked late and although it was never a spoken thing, I tried to stay as late as I could to impress her. Also I was busy and I loved my job.

Charlie would turn up when it suited him, usually between bongs at about five-thirty or 6 pm. Barely anyone left before 7 pm, so when he'd call me the knot in my stomach would morph instantly into a large stone. 'I'm here, come down now,' he'd bark.

'But wait, I can't leave yet because —'

He'd hung up on me.

Every day, I was torn. I didn't want to risk raised eyebrows from my colleagues for leaving before they did and I was terrified that Lisa would see me scampering to the lift and think I wasn't committed to my job.

The alternative was equally hideous. If I kept Charlie waiting for more than a couple of minutes, he would explode as soon as I got into the car. My car. Filled with petrol I had paid for.

'Where the fuck have you been?' he'd rage. I'd calmly try to explain that I couldn't just bolt out the door as soon as he called but this only made him more angry. I learned that the best way to deal with it was to just shut up and shrink into my seat.

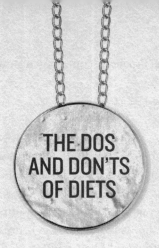

THE DOS
AND DON'TS
OF DIETS

Voicemail to Charlie from me:

'Charlie, I'm at the airport, have you forgotten to pick me up?
It's 11.45 and I'm waiting outside ... should I get a cab? Call me,
will you?'

One of my early responsibilities, soon after I started at *Cleo*, was
to help produce the annual diet special. This was a 'best-of'
compilation of the hottest diets the magazine had published
during the year and — sadly — it was always a bumper-selling
issue.

I say sadly because even then, publishing diets made me
uncomfortable. I've always thought they were evil. Perhaps this is
because I was never able to stick to one. Or maybe because in
my teens I saw so many girls torture themselves trying to follow
some kind of punishing food regime. A few of them tumbled
from dieting into eating disorders as issues of food, control and
body image twisted around in their minds.

But I had nothing concrete to support my gut feeling that
publishing diets was wrong. The first year, I just shut up and did
as I was told, putting my amateur opinions to one side and

carefully retyping the year's hottest diets into the new compilation feature.

There were some doozies in there including the Fish Diet, the Fruit Diet and my personal fave, the Drop A Dress Size By Saturday diet — which, as you may imagine, required fairly extreme measures to execute. Would you like some stir-fried air with that?

The second year, when diet-book time rolled around, I went to the features editor with my concerns. 'I think these diets are terrible,' I told her earnestly. 'In fact I think all diets are terrible. You have to practically starve yourself to drop lots of weight quickly and you just end up putting it back on anyway. Most girls can't stick to them and it makes them feel even worse about themselves.'

I paused to draw breath, unsure whether to continue. How far could I push it?

'All that stuff about calories just makes girls obsessed with food — in a bad way. And it makes them feel terrible about their bodies. Shouldn't we be trying to encourage them to treat food as food and not numbers?'

My arguments were simplistic, unscientific, personal and emotional. More importantly, they completely ignored the fundamental principle of commercial publishing: give readers what they want, not what you think they should have. And how do you know what they want? By watching circulation.

The circulation of the diet-book issue was always up on the average, which proved conclusively that I didn't know what I was talking about. Women wanted diets. In my passionate naïvety, I didn't understand that editors couldn't use their magazines to push their personal beliefs — not if those beliefs were in direct opposition to the bottom line.

A magazine is a business, not a community service announcement. And the objective of that business is to make money, not push a wheelbarrow or launch a crusade. In the future, I would come to better appreciate the difficulty editors sometimes face in balancing their private views with what they know will sell.

It was too late to drop the feature that year — it had already been promoted in previous issues and advertising pages had been booked around it — but by the following year it was significantly reduced in size and emphasis. The year after that it was gone.

I'd like to think this was due to my convincing speeches (of which I made several more), but in reality it was probably because it no longer spiked sales. Like any editorial gimmick, crash diets lost their potency in the nineties after being wheeled out enough times. They'd be back.

At home, even my job was the cause of argument and angst between Charlie and me. I was sometimes assigned to interview male models or celebrities and to help compile the annual eligible bachelor list. And although I carefully tried to hide these assignments from Charlie, knowing the reaction they'd provoke, he'd invariably pick up a copy of *Cleo* lying around at home, see my by-line on an interview with, say, Julian McMahon and accuse me of using my job as a way to meet men. Oh yes, that's why I'd chosen to work at a women's magazine as a beauty editor. To meet men.

One time, I was sent around Australia as a judge in a model competition for a week. My head was in such a mess by then — about nine months into our relationship — that I spent the trip desperate to come home.

My plane landed at 11 am on a Sunday morning and since I'd been travelling back from Perth straight from a shoot, I'd carefully packed a change of clothes for the last hour of the flight so I could arrive looking nice. I crammed myself into the aeroplane toilet and got changed into my new outfit. Did my hair. Put on make-up. I was excited to see him.

I've always loved an airport reunion and as I walked to the baggage area, I looked around expectantly for Charlie, imagining a big hug and a smiling face.

But he wasn't there. I tried his mobile but it was switched off. No answer at home either. So I sat on my bag outside the airport like a backpacker and I waited. An hour and a half later, he turned up, ambling towards the terminal, looking like hell. No apology.

'What happened?' I asked, my anticipatory buzz already dead, replaced by a deep disappointment.

'Look, don't hassle me, okay?' he snapped. 'We had a gig last night and then I went out and had a huge one. Everyone came back to our place and I didn't get to sleep until six this morning.'

'But you knew I was arriving at eleven …' I said plaintively.

'Fucking give me a break, will you?' he exploded. 'I'm here, aren't I? And I'm bloody exhausted, all right?'

I was shattered. He had no money to pay for the parking so I had to go back into the airport, find an ATM and withdraw some cash.

I was silent during the drive. When we arrived home, though, we had a screaming argument and I fled to my parents' house because I was so desperate for someone to be pleased to see me. But I didn't tell them what had happened with Charlie. I never did. I wasn't yet ready to be told I should leave.

GREENER GRASS
AND
CUSTOMS DOGS

Voicemail to me from a headhunter:

'Yes, hello. This is a message for Mia Freedman. My name is Josh Bradley and I'm calling about a potential job opportunity. Would you be able to give me a call back so we could discuss it further?'

With my home life so messy, *Cleo* was my refuge. I was still very young and fiercely ambitious. I was also impatient. So when a rival publisher approached me about the editor's job at *Girlfriend* magazine, I was excited. We had a few secret meetings and I thrillingly mulled over the prospect of being an editor at twenty-one. It was tempting. Lisa had become editor of *Dolly* at twenty-one. I was keen to do the same. Competitive — me?

Ego fought with pragmatism. The idea of saying I was an editor and actually being one? Being the boss of a magazine? With my own staff? That was a sexy proposition. But compared to *Cleo*, teen mags weren't the main game, they were off-Broadway.

Could I still reach my goal of editing *Cleo* at twenty-five if I diverted to the teen market first? Possibly. I'd have a few years of editing experience on my CV by then, which would help. Or would it? I hadn't been at *Cleo* very long but I knew I had so much more to learn if I was to lay proper foundations and be a successful editor at any magazine.

Still, I was torn. As negotiations with the other publisher intensified, I knew I had to tell Lisa. Also, I wanted to impress her with the news that I'd been offered an editorship. To my surprise, she made a counter offer.

'We've been thinking of doing *Cleo* in New Zealand. Would you be interested in moving there to edit it?'

New Zealand? Like the teen market, New Zealand was away from the main game, even though I'd be able to keep working closely with the brand I still felt so connected to. It was an invaluable opportunity to launch an established magazine in a new country. Even I could see that. But I wasn't convinced.

'Why don't you go over for a few days to see what you think and meet the team?' Lisa suggested.

'Let me think about it over the weekend,' I replied and went straight home and told Charlie. He responded to the idea of me moving to New Zealand by withdrawing emotionally and I responded by scampering after him.

'Come with me to Auckland for a few days,' I urged. 'We'll make a holiday of it. I'll pay for everything.'

He agreed and a week later we were at the airport.

Small problem, Charlie didn't know how he'd survive four days without dope. By now he was seriously addicted although he'd never have admitted it and I didn't dare point out the obvious.

An hour before our flight was due to leave, Charlie was crouched behind a car in the airport car park, sucking back deeply on a joint. It was enough to get him onto the plane and through the two-hour flight. He was still pretty mellow when we arrived in Auckland.

At the baggage claim, we noticed a couple of customs dogs sniffing passengers and luggage. We giggled about how funny it would be if they bounded over to us. And then they did.

While Charlie stood laughing in disbelief, one of the beagles began sniffing around his crotch. My giggle disappeared as it occurred to me we were in deep shit. Quickly, an airport official came over and discreetly yet firmly ushered us away from the baggage carousel. 'Are you carrying any illegal substances?' he inquired of Charlie quietly. 'No!' Charlie exclaimed.

The official briskly instructed us to collect our bags and then join a small queue away from the main customs lines. As we waited, Charlie put his hand in his pocket and discovered a tiny stray bit of marijuana from his pre-flight joint. 'Oh fuck,' he murmured and tried to discreetly drop it on the floor.

Having seen something suspicious through the one-way mirrors opposite where we were standing, another official soon appeared and took Charlie away for questioning. I was left alone to have our bags searched and consider how the hell I would explain this disaster to Lisa. After about fifteen minutes, Charlie returned, having been strip-searched. He had nothing on him — he wasn't that stupid — but he was a bit shaken and now strung out on adrenaline.

As our bags were painstakingly checked, he started babbling to the customs official. 'We've been sent here by Kerry Packer, you know. My girlfriend works for ACP and she's here for a job interview.'

I wanted to die. After I killed him.

The inspection finished and we were allowed to go. As we walked through the gates, now two hours past our expected arrival time, I caught sight of someone from ACP's New Zealand office waiting to greet us. 'Don't say a word about what just happened,' I hissed to Charlie, mortified.

'Guess what? We just got searched for drugs!' was the first thing out of his mouth. My colleague blanched visibly.

The next few days went steadily downhill, if that was possible from the starting point of a strip-search. Without dope, Charlie became increasingly agitated. His nervous energy — which he usually calmed with a cone, or three — had nowhere to go and while I had meetings at the office, he climbed the walls.

Not surprisingly, I didn't take the job. I think I'd already made my decision before boarding the plane and that's probably why I took Charlie with me. I wanted to make sure I wouldn't be seduced by my Auckland trip — I knew ACP New Zealand would make the job seem as attractive as possible — and with Charlie along for the ride, it was always going to be a disaster. I wasn't ready to move there and launch *Cleo*, but I was conflicted because the offer was an amazing opportunity. So I used my floundering relationship to sabotage it.

I didn't want the *Girlfriend* job either. I wanted to stay working closely with Lisa and my other mentors and learn more before making the leap to editor.

So two years after starting at *Cleo*, in the space of two months, I had been offered two incredible jobs and turned them both down. Somehow, I had not managed to convert either of these opportunities into more money or even a promotion. After all the excitement and flattery, it was business as usual at my small brown desk in the ugly brown features office. Part of me was relieved. Part of me was deflated. But I never regretted either decision.

The best thing about my New Zealand experience was that it marked the beginning of the end for Charlie and me. Back home, it continued to deteriorate until I realised I wasn't in love with him. I never had been. It had taken me more than a year to understand the difference between passion and abuse — although

I still didn't call it that. The fact I cried so often didn't mean it was deep and complex; it meant that it was destructive and ugly.

On paper, there was no reason not to end it. The apartment lease was mine. The car was mine. My friends and family were behind me. He had none of that.

Ironically, this made dumping him harder. I felt sorry for him. How would he support himself financially? How would he cope emotionally? Where would he live? The band's gigs weren't leading to anything substantial, and I knew he'd be devastated if he had to move back with his parents in Brisbane. So I put his wellbeing before my own and sucked it up for a few months more, waiting for an escape route to present itself.

A couple of months before Christmas, an opportunity arose for the band to travel to London. There had been a sniff from a record company who thought they had potential and wanted them to start touring in Europe to build up a following. It was an open-ended trip with the possibility of Charlie staying away as long as a year — longer if things worked out.

His physical presence and personality were so forceful that I felt powerless to end the relationship while we were living together. But I knew if I had some mental and physical space, I'd have a chance to close the door behind him permanently. So I encouraged him to go.

At first, he was suspicious. 'Are you trying to get rid of me? Is there someone else you're waiting to jump on the second I'm gone?' But I promised to visit in a couple of months and repeatedly reassured him that this was an amazing opportunity. 'You should grab it with both hands,' I said. Which of course he was always going to do, with or without my blessing.

I lied, telling him my lease was up and I'd be moving in with my friend Karen for a while. 'It might be a good idea if you put your stuff into storage while you're gone,' I suggested. He bought it.

And so he left. Suddenly I could breathe again. Within days of him boarding that plane, I could feel my strength returning. He phoned me regularly and I'm sure he sensed the change in my voice each time we spoke as I pulled away.

After a month, I told him it was over. His response was far easier to deal with across a different time zone. I no longer had his anger in my face, his clothes in my cupboard or his bong on my coffee table.

He called me at all hours, sometimes in tears, sometimes shouting, always begging for another chance. But once that door in my head had closed, there was no possibility of it opening again. As insurance, I began to cautiously tell my friends and family the truth about Charlie. I knew once they understood what the relationship had been like, they'd stop me if I ever tried to go back.

It's strange but when I did see him again — he came home to visit his family six months later — all the power he'd once had over me had evaporated. I wasn't scared or intimidated any more. It was over and I was relieved.

And then I was angry. The emotion was overwhelming and refused to dissipate. I was furious with him for being an arsehole and with myself for letting him treat me like shit. All the anger I'd never allowed myself to feel when we were together came bubbling up to the surface. Along with it came bitterness. Bitterness that I'd allowed such a destructive situation to continue for almost two years. And for what? Bong-water stains on my carpet?

Thank God for Alanis. She understood. One of the best parts of this break-up was my timing. It was the early nineties and *Jagged Little Pill* had just been released. Alanis Morissette's rage-fuelled album of vengeful anthems was empowering.

Jagged Little Pill was my soundtrack and solace in the months after the break-up. I played it so much it virtually embedded itself in my DNA. The shouty angst propelled me through the impossibly complicated tangle of my emotions and out the other side. The anger faded and I became simply sad for the person I'd been in those two years.

It took me a long time to understand this, but my relationship with Charlie was an extremely valuable one because it helped me calibrate what I was looking for in a partner. It taught me what I didn't want. What I wouldn't accept. What love didn't look like.

Had I not obliterated fantasy about the allure of the bad boy by experiencing its full destructive power, I never would have appreciated my next relationship for what it was: the best thing that had ever happened to me.

BREAKING UP WITH BEAUTY

Voicemail to Kim from me:

'Hi Kim, it's Mia calling again. I just wanted to say thanks so much for what you did with the shoes. I do feel dreadful about that. I hope you didn't get into any trouble because of me. Anyway, I also had an interesting idea I'd love to talk to you about. My job! Do you want it?'

'If I have to go to one more beauty launch I'm going to impale myself on a mascara wand,' I announced dramatically as I plonked into a chair across the desk from my boss. 'I swear, Lisa, I cannot stand it for another single second!'

Two years of beauty had taken their toll. I was over it.

She smiled indulgently at my theatrics. She knew this day would come. If you really want to be an editor, you tire of the beauty gig fairly quickly. Two years is maximum tenure before you become stuck, typecast, dizzy from champagne and fragrance fumes.

More importantly, I'd run out of space to stash beauty products at home. As a beauty editor you receive a truly obscene amount of stuff. Every day there would be at least half a dozen courier deliveries. As if the products themselves were not enough, PR companies would try to give their client an edge by sending a gift with the beauty products. Not to be photographed, just for the beauty editor to keep.

A range of make-up with an urban theme might come with an iPod or half a dozen CDs. A Valentine's Day lipstick collection might come with a huge vase full of white Lindt balls. A winter skincare range might be wrapped snugly in a pale blue pashmina. It was endless and excessive.

Beauty editors have lockable cupboards near their desks full of products they've been sent. They choose which ones to photograph for their beauty pages and then they're supposed to put everything back in the cupboard to distribute among the staff at one of the regular 'beauty sales' that happen every few months. Everyone pays a token fee, say ten dollars, and gets to take home hundreds of dollars worth of gear.

Of course, by sale time, the beauty editor has already taken home all the best stash for herself. I did. Some magazines use their beauty sales to raise money for charity or for their Christmas parties. At *Cleo*, we used it to sponsor a child from overseas. The contrast between the image of the sweet little brown-faced boy we'd stuck up on the communal fridge and the lavish superficiality of the beauty industry would sometimes make my brain hurt. But then I'd be distracted with yet another delivery from the courier dock. More flowers? More eye cream?

Sharing the cramped office with me and the beauty cupboard were three other staff including Wendy, *Cleo*'s features editor. Since arriving at *Cleo* via *Elle* magazine, where she'd done a brief beauty stint, she'd become an important mentor as well as a friend.

We'd bonded one day while at the launch of a new skincare

range. As we sat in front of yet another plate of poached salmon, watching yet another interminable presentation and hearing the 'scientific evidence' that this cream would change our lives, Wendy nudged me and whispered, 'Isn't all this stuff just Sorbolene in fancy packaging?' I stifled a giggle. Then the voice-over on the video intoned gravely, 'Every facial expression you make — every frown, every smile — is creating more lines on your face.'

'Note to self,' Wendy whispered. 'Must stop making facial expressions. Will appear boring and vacuous but youthful.' That was it. I loved her. So I was excited when Lisa appointed her features editor soon afterwards and plonked her next to me permanently. Having begun her career in newspapers, I learned so much from Wendy about writing and journalism, and how they could occasionally co-exist within the beauty gig.

A few months after arriving at *Cleo*, she gave me a wake-up call after overhearing me talking on the phone to a beauty PR.

'Mia, you really must get out of beauty,' she said when I hung up. 'Do you have any idea how insincere you just sounded?'

I looked at her blankly.

'The moment you picked up the phone you started talking in this fake sing-song beauty voice. It was awful. You don't want to be that person.'

She was right, I didn't. I hated fake beauty me. And there are only so many times you can arrange your face into an expression of rapt amazement while someone in a pretend lab coat gives a PowerPoint presentation about the revolutionary addition of free radicals to a neck cream. I never understood what free radicals were, anyway. And frankly, I didn't give a rat's.

All this I explained to Lisa and she listened calmly, as she always did. 'Okay,' she said finally, when I'd run out of rant, 'how about I make you lifestyle editor and you can start writing more features, move away from beauty and learn more about how the magazine is put together —'

'Yes!' I interrupted, beaming.

'One thing, though,' she smiled. 'You have to help me find a beauty editor to replace you before you get your promotion.'

'Done!' I promised, bouncing out of her office, straight to my phone. I was a girl on a mission. And the first person I thought of was Kim. There was no one else. She was perfect.

I'd known Kim socially for a couple of years through the industry and our paths had crossed again just recently. She was working as a fashion PR and a few weeks earlier I'd had to call her to apologise for losing a pair of shoes I'd borrowed to photograph for one of my pages. She could have been a bitch about it but instead was very kind. 'Don't worry,' she'd reassured me as I grovelled. 'I'll sort it out.'

I knew Kim used to work in magazines before PR and had been a PA to a couple of important editors. On the off-chance she'd be interested in returning to magazines, I asked if she wanted to apply for my job. She did. Lisa loved her and within a few weeks Kim was installed alongside me and Wendy in the small brown office.

Kim was incredibly glamorous — always immaculately dressed for work and perfectly groomed. I tried hard to work a look but 'try-hard' was exactly how I came across. Fashion just wasn't in my DNA like it was in Kim's.

She was a natural at beauty, had a prodigious talent for styling beauty shoots and quickly became a far better beauty editor than I'd ever been.

Like my other friends and workmates, she wasn't fond of Charlie and she'd been dismayed to see the effect he'd had on me. I tried to hide it but we worked two metres apart and even when she managed not to overhear my tense phone conversations with him, she couldn't miss the part where I was in tears afterwards.

She and Wendy were instrumental in encouraging me to kick his arse to the kerb and they were delighted when I finally did. How appropriate then that they were both witnesses to what would happen next.

USING CARAMELLO KOALAS TO OPEN DOORS

Voicemail to Kim from me:

'The Caramello Koalas worked. I have a meeting with Bernie Leser tomorrow at 3 pm. Could I really live in New York? Poppy King's here at the moment and we've been hanging out. She wants to move here too. I'll try to catch you tomorrow to fill you in on my meeting.'

The closer I'd risen towards my dream job of editing *Cleo*, the more disillusioned I'd become. From that first moment I'd sat in Lisa Wilkinson's office for my work-experience interview, I'd known, just KNOWN, that I'd be the editor of *Cleo* before I turned twenty-five. It was destined.

Such unshakable arrogance was perhaps unremarkable for a nineteen-year-old, but for a few years, it looked like I might be right. My rise through the magazine ranks at *Cleo* had been relatively swift. I'd been promoted from work experience to beauty writer to beauty editor to lifestyle editor to features editor within the space of five years. I'd risen from unpaid serf to one of the most senior roles on the magazine. And then, quite unexpectedly, everything stalled.

Pregnant with her second child, Lisa decided to leave *Cleo* permanently. Her first son was not yet two and she was about to have another baby. After ten years as the magazine's most successful editor, it was time. The end of an era. She was done.

As we prepared to farewell Lisa, the new editor was announced. It was Wendy, at the time *Cleo*'s deputy editor. When Lisa called the staff together to make the announcement, I was happy. Wendy's elevation cleared the next rung on my own ladder. I was going to be deputy editor.

So I was puzzled and annoyed that Lisa didn't announce my promotion at the same time she announced Wendy's. It was obvious, wasn't it? If number two was moving up to number one, then as number three I was in line for the number-two job. Right? Wrong. Wrongity wrong.

The hierarchy of magazines is not like a bank queue where the next person in line automatically steps up. Just because you're good at your job, it doesn't mean you have the right skills or personality to do the one above you when it becomes available. Even if you do, there's probably someone who can do it better.

Correctly, Lisa allowed Wendy to choose her own deputy, and right away my friend warned me that I might be disappointed. 'You and I are too alike,' she explained as I sulked and fumed. 'Our strengths are too similar. I need someone who can complement me and do things I don't want to do.'

There was another crucial reason she didn't promote me. She thought I wasn't ready. This was hard to hear and impossible to believe. You need more experience in features,' she explained. 'You have to do the time. It's too soon.'

I was so gutted to have my ambitions thwarted, I could barely look at her as she spoke but I've always remembered her advice. 'As an editor, you have to be able to commission writers and if you haven't had enough experience writing features yourself and editing other people's, the writers won't respect you and you'll do a lousy job.' Of course Wendy was right, although I couldn't accept it at the time.

Soon afterwards, when she appointed someone from newspapers to be *Cleo*'s deputy, I had a tantrum and threatened to resign. 'Please don't,' she urged me. 'I know you don't want to hear this but I'm doing you a favour. One day you'll be an editor and you'll be commissioning me. I'm just trying to help you build those foundations properly.'

She was right about that too, although it didn't stop me feeling humiliated and pissed off. Eventually, I got over it. The new deputy was a journalist who really did have different strengths from Wendy and me — the key one being an attention to detail that was vital in a good deputy. I learned an enormous amount from both her and Wendy.

It was a rough year for Wendy who never sat comfortably in the editor's chair. She was not a *Cleo* girl and had never had aspirations to edit it. She had been conscripted into the role almost against her will. She was particularly uncomfortable with being the public face of *Cleo* and — unlike most editors today who cultivate their public profiles as part of their jobs — she cringed every time she saw her photo on the editor's letter page.

One month, a decision was taken to give away a condom with every issue but it couldn't be stuck on the cover due to censorship restrictions. So it went inside the magazine, on the editor's page.

Unfortunately, when the magazines were stacked into piles, the weight caused many of the condom packets to burst open. The first we knew of this was a shriek coming from Wendy's office. We rushed in to find her with a newly printed issue open on her desk at her ed's letter. 'Look! There's a condom on my face!' she wailed. And there was. When the plastic packaging burst, the condom slid on its lubricant across the page and onto Wendy's face.

Just another day at the office.

A few months later, when Wendy announced she was leaving *Cleo* to edit another magazine, for a brief and hopeful moment I wondered if I might be appointed the next editor.

Nope. ACP decided to bring home the Australian editor of Singapore *Cleo* to do the job. That was it for me. In an instant, I knew I was done. The new editor was about my age and had never worked on Australian *Cleo*. I felt humiliated and infuriated all over again. The disappointment was crushing. My dream was flushed away.

This time, I did resign. At one emotional and irrational point I decided to abandon my magazine career altogether and go work for the RSPCA. It was the furthest thing I could think of from my ambitions to edit *Cleo*. 'Hey, I love animals,' I reasoned. 'Animals won't fuck me over like the magazine industry.'

With Lisa and Wendy gone, I'd lost my mentors and the magic years I'd had at my favourite magazine were well and truly over. As I worked out my three-month notice period, the new editor tried to talk me into staying on as her deputy, but I wasn't interested.

Instead, I decided I was going to move to New York and get a job in magazines over there. 'That will teach them!' I thought spitefully, although who 'them' was was never clear, even to me.

Anyway, I was twenty-three, single and had no anchor embedded in Australia that would preclude me from heading to the magazine capital of the world. I'd almost done it before. Two years earlier I'd gone to New York by myself to explore the idea and had taken a portfolio of my *Cleo* work. The head of America's biggest glossy magazine company, Condé Nast, was an Australian called Bernie Leser, and while I was there I'd taken a chance and hand-delivered my portfolio to his office — unannounced — along with a handful of Caramello Koalas and a letter of introduction.

Impressed by my chutzpah or perhaps just nostalgic for Australian chocolate, Mr Leser had his secretary call me up the next day and invite me in for a meeting. I told him I wanted to work in New York and named the magazines I believed I was best suited to. He organised for me to meet with the head of HR, who in turn organised meetings at *Allure*, *Glamour* and *Self* magazines and sent me to see an immigration lawyer.

The message was the same from everyone. There was a good chance I'd secure a job but I had to be there, on the ground, living in New York with the right visa. It couldn't be done from Australia. I had to take a leap and make the move before anyone would offer me work.

At the time, I hadn't been ready to take the risk and move to New York. Now I was. So I resigned from *Cleo* and made plans to go.

At my farewell dinner at a Thai restaurant, Lisa came along to give the speech. I was chuffed. 'Mia is a lot like a puppy,' she said. 'She's full of enthusiasm and energy but every so often she'll get over-excited and jump on the furniture and wee on the carpet.'

I laughed a lot. It was a good night. I had *Cleo* closure. I was ready to make my name in New York.

ENTER CUPID

Voicemail to me from Kim:

'Hi, it's 4.30 and this shoot is so bloody boring I'm ready to top myself. I think the model is bulimic. She keeps running to the toilet and has really bad breath. And her eyes keep watering which is pissing off the make-up artist because he has to keep re-doing her mascara. The photographer keeps saying, "Don't worry, we'll fix it later with Photoshop," but I really don't see the point in fixing everything later; I want to fix it now. Oh wait, the model's boyfriend just turned up — or is it her drug dealer? Oh God, just let this be over. Anyway, I can't remember if I told you about lunch on Sunday. Casual at our place. Just a few people. I think you'll know everyone. Karen is coming. And Andy. Bring a cossie. I'd better go. The photographer's assistant is cracking on to my work-experience girl and she's only fourteen. Speak tomorrow.'

Having just emancipated myself from Charlie and the worst relationship of my life, I wasn't looking to jump into a new one. Or was I? Being single has never been my natural state, it's true. I wasn't great on my own.

One weekend, Kim and her boyfriend decided to have a

Sunday barbecue and invited me along. I knew most of the people there, except for one.

I was sitting in the garden when Jason arrived. I looked up and saw him standing on the balcony. He seemed instantly familiar. I knew we'd never met and that I'd never seen him before but it felt uncannily like I had.

When it came time to eat lunch, he sat next to me and our conversation was easy and natural. My usual style when attracted to someone was to try too hard. I'd make a big effort to sparkle and be sexy; I'd flirt self-consciously and become intensely aware of every word and gesture.

With Jason, it could not have been more different. It didn't occur to me to flirt or try hard, nor was I aware of him flirting with me. I simply felt happy and relaxed, two things I'd never associated with burgeoning attraction. I do remember noticing how grounded he was, how quietly confident and comfortable in his own skin.

After lunch, we all jumped in the pool and the afternoon passed in a delightful, mellow mix of swimming and talking and eating. When it was time to leave, Jason and a guy we both knew said they were going to the movies and asked if I wanted to join them.

For an instant, the goat in me wanted to return to my track. I'd planned to go home and eat my comfort food of corn, tuna and rice in front of '60 Minutes'. Because I was so often 'on' in social situations, I needed to retreat frequently to the sanctuary of solitude. But something in me that day said 'fuck it', and to them I said, 'Sure, why not?' We went to see some gangster film and it felt very natural sitting next to Jason while we munched on popcorn together.

Still, I didn't really think about him that next week, which was also unusual for me. Normally, I'd try to engineer another meeting or analyse to death if, when and how he might call.

The following Friday night, my friend Karen asked me to come with her to a party. We went for a drink somewhere first and for reasons I can't remember we were both grumpy. We then proceeded to bitch and snark and grumble and complain our way through the evening.

We arrived at the party around 10 pm. 'I just want to go home; I'm over tonight,' I whined.

'One drink and we'll go,' Karen promised.

'All right, but I've got to get away from this bloody music,' I shouted, making my way towards some couches. The first person I saw was Jason. He came straight over and led me to a quiet corner. And suddenly, I didn't want to go home any more.

A few hours later, we left the party together and he dropped me home in a cab.

I woke up the next morning thinking about him. We still hadn't even exchanged phone numbers but I knew he could get mine from Kim in a second.

Sure enough, later that afternoon he called me and invited me out to dinner. After that, we pretty much moved in together.

My relationship with Jason was unlike anything I'd experienced before. Naturally, it was intense and fast. That's the only way I know how to do things. And he seemed equally smitten. Our pace and infatuation was in sync. Imagine that. But still, it was just so different from my other relationships.

'He has a car!' I marvelled to my friends. 'And a wallet! And a job!' I hadn't dated a guy in years who had any, let alone all, of these things. One thing Jason didn't seem to have was a bong. Was this possible? Indeed it was.

I kept waiting for the catch but it never came. Our relationship was healthy and supportive. We were equally matched financially, intellectually and socially — we were both past the partying stage and happy to stay home. We were ambitious and close to our families.

Within a month, our delighted parents had organised to meet each other for lunch. Our friends thought this was hilarious. Some of them had been together for years before their parents met.

We seemed to be a great match. He was supportive of my career, interested in my friends, keen to meet my family. Within a month or two, his lease ended and we moved in together at my place. He was wary about this because he was very independent, but it seemed like the most sensible option and we were dying to live together. He did it on the proviso that he'd be paying for everything — bills, groceries, going out. This was new. I'd always been the responsible one, the nurturer. Who knew it was possible to have a mutually supportive and equal partnership?

The physical, mental and emotional connection between Jason and me was extreme. I was giddy. In love. Deliriously happy. Besotted. Secure.

So it was hardly a surprise when we bought our first house together. We'd known each other less than a year.

DOING INTERVIEWS IN MY PYJAMAS

Voicemail message to Tracey Cox, 'sexpert' and friend, from me:

'Trace, help. Major dilemma. Only you can understand. I need to workshop my life over coffee. Any chance you're free this arvo?'

'What should I do?' I asked my friend Tracey over a berry muffin and a cappuccino. 'Really, what should I do?' It was an insane question. I'd just been offered the editorship of *Cosmopolitan*. And I was dithering. It's rarely easy being a Libran when you're faced with a decision, but even for me this should have been a no-brainer.

The correct answer, of course, was 'grab it with both hands you silly moron', but Tracey was circumspect, which is why I'd sought her counsel. She'd been *Cosmo*'s deputy editor but had left two years previously to concentrate on a new career as an author. Better than anyone, I thought, she could understand my reticence at the idea of going back into That Building and climbing back on the magazine treadmill so soon after jumping off it.

Now that I'd fallen in love and had no immediate intention of moving to New York, I was freelance feature writing for a handful of women's magazines including *Marie Claire*, *New Woman*, *NW* and *Cleo*. I had lots of work and after five years cooped up in a windowless office, I was relishing the freedom of working from home. Sort of.

I began with excellent intentions and a strict set of rules. No daytime television. No spending the day in pyjamas. No bare feet.

My fear about working from home was that it would turn me into a sloth and a slob. With no one to see me and fairly loose deadlines, it was highly likely. To counter this possibility, I made myself go to the gym each morning before returning home to shower, get dressed and blow-dry my hair. I put on make-up. And shoes. No 'Oprah'. I never went out for lunch or coffee because I was fearful I might never return to my desk.

This worked splendidly for a brief period. Soon enough, I was sleeping in and doing phone interviews for my articles from bed, sometimes with my eyes still shut, half asleep. This was bad. Also bad was my growing sense of isolation. It would be years before texting, email and the internet transformed the working-from-home experience. I was lonely. 'This would be a great lifestyle if I had a baby,' I thought most days. 'But since I don't, I'm just a bit … bored.'

Once the novelty of not sitting in an office all day wore off, I discovered being at home alone all day made me a bit crazy. Life as a freelancer was more precarious than full-time employment and was a breeding ground for insecurity. I was terrified to say no to any commission in case I never worked again. When I'd submit a feature idea and didn't hear back immediately — or sometimes at all — I'd become paranoid that the features editor hated it. And me. Invariably, it was just at the bottom of her in-tray and she didn't have time to call me and discuss it. Magazine people are busy and don't have time to stroke fragile freelance egos.

All my friends were busy too — at work. They envied me for being my own boss but I was lonely at home which made me needy. When Jason arrived back from the office each evening, I'd greet him at the door. 'What happened at work? Who did you see? What did you do next? Where did you have lunch? What did you eat? Then what happened?'

I was desperate for information and conversation. For stimulation. For company. He was desperate for a little space so he could breathe at the end of a stressful day. It wasn't an ideal combination.

Overwhelmingly, I felt like I'd stopped running before I'd reached the finish line — the finish line being my ambition to become an editor. I was only twenty-four. Had I given up too easily?

And then the new *Cleo* editor — having agreed to pay me a certain amount for a regular monthly feature — tried to cut my word rate. This infuriated me and provided the impetus I needed to go see the editor of *Cosmo* about doing some freelance work for her.

For the first few months after leaving *Cleo*, this would have been inconceivable because I was fiercely loyal to the magazine I'd lived and breathed and loved and reluctantly left. After all those years of intense competition with *Cosmo*, it was hard to shake the sentiment that they were the enemy. Until *Cleo* fucked me over and suddenly, the enemy looked rather appealing.

I went in to *Cosmo* expecting to talk about possibly becoming a regular contributor and came out with a job offer to be the editor.

The current editor, Pat Ingram, had been looking to replace herself for some time. She'd edited *Cosmo* for many years and was taking on more responsibility with a new role as Editor-in-Chief of several of ACP's women's magazines. She told me she'd followed my work over the years I'd been at *Cleo*. 'You know I'm looking for an editor,' she said casually, after we'd been chatting for a few minutes. 'What do you think?' We'd clicked straight away — she was warm and smart and motherly — but her question absolutely floored me. In my myopic mission to edit *Cleo* before I turned twenty-five, I had totally missed the fact there was an almost identical magazine in the same company with a vacant editor's chair. Duh.

'I'm not really interested,' I said quickly, without thinking. 'I've just left ACP after five years and I'm not looking to come back right now.' What I didn't tell her was how much I'd loved *Cleo*. How my heart had been broken by *Cleo*. How it hadn't occurred to me to jump into another relationship, I mean job.

If Pat was surprised by my response, she didn't show it. Well within her rights to say 'Get out, you arrogant little shit,' instead she kept chatting with me about the two magazines, commissioned all the features I'd pitched to her and suggested I stay in touch.

At home over the next few days, thinking about it more, it slowly dawned on me that I was nuts. I was being offered an incredible opportunity, one I arguably wasn't even ready for. Editor of *Cosmopolitan*. And I'd turned it down flat. So I called Pat and asked if we could have another chat about it. We did. And then I called Tracey.

'Here's what you need to do when you can't make a decision about something,' she advised while spooning sugar into her long black. 'Think to yourself, "Yes, I'm definitely taking the job," and see which emotions immediately come up. Do you feel excited? Sick? Trapped? Happy? Spend half the day thinking that you're going to do it and monitor how that makes you feel. Then, say to yourself, "No, I'm definitely not taking the job," and see how you feel about that. It's a great way to cut through all the surface shit and get in touch with your base emotions, your gut.'

It was genius. And it worked. When I thought about taking it I felt scared but excited. The idea of not taking the job made me feel slightly relieved but predominantly disappointed. I talked it through endlessly with my close friends Jo, Jen and Karen, and I confided in Wendy and Kim. Do it, they all urged. Why wouldn't you?

Jason was also supportive. One hundred per cent behind me. I imagined briefly how Charlie would have reacted in the same situation, how threatened he would have felt, and I was reminded yet again that this relationship was the happiest and healthiest I'd ever had.

So I said yes, and Pat and I agreed on a start date. Two months before my twenty-fifth birthday. Ha! By finally loosening my hands from around the throat of my dream to edit *Cleo* by twenty-five, I'd made space for a slightly different dream to come true. As it turned out, this one was far better.

AND THEN SHE CALLED ME PUSSYCAT

Voicemail to Wendy from me:

'Hi, it's me! I just met Helen Gurley Brown and OH. MY. GOD. You have no idea. She's unbelievable. Will fill you in on every detail when I'm home. Do you want anything duty free? Anything except cigarettes. When are you going to quit that disgusting habit?'

I was about to be crowned the new editor of Australian *Cosmo* — only the third in its thirty-year history. However, before I could officially be presented with my sash and my staff, I had to pass one important test. I had to meet *Cosmo*'s founder, the iconic Helen Gurley Brown.

Currently, *Cosmopolitan* has fifty-eight international editions, is printed in thirty-four languages and is distributed in more than one hundred countries with seventy-eight million readers globally. And like most of the international editions, Australian *Cosmo* is a joint venture between the brand's owner and publisher, US media giant Hearst, and a local publisher, in this case Australian Consolidated Press.

Because we are voracious magazine readers, Australian *Cosmo* has the highest circulation per capita of any *Cosmopolitan* in the world and Hearst has always had an excellent business relationship with its Australian partners. Hearst had complete trust in my predecessor, Pat, and since she had chosen me as her replacement, I came well recommended. But I still had to be vetted by Hearst.

This meant flying to New York for two important interviews. The first was with the Vice President of Hearst International who quizzed me on what I thought about *Cosmopolitan* as a brand and where I might take it in Australia. I could talk about magazines under wet cement so that part was no problem.

Next, I was taken to meet Helen Gurley Brown. As the editor of US *Cosmo*, Helen didn't have direct control over editorial appointments on the international editions but in every other way, she *was Cosmopolitan*. She had literally invented it.

She was born in Arkansas some time around 1922 (it's hard to get a lock on her exact age) and started her working life as a secretary but shot to fame upon the release of her first book, the controversial *Sex and the Single Girl*. Helen was about forty years old when it was published in 1962 and the book became an instant bestseller. Full of advice for single girls, its most sensational premise was that a woman didn't need to be married to enjoy sex. In fact, she didn't need to be married at all.

It wasn't just the sex part that readers could relate to. They also identified with the idea of the 'mouseburger' as Helen called herself, a woman who had not been born rich or well connected, particularly clever or especially beautiful, but who had made it anyway, via hard work and determination.

Soon afterwards, Helen pitched the idea of a magazine for women to US publishers based on the messages of *Sex and the Single Girl* and was invited by Hearst to take over their ailing title *Cosmopolitan*. Her first issue appeared in July 1965, and Helen's philosophy for *Cosmo* was the same one she applied to her own life: self-improvement. What woman doesn't want a better relationship? Better sex? Better hair? A better job? A better wardrobe? A better body? *Cosmo* was the original self-help manual, decades before the genre would spawn Mars & Venus and Dr Phil. The *Cosmo* girl, as created by Helen, saw no conflict between loving men and being ambitious. She wanted to please men and herself. Deep-cleavage feminism, some called it. The formula worked.

Helen's *Cosmopolitan* would go on to become the most successful magazine in the world.

I knew virtually nothing of this impressive legacy as I waited outside Helen's office. My knowledge of Helen Gurley Brown was based on her more recent press, which had been equally controversial — and not for pushing socio-sexual boundaries in a good way.

Around the 1980s, Helen had begun to be seen by some not as a feminist pioneer but as someone worryingly retro in many of her views. In particular, that straight women couldn't contract HIV and that sexual harassment in the workplace was harmless fun.

There was also disquiet from some of Helen's contemporaries about the man-pleasing aspects of her *Cosmo* philosophy. Feminist icon Gloria Steinem told the *New York Times* in 1996: 'She deserves credit for having introduced sexuality into women's magazines — *Cosmo* was the first. But then it became the unliberated woman's survival kit, with advice on how to please a man, lover or boss in any circumstances, and also — in a metaphysical sense — how to smile all the time. The *Cosmo* girl needs to become a woman.'

There was some truth to this. The flip side to the empowerment message of self-improvement is that women's magazines like *Cosmo* are essentially sold on angst. The idea is that the mag tells you that you have a problem, and then helps you fix it. By perpetuating feelings of inadequacy, it cements its role in making you feel better. Helen had invented the formula and used it with wild success. Now it was my turn to take the *Cosmo* baton in Australia.

I was ushered into Helen's office, which could only be described as teenage girl's bedroom meets bordello. It was wall-to-wall leopard-print carpet with gilt-edged antiquey-looking furniture and a sofa decked in chintzy rose fabric. There was a stuffed lion, a teddy bear wearing a pearl necklace, and an embroidered cushion that said, 'Good girls go to heaven, bad girls go everywhere'.

While I was trying to take all of it in, a tiny bird-like creature stood up behind a small desk where she'd been obscured by a large typewriter. Helen.

As she skipped towards me — actually skipped — I felt my eyes widen. It was a visual riot.

Helen was wearing a black micro miniskirt and black fishnet stockings with black patent slingbacks. Her shirt was hot-pink satin with unbuttoned flashes of black lace bra underneath. And cleavage. She was wearing lots of very fancy gold jewellery and she was the size of my little finger. There was lots of make-up, artfully arranged brown hair and a face that was the disconcerting result of too much surgery.

In the future, she would happily talk to me — and anyone — about her facelifts and other procedures, even the breast implants she'd had in her late seventies. Her husband was not happy about those. 'He liked my bosoms,' she said fondly. 'He thought it was unnecessary.'

I'd never met an icon before and had no idea what to expect. Helen was the most charming and flirtatious person I'd ever met. As she blinked up at me from heavily made-up eyes, I felt like a large gargoyle. I am not a tall person — in fact, I am moderately sized — but Helen is a sparrow.

Her coquettish manner was instantly disarming as she shone the full light of her attention on me, and I quickly understood it was merely the window-dressing for an extremely sharp business brain. She was familiar with the Australian magazine market and asked me about *Cleo* and my time working there. She knew who Lisa Wilkinson was. She also wanted to know all about my personal life. Did I have a boyfriend? How long had we been together? And then she called me Pussycat.

'I don't have any children so you can be like my daughter, Pussycat,' she said as she gently steered me out of her office after about twenty minutes. I wasn't sure of the correct response. Should I purr? Rub myself against her legs? Clearly I'd made a good impression if she wanted to adopt me. Later, I'd learn that it was one of the standard lines she used with any editor under fifty. Still, I was chuffed. And, it seemed, anointed.

LET'S NOT TALK ABOUT SEX

Voicemail to Pat from me:

'Hi, sorry to call you on the weekend but I was just really keen to tell you about my new Cosmo *idea. It's about sex and relationships and I think it could be really amazing. I'll make a time to see you first thing on Monday to explain.'*

On my first day as editor of *Cosmo*, I noticed I was the youngest person there. By decades in some cases. I was a couple of months shy of my twenty-fifth birthday and my team of twenty staff ranged from mid twenties to late forties.

This should have made me nervous or self-conscious or possibly insecure. It didn't. The older I get, the more I realise I don't know. But back then? I thought I knew rather a lot. Everything, in fact. Gen Y didn't invent over-confidence, they merely picked up the baton when Gen X dropped it after growing up and realising there was an infinite amount more to learn.

My over-confidence got me into a lot of trouble that first year. I made many mistakes. Some were with staff. Like the way I blithely reassured a pregnant staffer, 'Sure, we'll work it out so you can go part time after the baby is born!' and then changed my mind when her daughter was a few months old. I had no idea at the time how much I'd messed with her life by being so cavalier about the terms of her employment. It was a disgraceful thing to do.

Other mistakes involved the magazine itself. Like deciding we should remove all the sex and relationship stories from *Cosmo* and toss them in the bin.

'All that stuff is so tired and old-fashioned,' I insisted to my boss with the supreme certainty of a twenty-four-year-old novice editor. 'So 1980s! Women are over it. We don't need to read about how to have a better orgasm or how to tell if he's about to dump you any more! Bor-ing!'

Regarding me carefully and no doubt thinking, 'Is this girl completely clueless?' Pat blinked a few times. Her out-loud response was a cautious green light. 'All right, let's give it a try but we'll have to watch sales very carefully.'

This clearly went against her better judgement because sex and relationships were the two most fundamental foundations of the *Cosmo* brand. Always have been. In every country of the world. Successfully. Australia included.

But since she'd hired me to ensure *Cosmo* stayed relevant to the next generation, she decided to listen to what I had to say and allow me to try some new things. Maybe, just maybe, I was right.

I was wrong. In what would turn out to be both my greatest strength and weakness as an editor, I was desperate to take *Cosmo* in a new, more modern direction. To position it away from its heritage. To make it different from *Cleo*. To reinvent the wheel.

With a huge, successful international brand of any kind, the key to remaining huge and successful is to change via evolution, not revolution. Don't scare the advertisers. Don't lose readers.

But I was impatient to make my mark and evolution sounded far too slow and dull. I wanted to prove I was a genius by making fast, flashy changes.

The lesson I learned was certainly fast: edit for your readers, not for yourself. How could I have forgotten this so quickly? Just because *I* was sick of reading sex and relationship stories (not helped by the fact I'd had to write so many of the bloody things over the previous five years), it didn't mean all *Cosmo* readers felt the same way. In fact, most of them felt exactly the opposite.

There was no denying I was nothing like my typical reader. I was settled and secure in a long-term relationship. And because I was in love, it made me immune to the angst upon which all sex and relationship stories are built. Most *Cosmo* readers were single and one of the main reasons they bought the magazine was for stories about sex positions and finding your soulmate.

Without any sex or relationship coverlines on that first issue, sales tanked. My U-turn was instant. As was the sharp reminder that I couldn't edit *Cosmo* for myself. Not if I wanted to keep my job. There's one other crucial thing this early misstep taught me: if you're going to take something away, you'd better replace it with something even better.

When Lisa made the controversial decision to ditch the famous *Cleo* centrefold in the eighties because she felt it had become tired and tacky, she replaced it with the equally iconic Most Eligible Bachelors feature. Sales didn't slide. They increased. Attracting new readers without losing all your old ones is a highwire act. You have to proceed with caution. Fortunately, Pat was my safety net. She consistently gave me the freedom to try things she didn't necessarily agree with but never to the long-term detriment of the brand or the bottom line. By doing this, she allowed me to learn practical lessons rather than just telling me what to do.

My biggest challenge was to find a new way to tell old stories. Messing with the fundamentals of *Cosmo* was obviously not an option. When anyone asked her about the fact *Cosmo* had been covering the same subjects for thirty years, Helen Gurley Brown always replied, 'Feelings like jealousy, love, low self-esteem, insecurity, they are universal and timeless.'

But something needed to change if we were to remain relevant to girls whose mothers had read *Cosmo*. One way we did it was with language. Regularly, Pat and I would stand in front of a wall of *Cosmo* covers, with sales figures in our heads, trying to work out what had caused particular issues to be winners or losers.

'Look at what all these covers have in common,' Pat suddenly said one day, pointing to four poor-selling issues. 'Orgasms'. She was right. Each of the four covers had the word 'orgasms' in large type as part of sex coverlines: 'Faster! Stronger! Longer! Orgasms Made Easy!' shouted one. 'Secrets of Women Who Have Orgasms!' shrieked another. 'His 'n' Her Orgasms: How To Slow Him Down and Speed You Up' promised a third. 'The Orgasm That Lasts 179 Times Longer: Come and Get It!' Gee, that sounded exhausting.

And perhaps that was the point. Women were tired of that word even if they still wanted the information. Every time the word 'orgasm' was prominent on the cover, sales went down. There were two reasons for this, we theorised. First of all, many *Cosmo* readers bought their magazines to read on public transport. Who wants to sit in a train full of strangers reading a story about orgasms? Ever since the spectre of HIV had entered the realm, a whiff of new puritanism had permeated society. For other readers, the opposite was true. Orgasm had become such an overused word on the cover of magazines that it was now a cheesy cliché.

Cosmo had to be surprising again. Within the boundaries of appropriate *Cosmo* subject matter, I had to freshen up our approach. Apart from using different words, like 'bonking', we began to use humour, an approach I stole from the UK men's market, which was starting to boom.

But the biggest change I would ever make to the magazine during my time as editor was a visual one. Ironically, that would be the most controversial thing I could have done.

THE
MAGAZINE
TWINS

Voicemail to me from *Cosmo*'s art director:

'Hey Mia, I'm at the printer and I've just snuck a peek at Cleo's next cover. Shit. They've got Jennifer Aniston too.'

What's the difference between *Cosmo* and *Cleo*?

I was asked this question, oh, about eight million times over the fifteen years I worked on both magazines. Depending on whom I was talking to and which magazine I wanted to favour, my answer varied. Even though the two titles and everyone who worked on them were fiercely competitive, both magazines were owned by ACP so you could never explicitly slag off your rival publicly. That would be unprofessional and could get you into trouble if word boomeranged back to your boss.

You had to do your slagging discreetly. Since the internal rivalry was so extreme, both magazines were excellent at the subtle sledge.

We did this with metaphors, some descriptive, some bitchy and some utterly nonsensical.

Cleo is more Australian; *Cosmo* is international.

Cleo is your sister; *Cosmo* is the slightly older girl next door.

Cleo is Cameron Diaz; *Cosmo* is Jennifer Lopez.

Cleo is a mirror to yourself; *Cosmo* is a window to the world.

Cleo is inspirational; *Cosmo* is aspirational.

Cleo is down to earth; *Cosmo* is sophisticated.

Cleo is younger; *Cosmo* is older.

Cleo is the beach; *Cosmo* is a cocktail bar.

Cleo is a bikini; *Cosmo* is a little black dress.

Cleo is the Logies; *Cosmo* is the Oscars.

Cleo is Coke; *Cosmo* is Pepsi.

Cleo is a one-night stand; *Cosmo* is a relationship.

Cleo is a condom; *Cosmo* is the pill.

The metaphors changed over the years and every editor and ad manager had her own bucket of neat one-liners to pull out for clients to make her own magazine look better.

In actual fact, it was all rubbish. Yes, there have always been small differences in tone and visuals between the two titles depending on the editors, but they were so subtle as to be almost indistinguishable without a magnifying glass.

Cosmo and *Cleo* have always covered the same subject matter in the same way and they put the same handful of celebrities on the cover month after month. Always have. They're aimed at the same women of the same age and income. They are essentially twins — non-identical perhaps, but still twins.

The two magazines are the same because, historically, *Cleo* was born from a business deal that suddenly turned on Kerry Packer. He transformed the unexpected setback into a revenge moment that became a stroke of commercial genius.

Back in the late 1960s, Hearst magazines realised that the winning editorial formula created by Helen Gurley Brown in 1965 could become an international one. The foundations of *Cosmo* — sex, relationships, fashion, career, beauty, health, friendship — were the same for women in most countries of the world. And so began the international expansion of the *Cosmo* brand that would eventually reach one hundred countries where Hearst would team up with an established local magazine publisher.

In Australia, Hearst chose ACP and the *Cosmo* deal was negotiated directly with Kerry Packer. A few months before the first issue was due to be published, Hearst changed its mind and instead signed with ACP's rival publisher, Fairfax. Kerry was not happy. Kerry was really, really not happy.

So he called a talented young journalist named Ita Buttrose into his office, gave her a copy of US *Cosmopolitan* and basically said, 'Here, do this. Fast.'

That's how *Cleo* was born. *Cleo* launched in Australia in 1973, several months before *Cosmo* and was an instant, massive hit. Fairfax launched *Cosmo* and it was also successful but *Cleo* had the edge in the market as a fully homegrown product.

Ironically, years later, Kerry would do a deal with Fairfax and Hearst to buy all their titles, including *Dolly* and *Cosmo*. The editor of *Cosmo* at the time of this transition from Fairfax to ACP was Pat Ingram, who would continue to edit *Cosmo* until she was ready to hand over the mantle to someone else. And chose me.

So that's how one company came to have two virtually identical magazines aimed at the same market, competing for the same readers and ad dollars. And that's how ACP came to control the young women's lifestyle market with the two dominant players.

Externally, this has been smart and profitable. Internally, it's been a little more complex. *Cosmo* and *Cleo* are like two intensely competitive siblings. They compete not only for readers and ad pages but also for the love and attention of their parents, I mean management.

Basically, each magazine has always been convinced the other had it easier. There was much mutual paranoia that the rival was getting preferential treatment, a better deal.

Over the years, management has played the role of patient parent, defusing squabbles and occasionally sending someone to their room for time out when things became too heated. In truth, the overall effect of such intense internal competition has been extremely good for business with each trying to outdo the other to prove that they are the better magazine.

Every few years another title would launch into the market — most notably *B* magazine in 1998 — but they never lasted long. *Cosmo* and *Cleo* were iconic brands and squashed competition very quickly.

After buying *Cosmo*, the first and smartest thing Kerry did was change the on-sale date of *Cosmo*, separating it from *Cleo* by two weeks.

This instantly spiked *Cosmo*'s sales because many women suddenly started buying both, almost as a fortnightly '*Closmo*'.

Before I began working for ACP, I was one of those women. But like most readers of both mags, I always identified more strongly with one. In my case, *Cleo*. It was more Australian and less sophisticated. I found *Cosmo* a bit remote. A bit harder to relate to. I was more of a beach than a cocktail bar. I was more of a cossie than a little black dress. And *Cleo* had Lisa, my idol, who I'd followed from *Dolly* like a loyal puppy. That sealed the deal and made my preference a no-brainer.

Ironically, I think my passionate devotion to *Cleo* and Lisa would have made me a lousy *Cleo* editor. I was too close to it. Conversely, my feelings about *Cosmo* had been ambivalent at best. As a reader, it had been a mag I bought but didn't love. As a *Cleo* staffer, it had been the enemy. Now, my allegiances had had to shift and *Cosmo* had become my passion.

A SLUMBER PARTY WITH SEX TIPS

Fax to me from Hearst:

'Dear Editors, we can't wait to see you all in Amsterdam next month. The itinerary for the conference is attached and attendance is compulsory.'

Every couple of years, all the international editors of *Cosmo* gather together for a conference. With more than fifty women from dozens of countries converging for several days of fun, wine and work, it's a bit like a Miss World contest meets a hen's night at the UN. They're a trip. Mentally and literally — the meetings are held in a different country every two years and Helen Gurley Brown is very much the reigning monarch. Symbolically at least. Like the Queen at the Commonwealth Games.

My first *Cosmo* conference was in Amsterdam and a lot had happened to both Helen and me in the few months since we'd met in New York for my job interview. I'd begun my new role as editor and I arrived at the hotel with six advance copies of my first issue packed carefully in my suitcase. Meanwhile, Helen was preparing to step down from the magazine she had created thirty-one years earlier. Her final issue as editor was about to hit news-stands and she wasn't happy about it.

Leaving *Cosmo* was not her idea. She was astonishingly, disconcertingly, heartbreakingly candid in private and public about the fact that she was going against her will. 'I want to keep editing *Cosmo*,' she told anyone who'd listen. 'I'm still a *Cosmo* girl.'

But Hearst could no longer ignore the fact that Helen was not a 'girl' any more. Their biggest and most profitable magazine, a magazine aimed at women under thirty-five, was being edited by someone who was seventy-five. At least. The maths just didn't work.

To continue pulling in the huge circulation and the associated advertising bucks, US *Cosmo* had to stay relevant to its target demographic. It had to evolve. And while you don't necessarily have to be exactly the same age as your reader to edit effectively … five decades older? That's pushing it.

So finally, the magazine icon had been tapped on her Pucci-clad shoulder. Hearst was careful to handle the situation with the utmost respect and diplomacy because Helen had brought the company massive profits, profits that continued to flow from around the world thanks to her winning formula.

A new role of International Editor-in-Chief was created as a parachute and as a way for her to keep contributing to the brand she had built from a blank page. She would continue to work full time in the Hearst building where she would critique all the international issues in personal letters to the editors every month. She would have an office, an assistant, a title. But someone else would be editing *Cosmopolitan* and she would have no input whatsoever into the US edition. It had to be that way if the new editor was to have any hope of steering the magazine forward. When there are too many drivers at the top, magazines quickly go off the rails and lose their voice. You can only have one vision if you want the magazine to be authentic. Editing by committee is a disaster. And so Helen had to go.

It was never going to be an easy transition for her. The magazine was literally her baby. She and her husband had no kids of their own. As with every aspect of her life, Helen was candid about why not. 'I never wanted to share my husband's attention with a child,' she'd say, admitting to feeling competitive at the very thought. She was happy for other people to have babies and always asked after them with interest, endearingly feigned, but she'd never much liked kids.

The Amsterdam conference was a hugely symbolic moment in *Cosmo*'s history and it was fraught with politics. It would mark the handing over of US *Cosmo* from Helen to its new editor, Bonnie Fuller. I had turned up in time to witness a momentous changing of the guard.

It was the opportunity for the foreign editors to hear Bonnie's plans for US *Cosmo* in detail, plans that would have a huge effect on our own editions. The licensing arrangements Hearst had with each country meant we had full access to the stories and images in US *Cosmo*, and we all used this content to varying degrees.

Hearst had always maintained that while the basic *Cosmo* formula must be applied to every edition of the magazine, it also needed to have the flavour of the country in which it was published. They never installed American editors abroad. Tone and content were adapted subtly by the local editor and her team to suit their market, everywhere from Pakistan to Taiwan, Israel to Kazakhstan. Wherever there were women, there was a market for *Cosmopolitan*.

However, depending on the size of the country, their expertise and their budget, an international edition might need to use up to ninety per cent of US *Cosmo* content each month. In Australia, it was closer to forty per cent and I would deliberately whittle that down over the years I edited the magazine. The bulk of US *Cosmo*'s readers came from middle America, making them older and more conservative than Australian readers. This made much of the content unusable in our market if I wanted to keep *Cosmo* relevant to young Aussie women and increase circulation.

Australia was one of the most liberal countries in which *Cosmo* was published and our relaxed attitude to sex meant we could get away with far more raunchy, edgy content than virtually any other *Cosmo* in the world.

In Amsterdam, while all the international editors had to remain respectful of everything Helen said, the future direction of our own magazines now depended on the new US editor. We were all impatient to hear what changes Bonnie had planned and what they would mean for us.

Bonnie Fuller was herself a publishing powerhouse who had edited several American glossies, including *Marie Claire*. She had just turned forty and was pregnant with her third child. Her changes to the magazine included increasing the fashion content and decreasing the word count in features. *Cosmo* would be a more visual, modern product. We were all excited.

Over the three days we had a variety of presentations and discussions. The schedule was intense. Editors who had experienced particular challenges or triumphs — from dealing with censorship to creating *Cosmo* TV shows — presented to the group.

There was very little free time, and each night we had a group dinner at a different location in Amsterdam. Between daytime sessions, Helen would zip back to her room to do sit-ups and tricep dips. This was something she did at the office too, several times every day. Her fear of fat drove her to exercise whenever she could, day or night.

'I exercise for an hour and a half minimum every day, except for when I had a hysterectomy,' she explained in her soft voice. Then she took two weeks off instead of the recommended six. 'I'm always hungry,' she added gaily, eating salad leaves daintily with her fingers. 'Being skinny is how I fight ageing. Being cute and slim, I can get away with things at seventy-five that I just know I couldn't do if I was heavy and flabby.'

Helen was nothing if not unique.

I felt enormously privileged to be included among a group of such accomplished, intelligent, ambitious women. Some of them had been editing *Cosmo* for several decades, although none as long as Helen. I was the newest and the youngest and I had a hell of a lot to learn. As I flew home, for the first time but not for the last, I felt daunted by the task ahead of me.

OOPS. TWO BLUE LINES

Voicemail to Jo, Wendy and Karen from me:

'Um, hi, call me. I have some news.'

I was pregnant. Surprised, ecstatic and pregnant. As I stood nervously in the doorway of Pat's office, waiting to go in and tell her my news, I practised my speech in my head while she finished talking on the phone.

She wasn't going to be happy. I'd only been in my new job for three months and now we'd have to discuss maternity leave. Fortunately, I wasn't going to need much of that.

'You won't even know I'm gone,' I babbled. 'I'll come in for features meetings and to do coverlines and I can read finals from home and the staff can come to my place for art meetings and I'll be back before you know it, I swear. I only need three months max and —'

I was still talking when she leaped up from her chair and rushed over to give me a hug. 'Darling, I'm so excited for you,' she said warmly, meaning it. 'But we need to talk about your plans, they're ridiculous.'

She was calm and wise. 'First, you're going to take four months off not three. And second, if you have all these arrangements to still be involved in everything while you're away I'm going to be very uneasy because when you find you can't actually be here things will fall apart. Better to set it up so that you can have some proper time with your baby.'

Right. Really?

'But what will I *do* all day?' I asked.

She laughed.

I wasn't kidding. 'Surely the baby will, you know, eat and sleep a lot and I'll have quite at lot of spare time, won't I?'

More laughter. 'Look darling, you'll be flat out but I'm thrilled for you. Being a mother will make you a better editor.'

At the time, I had no idea what Pat was talking about. I thought she was just being nice. But in time I'd realise she was right. I'd become more efficient with my time and I'd have better perspective.

Now I just had to get through the next six months until I gave birth.

I had a lot to do. First on my list was coming up with a signature *Cosmo* event that would make the magazine cooler and sexier. Something that could compete with — or even overtake — *Cleo*'s Most Eligible Bachelors party as the most iconic magazine event of the year.

When I arrived at *Cosmo*, there was … nothing. No annual event. No branded list or annual feature to generate PR. Instantly competitive and determined to manufacture some media attention for *Cosmo*, I decided to start with a calendar of male models, attached to the January issue of the magazine. This meant I got to spend my first few weeks on the job casting hot men along with my fashion editor. We saw dozens of them to the point where all those abs and waxed chests began to blur. If only that had been as much fun as it sounded. Even if I'd been single, it would have been a wasted gift. Male models just aren't my thing. They're too … obvious.

With a nonexistent line in the budget for events that year and all available marketing dollars diverted into printing the calendar, all we could scrape together to launch it were a few party pies, some bad wine and a straggle of media at Planet Hollywood. It was all contra. I persuaded Planet Hollywood to provide the venue, food and alcohol in exchange for some coverage of the party in a subsequent issue. More magazine deals are done this way than you could possibly imagine.

The following year, I thought more carefully about how I wanted to position *Cosmo*. I realised it was futile to try to compete with *Cleo*'s bachelors. My male models had flopped. I needed to go in a completely different direction if I wanted *Cosmo* to be something other than me-too.

Working on the premise that — as with bachelors — the media love a list, I came up with the idea of *Cosmo* naming 'Australia's 30 Most Successful Women Under 30'. I wanted to position *Cosmo* as more than just a mag about sex, angst and beauty tips. I wanted to stop peddling insecurity and start selling aspiration while also injecting some reality into the mix. So I went worthy, by naming, photographing and celebrating the most talented young women in the country in areas as diverse as medicine, social work, comedy, acting, science and business.

I recruited some high-profile judges and scoured newspapers around Australia for young women who were achieving big things in their chosen fields. In my editor's letter, I referred to our collective waning love affair with supermodels and how it was time to look to women of substance for inspiration: 'None of these women is engaged to Johnny Depp, has a wardrobe full of Gucci or gets paid millions to endorse lipstick,' I wrote. 'But each one has used a unique combination of talent and hard work to achieve a level of excellence in whatever she does, at a remarkably early age.'

From the hundreds of nominees, the judges whittled the list down to thirty. I was adamant that I didn't want a winner because I felt it was impossible to compare an up-and-coming actor with a scientist or surfer.

The first step towards gaining publicity for the magazine was when the list was released. This meant me doing print and radio interviews. The next step was generating some pictures for TV and the social pages, which meant an event. We threw a cocktail party when I was already three months pregnant. Nobody knew yet and I had to keep excusing myself to run to the bathroom and vomit due to the 'morning' sickness that was plaguing me every evening.

The issue sold okay but not fabulously. Still, I felt the annual list was an important aspect of *Cosmo*'s rebranding so I repeated it for the next couple of years. In year three, I added thirty men under thirty and tried to ignite more media attention by announcing winners — a female social worker and the actor Alex Dimitriades, in hindsight, a perfectly bizarre combination. But worthy didn't sell and in 2000 I euthanised the concept.

My next approach was if-you-can't-beat-'em-join-'em. I abandoned worthy and went sexy. I needed a reason to have an event; something to peg a party on. Rather unoriginally, I chose Christmas.

Cosmo had its first sexy Christmas party in 2000, held in a groovy bar with male and female models in bikinis and budgie smugglers serving cocktails and taking Polaroids of guests as souvenirs. There were Christmas trees decorated with plastic handcuffs — which were all quickly swiped — and in the gift bags were Kama Sutra sex positions made out of chocolate. It was raunchy and enormous fun. The following year we had male strippers and the year after that the party was held in a strip club with pole dancers. My last Christmas party as editor and host culminated with the Kylie drag performance. It was a good time to leave.

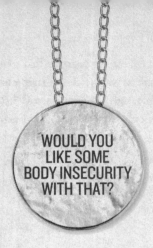

WOULD YOU LIKE SOME BODY INSECURITY WITH THAT?

Voicemail to the *Cosmo* fashion editor from me:

'Thanks for leaving those shots on my desk. The clothes are beautiful and I love the location but the model is too thin. I can see her ribs and she looks about fourteen. How old is she actually? I'm afraid you're going to have to reshoot. Are there any bigger models around? When you're back from the studio this arvo can you bring me some model cards? Sorry, I know you put a lot of work into it but we just can't publish those pictures.'

It didn't take me long to start beating my body-image drum. While I was wary of repeating my sex and relationships mistake and deleting any key component of the *Cosmo* philosophy, I was keen to add something new.

My third issue of *Cosmo* screamed: 'STRONG & SEXY: THE BODY ISSUE! Forget waifs! What REAL women weigh'.

In my editor's letter, I wrote about going to a Korean bathhouse in Sydney and how the experience of being among dozens of differently shaped naked women of all ages and ethnicities had been both confronting and fascinating.

Big breasts, flat bottoms, flat chests, scars, curves, bits that wobbled, natural blondes, women who worked out, women who didn't, mothers, grandmothers — nudity is the ultimate equaliser. Take away the layers of clothes, the make-up and the accessories and suddenly there's just … our body. And our paranoia about it.

I went on to address the pink elephant in the corner of any discussion about women's magazines and stated my aim to tackle that elephant responsibly.

Magazines are often accused of promoting this kind of insecurity in women. And once upon a time — back in the dark days of 'wonder' diets and waifs — that may have been true. But at Cosmo *in 1997, we pride ourselves on presenting a more balanced, healthy image of women. Yes, you may sometimes find slimmer-than-average models on our pages, but you'll also find a variety of differently shaped women whose income doesn't depend on fitting into a size ten dress.*

How ironic that the cover of this issue was retouched half to death. The model in the shot I chose was rather masculine looking and we shaped her jaw to make her look less like a transvestite. I also changed the colour of her dress. None of this struck me as remotely hypocritical at the time, although in hindsight I'm mortified. While I recognised the impact wall-to-wall skinny models could have on a reader's psyche, details of face, hair and dress colour didn't worry me. In the years to come, I would regularly alter the cover image in a bid to make it as appealing as possible — although I never made cover models thinner. In fact, I often fattened them up.

The next thing I did was ban diets. I thought I was being terribly brave. A maverick even. Women's magazines had always survived on a diet of diets. So I was slightly deflated when my grand gesture went unnoticed. No one really cared. Or more to the point, no one was going to buy a magazine because of something I'd taken out of it. Diets had never been a huge feature of *Cosmo*. It was far less of a body-focused magazine than *Cleo* whose heritage was all about the beach and that Aussie outdoor sexiness.

I slept better at night knowing I'd abolished crash diets from *Cosmo* but if I wanted to make a difference — to women or to circulation — I needed to be proactive about promoting a more positive body image. Articles urging women to 'Love Your Body!' just weren't going to cut it. I'd always found those kinds of stories tokenistic, hypocritical and condescending, especially since they were invariably sandwiched between pages of size six Amazons and usually illustrated with a skinny model jumping in the air.

My first significant step into new territory came after I picked up an issue of UK *Vogue*. They'd published a fashion shoot that had attracted quite a lot of media attention. The model was an art student who'd been scouted by a fashion photographer at McDonald's. She was about size sixteen to eighteen and the pictures were striking.

I won't pretend I was the first to feature a larger model in an Australian magazine. Others had before, usually once a year in a token 'Big Girl' story designed to generate some ad revenue from plus-size fashion labels. Unfortunately, it seemed most magazine editors thought there was only one acceptable way to shoot a model larger than a size eight: drape her in ugly cardigans, sensible shoes and shapeless separates.

The UK *Vogue* shoot was a revelation because the model was portrayed as a sexy woman. The clothes were tight — black dresses mostly — and the hair and make-up was vampy. It was the first time I had seen a larger model do sexy. She was someone to aspire to instead of someone to pity.

You certainly couldn't just flick past these pages on your way to the standard slimline fashion stories. These images demanded your attention. And because they were so different to anything else in the magazine — and anything else in any other magazine I'd ever seen — they were a visual jolt in an endless sea of skinny. As a reader I knew this was rare and unexpected as you flicked through the pages. As a feminist I felt it was a wonderful thing for women.

And as an editor? Well, I'd love to say I always knew featuring larger women in *Cosmo* would lead to higher sales. But I didn't. I hoped it would but I wasn't sure. What I did know was that it would start people talking. And this was my first priority.

In the early nineties, *Cosmo* and *Cleo* had lost their edge. Publishing a sealed section was no longer daring, it was predictable. All the allegedly risqué sex advice, angst and insecurity upon which the magazines had traded so successfully had started to feel old school. Everyone knew what they were getting when they picked up *Cleo* or *Cosmo* and that was not conducive to repeat sales, let alone new ones. I wanted *Cosmo* to be surprising. Unexpected.

I was looking for the 'pass-around factor'. Something that would make the reader say to a friend, 'Hey, look at this.' I wanted to generate new buzz around an established brand that was decades old. This drove me creatively for those first few years as I tried desperately to jolt people out of the idea that *Cosmo* was tired and formulaic.

So I ripped off the UK *Vogue* story immediately and unashamedly I found a larger model through an agency called, appropriately, Big Gals, because they were the only ones who had larger models on their books. I handed my fashion editor a copy of the *Vogue* story and instructed her to dress the model in similar sexy clothes, including one shot in lingerie.

Was this plagiarism? Stealing someone else's intellectual property? Staggeringly unoriginal? I didn't care. My job was to make Australian *Cosmo* the best magazine I could and if that meant 'borrowing' ideas, well, I could live with that. An editor once told me 'There's no copyright on ideas' and I've never forgotten that. Provided you did your own version, I saw nothing wrong with being 'inspired' by other sources. Most *Cosmo* readers didn't have access to foreign magazines so what we were doing, in effect, was cherry-picking some of the best ideas in the world and reinventing them locally.

Editors get many of their best ideas from other magazines. This isn't as bad as it sounds. One of my favourite parts of the job was being paid to read magazines. Hundreds of them every month. To stay on top of what was going on in Australia and overseas, *Cosmo* subscribed to around sixty titles, some monthly and some weekly, which meant I had at least 150 magazines plop into my in-tray each month. That's a lot of 'inspiration'.

I think it would be fair to say there's not an editor alive who's never given a staff member a copy of another magazine's story and said, 'Here, do this.' What the editor means, of course, is 'Do your own version of this', but more than one editor has been caught out by a writer who took her instructions to mean 'Plagiarise this' — which she certainly didn't intend the writer to do.

Anyway, the big-girl shoot hit a roadblock almost instantly. 'No one wants to give me clothes,' announced my fashion editor, slightly smugly, one afternoon.

'What do you mean? Don't they have clothes big enough?'

'Oh no, that's not it; they all go up to size sixteen or bigger,' she replied. 'They just don't want their labels appearing on a large model in *Cosmo*. Or anywhere in the media.'

I was stunned. 'So they're happy to take money from size-sixteen customers but they want their public face to be a size-eight one.'

'Yep,' she nodded. 'And did I tell you that the photographer I want to use has finally agreed to do it? But he doesn't want his name on the story.'

Unbelievable. Eventually, the story went ahead and the uncredited photos turned out beautifully. My boss wasn't sure that it was very *Cosmo* but she let me do it. I called the story something unintentionally condescending like 'Modern Curves' and was very proud of the result.

Encouraged by the positive reader reaction when the issue came out, I gaily made plans for more big-girl shoots. My fashion editor was horrified and told me so. At length. Fashion editors are not bad people, they are just pure aesthetes. They don't really see models as people; they see them literally as coat hangers. And coat hangers are best without padding because those pesky female lumps, bumps and curves 'spoil the line'. That's the exact phrase fashion people use. I've heard it a hundred times. They are oblivious to how a woman might feel about herself when she looks at a photo of a six-foot-tall, size-zero, sixteen-year-old model and automatically compares the image with her own body.

By asking my fashion team to shoot bigger models, I was making their jobs much harder. For one thing, there were very few large models to choose from. Modelling is generally not high on a list of jobs you'd choose for its security or stable income, even if you are as skinny as a stalk of asparagus. Hardly any Australian models of any size are able to make a full-time living from modelling.

The editorial day rate for a model working for a magazine — whether she's shooting a fashion story or even a cover — is $190 per day or $120 for a half day. From this, the model has to pay twenty per cent to her agent, leaving her with about $150 for a long day's work. Out of this money she must also spend a significant amount on maintenance — haircuts and colour, manicures and pedicures, facials and fake tans.

The work itself can be hard. Not compared to, say, being down a mineshaft, admittedly, but it's not as absolutely fabulous as you might imagine.

The average day on an editorial shoot starts at 5 am for a weather check and doesn't finish until you lose light at the end of the day — even later if you're shooting in a studio. Because of long magazine lead times, magazines shoot bikinis in July and winter coats in December. A model may be sent home unpaid if she turns up with pimples or doesn't fit into the clothes. She'll have to hold uncomfortable positions for hours, and to make the clothes look better they'll probably be pinned and held together with bulldog clips down the back. All for less than fifteen dollars an hour.

The real bucks only kick in for advertising jobs when a model's day rate can be anything from $500 to $5000. Even $10,000 if you're 'super'. But there aren't very many of those jobs. Not nearly enough for all the girls who call themselves models.

The market for larger models is even smaller and more specialised. The only advertising work available is for plus-size fashion labels — of which, in Australia, there aren't many. Sadly, no campaigns for food products or cosmetic products are ever fronted by models larger than size ten because advertisers believe that women won't buy products if they see them on non-skinny models. I'd be shocked to meet even one Australian plus-sized model who could support herself purely from modelling.

If clothes and models weren't hard enough to find, photographers are notoriously negative about shooting pictures of bigger girls, as *Cosmo*'s fashion shoot had proved. They believe it's simply not cool. Even make-up artists have been known to ask for their credits to be removed when the photos are published.

Still, I persevered, ignoring the eye-rolling from some of my staff who thought I was insane for being so enthusiastic about shooting bigger models.

But the images in the fashion stories weren't the only thing I had to change. I wanted *Cosmo* to feature more articles about body image and to become a strong voice of advocacy for non-model-sized women. This was new territory and straight away I stumbled. My intentions were good but the way I went about executing them was clumsy.

So eager was I to atone for the past sins of magazines like *Cosmo* in featuring only skinny models, I went too far the other way. I accidentally started skinny bashing.

Intros to fashion stories and features enthused that 'real women have curves' and declared 'men prefer some meat on your bones'. We made many references to skinny vs 'normal-sized' bodies. Big mistake. Don't piss off the skinny chicks. Dozens of furious letters arrived from thin women saying how insulted they were at the implication they weren't 'real women' because they had no curves. Skinny can be normal too, they harrumphed.

In my haste to make some women feel better about themselves, I'd made other women feel lousy. So I quickly modified my approach. All sizes could be sexy, *Cosmo* now preached. Diversity was something to be celebrated. 'Real women' came in all shapes and sizes and no one type of woman was better or worse than any other. 'Healthy' was a better pursuit than 'skinny'.

After about a year the regular inclusion of larger models in fashion shoots was being well received and had begun to generate the buzz I'd hoped for. Sales were starting to climb. But we still weren't reflecting enough diversity on the pages for my liking. Frustratingly, there was, and still is, a big hole in the modelling market for girls who are size ten to sixteen. The models represented by major agencies are overwhelmingly sizes six to eight. Meanwhile, plus-sized models are usually around size sixteen. Given that the average Australian woman tends to hover around size fourteen, this hole in the market is rather ridiculous, since it covers the majority of the *Cosmo* demographic.

So after a few months, I realised I had to broaden my strategy. As a reader, I'd always loved looking at images of 'real women' in magazines — that is, women who weren't models. So we started shooting lots of them. We found them in the street and via call-outs in the magazine. We shot them in lingerie and swimsuits in line-ups that preceded the famous Dove 'real women' campaign by several years but looked virtually identical.

Perhaps Dove ripped us off? Oh well. That would be karma. There's no copyright on ideas.

There was no body type, shape, size or nationality we didn't shoot. If you wanted to be in *Cosmo* and could get yourself to Sydney to be photographed, you could appear in the magazine. No problem.

We still used professional models in fashion shoots in most issues but we always balanced this with plenty of diversity elsewhere. So you could pretty much be guaranteed to see a body that looked like your own somewhere when you flicked through the magazine.

Gradually, I formalised this into *Cosmo*'s Body Love policy. '*Cosmo* will guarantee that we'll feature women size six to sixteen every single month.'

I felt passionately that this was the right thing to do from a socially responsible point of view, but to me it also made business sense. I knew from experience that flicking through a magazine filled with models who looked nothing like me left me feeling hopelessly inadequate. Fat, short and ugly. I didn't want my readers to feel that way after reading *Cosmo* because I genuinely didn't believe it would make them want to buy the next issue. Why would they? For more punishment?

When they're asked about why they don't use larger models in their magazines, I often hear editors claim one of two things. Usually, they ramble on about 'aspiration and fantasy', claiming that a magazine is meant to be about glamour and not real life. Frankly, this is insulting. Who said only skinny white woman can be aspirational and glamorous? Sometimes they'll say that 'Women don't want to see bigger women — we're our own worst enemies.' Again, bullshit.

How can they possibly know what women do or don't want when they serve them the same diet of tall, skinny, white models month after month with little alternative?

For the record, when *Cosmo* began to feature women of different shapes, sizes and skin colours throughout every issue of the magazine, sales went up. Readership went up. And advertising revenue went up. Dramatically. It was my proudest career achievement and a pie in the face to anyone who said it couldn't — or shouldn't — be done.

THE BIG BABY FREAK-OUT

Voicemail to Jen from me:

'Ugh. I feel like shit. How is it possible that I felt fine yesterday and today I feel like a hundred-year-old swamp creature? Everyone who warned me that the last four weeks of this pregnancy would be tough was right. Anyway, thanks so much for organising the baby shower yesterday. Thank God I hadn't yet hit the wall and could actually enjoy it.'

Like so many first-time mums, I'd been to birth classes with my partner and read seven hundred books about pregnancy and birth but knew approximately nothing about What Happens Next. A couple of weeks before my due date, I realised there was a small gap in my knowledge. Namely, WHAT THE HELL YOU DO WITH A BABY.

All the classes and books and magazines know this will happen to you so they all sneak in a token amount of info at the end to cover the basics of that first six weeks.

Of course I'd resolutely ignored all of it. Baby? What baby? I wasn't having a baby. I was having a pregnancy and then I was having a birth.

One night, at about week thirty-eight and counting, I sat in my new feeding chair and dared to turn to the 'Afterwards' chapter in *What To Expect When You're Expecting*.

I became upset very quickly.

'What's wrong?' asked Jason.

'I don't understand any of this!' I wailed.

'What do you mean? What don't you understand?' he asked carefully, like a hostage negotiator talking to a crazed gunman.

'This BABY STUFF! All about feeding and sleeping and changing nappies and something called swallowing or swaddling or something!'

I was working my way towards hysteria, rocking faster in my chair. 'It's like a whole other language I don't understand!'

Jason took a breath. 'But you didn't understand pregnancy at first and you learned about that and now you could do a whole PowerPoint presentation on the subject.'

'This is DIFFERENT! This involves an actual person OUTSIDE MY BODY and if I don't care for it properly IT MIGHT DIE!'

'Cup of tea?'

He retreated from the crazy lady into the safety of the kitchen to find emergency chocolate, momentarily diverting me with a king-size Crunchie. A few bites and I was ready to resume my rant. Slightly calmer but still impassioned.

'It's like my brain is FULL. Everything I've had to learn about pregnancy and birth has taken up every available brain cell and there are none left to learn anything about what to do with an ACTUAL BABY.'

I was overwhelmed. And scared. I didn't like doing new things unless I knew I would be really good at them. A mature approach to life that would no doubt be a terrific lesson to pass on to my future child. Once I worked out how to change its nappy.

I'd not had any exposure to babies in my life. I had no younger siblings or cousins. No nieces or nephews. No godchildren. And my close friends were years away from having babies. They were still dancing on tables in nightclubs and dating inappropriate men.

At my baby shower, one girl who'd had a baby five weeks earlier brought him along and there was that awful moment I always dread when a mother asks, 'Would you like to hold him?'

My head screamed 'NO! I would not! I don't know how! He will cry!' My crap maternal skills will be on public display and everyone will shake their heads and take their presents back and then call DOCS to warn them about the impending danger to my unborn child!

'Um, oooh, yes, I'd love to,' was what I actually said and she carefully transferred the peacefully gurgling little boy into my awkward arms. It felt like a test I hadn't studied for.

I'd hoped that since I had my own baby inside my body at this point, a mere five weeks away from being outside my body, somehow the maternal secrets of the universe would be unlocked and it would all suddenly feel magically right. It didn't.

I was self-conscious and uncoordinated. I rocked back and forth a bit and made the requisite cooing noises as I madly wondered how long was enough time before I could give him back. Naturally, he began to cry and any shred of confidence I had was obliterated. This mother business was going to be harder than I thought.

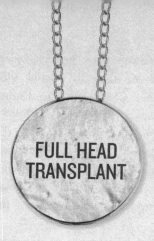

FULL HEAD TRANSPLANT

Voicemail to *Cosmo*'s art director from me:

'Hey, I need you to chop off Alyssa's head again. We need to run her for the Feb cover. Come see me when you're back.'

The most important part of an editor's job is choosing the cover. Nothing has a bigger impact on sales. So oddly, there is surprisingly little research about what works. It's a frustratingly inexact science although every editor has her theories. Generally, if an issue sells well, the cover takes the credit. If it's a flop, the cover is blamed.

There are other factors that come into play too. What your competitors have on offer that month, for instance. Your cover may be a killer but if another magazine has something better — a mascara stuck on the front or a jumbo-sized issue or exclusive photos of Angelina Jolie with new babies — this can impact negatively on your sales.

Readers might also be turned off (or on) by a coverline or the size of your magazine. The colours you choose might appeal or not. Then there's the cover price. Australian magazines are notoriously expensive and the best way for a new mag to gain a fast foothold is to launch with a bargain cover price. *Glamour* launched very successfully that way in the UK, as did *OK!* magazine here. But in most cases, bad sales are due to a lousy cover. So it's crucial the editor chooses the cover very carefully.

Up until the early 1990s, ordinary 'models' appeared on the covers of *Cosmo* and *Cleo*. No one knew their names. You didn't have to. It was all about how they looked, a feeling, not who they were dating or which cereal they ate. Usually, the cover photo wasn't even a separate shoot, it came from one of the fashion stories inside the magazine.

In the mid nineties this changed and suddenly any old model just wouldn't do. You needed a supermodel. For the magazines that relied on shots of the half-dozen or so supermodels who moved copies, this effectively meant the end of shooting your own covers. You had to buy them from international photographers. It wasn't so much the price that was prohibitive (the same editorial day rate was paid to all models, even the super ones) but the access. When you're Cindy Crawford and you can spend your day shooting a cover for US *Vogue* (huge prestige), a Revlon commercial (huge cash) or the cover of an Australian magazine (no prestige, tiny cash), three guesses how you're going to allocate your time.

For a few years, *Cosmo* and *Cleo* alternated a very small roster of supermodel cover girls: Cindy Crawford, Claudia Schiffer, Daniela Pestova, Laetitia Casta, Karen Mulder and Elle Macpherson. Not all supermodels sold magazines and the only way to discover this was through trial and error. As another editor once told me: 'The first time I put Helena Christensen on the cover and it was a dog I thought surely it couldn't be Helena's fault. The second time, I thought maybe it's Helena's fault. The third time I knew Helena barked.'

Why? Who knows. With Danish–Peruvian parents, perhaps she looked too exotic. All the bestselling supermodel cover girls were white almost to the point of Aryan. It's a dirty little secret in magazines that covers of Asian or dark-skinned women don't sell. Famous, super or not. This is disappointing and disgraceful and most editors wish it wasn't the case. But does that mean they can afford to do the right thing by opting for more visual diversity and putting Asian and dark-skinned women on their covers? Not if they want to sell magazines and keep their jobs.

It comes back to the rule about giving readers what they want, not what you think they should have, even if you're not always happy about it. Even if you're sometimes ashamed.

About a year after I began editing *Cosmo*, readers decided they didn't want supermodels any more. Cindy, Claudia and their genetically freaky peers stopped selling like they used to. An era was ending. Magazines all over the world had ridden the supermodel wave to great effect, and at *Cleo* I'd had to write a bazillion fawning stories about them.

We had dissected everything from their beauty regimes to their wardrobes, relationships, hairstyles, diet secrets, travel tips, exercise routines, bank accounts and even their sex lives. The genre peaked — or bottomed out — when I wrote a story called 'Lesbian Supermodels' that delved into 'the secret world of the supermodels who sleep with each other'. Of course it was all based on rumour but it made a cracker of a coverline.

In the course of reading and writing so much about the dozen or so supermodels with whom our readers were on a first-name basis, inane knowledge had implanted itself in my brain. Niki Taylor had a tattoo of a daisy on the top of her left foot. Linda Evangelista only wore G-string underwear. Claudia Schiffer drank a cup of hot water with lemon every morning. Cindy Crawford liked to squeeze her pimples in the bathroom on aeroplanes. Vendela's biggest regret in life was that her nail beds were too short.

Riveting it wasn't. So I was hardly surprised when readers collectively tired of reading such inanity and looked for new pretty things to gaze at.

It was the dawning of the age of celebrity. Actresses and pop stars like the Jennifers (Lopez and Aniston) kicked Claudia and Cindy off the cover of *Cosmo* and *Cleo* never to return.

I was delighted by this for a couple of reasons. As a reader myself, I was bored stupid with looking at the same handful of genetically gifted freaks month after month. As an editor, I was sick of competing with every other magazine on the planet for the same pictures of them. As a feminist, I was jubilant that having celebrities on the cover meant that *Cosmo*'s covergirls finally had a skill other than being tall and slim with prominent cheekbones. They could act. Or sing. They also were a more diverse bunch. From Natalie Imbruglia to Jennifer Aniston, Cameron Diaz, Jennifer Lopez, Gwyneth Paltrow, Madonna, Alyssa Milano, Jennifer Love Hewitt, Kylie, Christina Applegate, Naomi Watts, Sarah Jessica Parker … suddenly there was a diversity of ages, nationalities and body shapes after years of brutally same-same supermodels.

Still, the celebrity covergirls were overwhelmingly slim. Not model-slim but slim nonetheless. I hoped and waited for someone larger to become famous enough for a *Cosmo* cover and the closest I got (apart from Sara-Marie from 'Big Brother') was Kelly Osbourne.

In 2002, when her family's reality show 'The Osbournes' was killing it in the ratings, Kelly was flown to Australia to present at the ARIA awards. Opportunistically, I grabbed the chance to buy a shot of her and put it on the cover to coincide with the visit. I shouldn't have. It was a disaster.

In the only remotely suitable shot I could find, Kelly was wearing a tight yellow top with dark jeans and a hot-pink leather belt to match her hot-pink hair. I knew I was straying approximately a million miles from traditional *Cosmo* cover territory but her pose was sexy and her make-up was beautiful. I thought it could work. Hearst was apoplectic. The verdict from Helen came via fax instead of snail mail, which meant she was agitated. Even so, it began in her signature iron-fist-in-velvet-glove style.

> *Mia dear,*
>
> *You put out a wonderful magazine and all those readers buy and advertisers kick in. Mia, Hearst is perfectly happy with the November cover and there surely is a lot to be happy about in the magazine — wonderful articles and all that advertising but I have a rough time with the cover because it isn't* Cosmo! *Yes, it's something Mia wants to do and Mia is a wildly successful editor but, Mia, you make it so hard on us with the rest of the countries. If Mia can do anything in the world she pleases (put Kelly Osbourne on the cover instead of a* Cosmo *model), why can't they?*
>
> *We are trying desperately to have all of these countries produce* Cosmo — *why? Because it works! It works all over the world. It's hard to tell them they can't go out there and do anything that possibly enters their head when Mia gets to do exactly what she wants to do!*

It went on for several pages like this and while she never actually said '... AND SHE'S FAT!' I could read it between every line. Helen didn't like fat in any part of life, heaven forbid on the cover of *Cosmo*. As it turned out, she was absolutely right. Not about the fat part but about Kelly Osbourne being a lousy cover choice. Sales tanked abysmally.

To this day, I don't believe it had anything to do with her size. Kelly Osbourne was just unlikeable. She was a foul-mouthed, obnoxious brat who had no obvious reason for being famous apart from her father being Ozzy Osbourne. Just to underline this point and kill my circulation definitively, Kelly appeared up on the red carpet at the ARIA awards and called Natalie Imbruglia a cunt, just as we went on sale. I can't even remember why, but it didn't win her many new fans. Lesson. learned. Ironically, Kelly's larger-than-the-average-covergirl size had blinded me to the fact that she was not AT ALL right for *Cosmo*.

What makes one model or celebrity cover gold while another seemingly similar celeb is cover poison? Again, every editor has a different theory.

For *Cosmo* and *Cleo*, the covergirl has to be someone you like, someone you'd like to be or be friends with. Someone a little intriguing too. An interesting personal life helps. So does a famous boyfriend.

Another factor is vulnerability. A *Cosmo* or *Cleo* covergirl should have some degree of realness. They shouldn't be impenetrably perfect. Nicole Kidman was widely acknowledged to be cover poison for all mags until she was dumped by Tom Cruise. That seemed to make her a more sympathetic, interesting figure and more editors used her after that. Still, I never risked her on *Cosmo* because her image didn't resonate with the *Cosmo* reader who was most likely twenty-three and single.

One thing that's clear though is that there are trends. Certain people sell magazines better than others and just when you've worked out who those people are, they inexplicably stop working. And occasionally, you can break all the rules and still somehow land a winner.

Pamela Anderson is the perfect example of an unexpected hit. You'd not normally think of her as *Cosmo* covergirl material. She's more of a men's-magazine type. But the key — I believe — to the success of our cover with Pamela was the coverline I stole from South African *Cosmo*, which ran the shot first. 'Why Is Pammy On Our Cover?' we asked, articulating what many readers would have been thinking and thus neutralising any negativity. It worked. The issue sold beautifully.

Even when you thought you knew who would sell well, securing the right shot was a nightmare. Getting access to the kinds of celebrities you needed for your cover — internationally famous ones — was virtually impossible for an Australian magazine. Occasionally, *Cosmo* could piggyback on US *Cosmo* and use one of their cover shots but this didn't happen often because *Cosmo* in the United States was still mostly using models on its covers. Easier and cheaper. Half their luck.

The majority of the time, *Cosmo*, like *Cleo* and most Australian magazines, had to trawl photo agencies and other publications, looking for cover shots to buy. This was hard.

Say Gwyneth Paltrow does a shoot for US *Vogue* to publicise her new film. The photographer owns the rights to this shot, not *Vogue* or Gwyneth. So if you want to buy it for your magazine's cover, you must approach the photographer's agency. While you negotiate a price — celebrity covers now sell for in excess of US$15,000 each — you must simultaneously approach Gwyneth's publicist for written approval to buy the shot. Without it, the photographer won't sell it to you because he doesn't want to piss off Gwyneth who can make him a lot of money in the future. To gain approval from the publicist, you must send a copy of the story you want to run with the cover shot, usually one you've bought from an overseas magazine or newspaper because Australia is low down the pecking order when stars grant interviews. Even when the story you submit to the publicist is suitably sycophantic, if Gwyneth does not have a movie being released in Australia at the time your issue goes on sale, the publicist will say no to prevent Gwyneth from being overexposed.

This is how Gwyneth controls her image and this is how editors become prematurely grey-haired. If you've ever wondered why the celebrity features accompanying covers are so utterly lame, now you know. Write a story about how Gwyneth has a rocky relationship, or say, a pimple and you're unlikely to get approval to buy any shot to go with it.

Okay, so by some miracle, the planets have aligned, you've secured approval and negotiated a price for the cover. Now the shot arrives and it's retouched to buggery. Bad luck. That's all you can use. Celebrities will not approve any un-retouched image of themselves. So even if editors wanted to run more realistic cover images, in most cases they simply don't have access to any.

I've been attacked many times over the issue of covers. 'You're the editor, you can decide who goes on the cover,' critics will say. 'So why don't you have more dark-skinned women or bigger women or older women or women who aren't just actresses, models and pop stars on your magazine?'

I once spoke at a body-image forum in front of several thousand schoolgirls. Even though I was there to speak about all the positive steps *Cosmo* had taken to portray a more healthy body image in the magazine, I unwittingly became a whipping girl for all the sins of all magazines, past and present. During question time, girl after girl stood up and abused me for the way magazines publish unrealistic images of women.

No matter how much I pointed to the good things *Cosmo* was doing to turn this around and agreed that there was still a long way to go and that magazines needed to be more responsible, they became more and more aggressive. Finally, one girl got up and shouted into the microphone: 'If you're so committed to changing things, why don't you put *me* on your cover?'

A cheer went up and I took a breath, which I possibly should have saved. 'As much as I would love to put you on a *Cosmo* cover — or, say, myself — it's likely that the only people who would buy those issues are our friends. And this would fall a bit short of the quarter of a million copies of *Cosmo* I need to sell every month.' There was booing from the back of the hall. I persevered. 'You need someone extremely famous to move that many copies of a magazine. You need to remember that magazines are not a school project or a public service announcement, they are a business. Sometimes I have to put my personal feelings aside because as much as I would like to put you or Natasha Stott Despoja or Cathy Freeman on the cover, I have to choose the person I think will sell the most copies, even if it's Jennifer Aniston — again.'

While some of my words were drowned out, lots of girls came up to me afterwards to say they loved what *Cosmo* was doing for body image.

I wasn't that flustered, really. I understood the anger and I liked the challenge of trying to disarm aggressive people, even if it didn't always work.

Had they known the truth about what routinely goes on behind the scenes of a cover, they would have thrown eggs.

Back before publicists and photographers got wise to the power they wielded over magazines that desperately need their photos to sell copies, you could get away with a few tricks.

I first learned this lesson when I watched an art director remove the stairs from the background of a shot and replace them with a beach. Next, she removed the model's knee from in front of her seated torso and replaced it with a belly button. Then she carved out a thinner waist. The model was Elle Macpherson and that issue sold very well indeed.

Years later, I would sometimes work my own black magic on covers. Alyssa Milano was a mysteriously popular covergirl, despite having only been on two moderately successful TV shows. Infuriatingly, Ms Milano didn't like doing publicity and shots of her were incredibly scarce. US *Cosmo* photographed her once for a cover and there were a couple of different outfits in the series to choose from. We used one and sales went ballistic, so a few months later I went back to look at the other shot. Frustratingly, she wasn't smiling and while the clothes and pose were terrific, her face was not.

Without a second thought, I asked my art director to take the head from the first image and put it on the body of the second. It was still all Alyssa but the image was artificially constructed. It didn't really exist. Editors did this not infrequently before photo agencies got wise to the practice and began issuing massive penalties for altering cover images. I paid a few of those. I know of certain covers of other magazines which have featured a celebrity's head grafted onto the body of one of the magazine's staff, shot from the neck down and wearing an outfit that the editor and art director liked more than the celebrity's original one. Of course if you've shot the celebrity yourself, as some mags do, you can do what you like. If it makes her look better, she won't complain.

It was a far milder transgression that landed me in the middle of a media controversy. I'd bought a shot of Cameron Diaz from an agency after it appeared on the cover of UK *New Woman* and, in designing the cover, we decided to change the colour of the background on the original shot. We also changed the colour of Cameron's dress. I'd done it loads of times. No big deal. Or so I thought.

When the cover came out, Australian *New Woman* decided to stir the pot by sending out a press release revealing what we'd done. The media pounced and readers were horrified. I received dozens of angry letters from women saying we'd misled and deceived them. But it's just a frock, I protested, missing their point entirely. They thought Cameron had been wearing a red dress when in fact it was blue. So what else might we be lying about?

A lot, as it turns out. Women are justified in mistrusting the images they see in magazines. In recent years, a new job has crept onto the staff list at the front of every magazine. It's usually called something like 'digital production' and it basically means retouching. Every image you see in a magazine has been digitally altered — every product and every person. Some, just for clarity or colour correction, others for 'unsightly blemishes' like stretch marks, pimples, pores, freckles, moles, pigmentation, cellulite or goosebumps.

Some images, particularly in fashion photographs, are altered to the point where the models are almost unrecognisable as human beings, so plastic looking and flawless are the skin, the hair, the teeth and the eyes. Some photographers and art directors will alter body shapes entirely, chopping into arms and legs, lengthening torsos, removing curves and bulges and waists.

Hypocritically perhaps, I had a line in the sand about altering images. A line that shifted. For some reason, I always saw a clear distinction between the cover image and the images inside the magazine. Inside, I always urged my staff to leave stretch marks, cellulite and other 'blemishes' in place. On the cover though, I had no problem with changing the colour of clothes or digitally thickening or lengthening someone's hair. Sometimes I did change bodies but only to make them bigger. Oh, and to attach them to different heads …

BIRTH DAY

Voicemail to me from Mum:

'Oh darling! I got your message! How exciting! I'm going to come over and make you tea! See you soon!'

The pains wake me up at 2.40 am but that's not unusual. This has been happening for the past few nights. It can't possibly be labour because it's not too painful, really. Other nights, I've just fallen back to sleep but this time I'm struggling a little. Could it be … nah.

I hoist myself, awkwardly out of bed, wrap a cardigan over my pyjamas, stuff my feet into ugg boots and take my book downstairs to sit on the couch and read.

For the next hour, I turn the pages distractedly. I'm aware that the pains are fairly regular, although I don't time them. Every five or ten minutes I'd guess. They're not getting stronger but they're not stopping either.

It's 4 am and I'm feeling tired now so I shuffle upstairs and climb back into bed. Ouch. Each time a pain starts, I open my eyes and look at the clock on my bedside table. They seem to be coming at seven-minute intervals. I try to will Jason awake but he's not budging, so at 4.58 am. I shake his shoulder.

'Babe, I'm not sure but I think something might be happening …'

Suddenly, he's awake. 'Right. Wow. Okay. Contractions?'

'Yep, I think so.'

'How often?'

'About every seven minutes … here comes one now.' I wince.

'Okay, I'll call the hospital.'

Nine hours later and I'm still at home. The midwife Jason spoke to explained that because this was my first baby, labour would probably take a long time and I might be more comfortable at home. So that's where we've been. Me in the nursing chair watching 'Video Hits', Jason manically cleaning the house, and my mum making tea for everyone while Jason's mum makes us toast.

I still don't feel like it's the real deal yet. I'm not able to focus on anything past the next contraction. I've been up for almost twelve hours with contractions almost every five minutes. Fatigue is settling over me like a blanket.

Everyone has left us now and I settle into our bathtub, which is underneath a skylight. Looking up, I notice it has become strangely dark, and soon lightning begins to flash.

A giant, naked pregnant person in a bath under a skylight during an electrical storm. And oh my Lord, the pain is bloody awful. I have a sudden and very strong sense that it's time to get to the hospital.

Jason helps me out of the bath and into my clothes. Despite my sense of urgency, I insist on blow-drying my hair because … why wouldn't I? I don't want it to go all wavy and frizzy. That would be unattractive. Vanity is a hard habit to shake, it seems. Even while in labour.

The drive to the hospital is interesting and not in a good way. Like many couples, Jason and I have very different ideas when it comes to choosing the best route between point A and point B.

Personally, I don't really care how many traffic lights there might be, I like straight lines and staying on one road for as long as possible. Keep it simple is my navigational mantra. I want to be able to tune out of the fact I'm driving and cruise along on autopilot. But Jason? He likes to keep moving. He must determine the fastest possible route between A and B.

To achieve this, he'll always go the tricky back way, the polar opposite of me and my preference for main roads. So naturally, the route Jason chooses for our early-afternoon trip to the hospital is along the road with the most speed bumps in Australia. Over we go! Another bump! In addition to being bumpy, this punishing road is windy because clearly I'm not suffering enough.

If you have ever been in labour, witnessed someone in labour or even just know what labour means, you'll understand that a contraction and a speed bump are not well matched. The only thing more painful than having a contraction is sawing your own arm off. Or having a contraction while going over a speed bump.

To make matters worse —Yes! Possible! — Jason decides it's a good time to call the hospital while we're driving along Speed Bump Boulevard to inform them of our approach.

It all goes down something like this:

Jason: *'Um, hello. I called earlier about my partner who's in labour.'*
[bump]
Me: *'FUCK. FUCK FUCK FUCK.'*

Jason: 'What? Yes, her name is Mia. Freedman. F-R-E —'
[bump]
Me: 'IDIOT. FUCK. I HATE YOU, JASON! FUCK.
FUCK. OW! FUCK! HATE YOU!!!! OH FUCK.'
Jason: '… Hang on, sorry, yes, that's it. Um, yes, we're about
ten —'
[bump]
Me: [trying to punch him while grabbing phone] 'HANG UP,
FUCK, SHIT, HOW COULD YOU TAKE THIS —'
[bump]
Me: … 'FUCKING BLOODY STUPID ROAD!
FUCKING FUCK!'

When the speed bumps, phone call and my need to swear are over, I lapse into silence.

I've discovered, as the day has progressed, that I am not a noisy labour person. None of those moans and groans and panting and shrieking like the labours I've watched in movies and birthing documentaries. For me, anything that involves my stomach muscles, like making noise, makes the pain worse. Speed Bump Boulevard is an exception — it seems fury trumps pain, and I regain my ability to shout — but now that particular nightmare is over, I retreat back into silence. This is Christmas come early for Jason, no doubt.

When we arrive at the hospital, we're shown to an exam room straight away and a midwife comes to see how dilated I am.

'Three and a half centimetres,' she announces.

I'm not quite sure how to react to this news. 'Can I have an enema?' I reply in the same tone I'd use to request soy milk in my latte.

'Why would you want that, pet?' she says, a little taken aback.

'Um, so … you know … I don't … you know, um, poo on the baby?'

I cannot quite believe I am petitioning for an enema. The midwife looks at me and reflects for a moment. 'Well, I suppose I can give you a suppository if you really want one,' she relents.

'Great! Yes please!' You'd think she'd offered to double my baby bonus, I am that grateful. I have officially crossed over to a parallel universe. One where you beg complete strangers to put things in your bottom.

Five minutes later, when the suppository does its work, I experience the unique sensation of my uterus contracting at the same time as cramps rip through my lower intestine. A double treat.

Did I really request this? Yes I did.

Mercifully it works quickly and the midwife is waiting for me when I go back into the examination room. Jason has gone back downstairs to remove our car from the ambulance bay and park it somewhere more legal and less selfish. I am not unhappy that he missed the enema conversation and its aftermath.

'Hop back up on the table,' the midwife says kindly, helping me. 'Dr Bob wants me to break your waters and get things moving along.'

Sounds good to me. Break away.

As I wonder about how the breaking part might happen, the midwife produces a nasty-looking implement that at first glance appears to be a stick with a metal hook on the end. At second and third glance, it's still that.

She waits until I'm between contractions and then the stick-hook and I become intimate. I hear a small pop and suddenly feel a release of pressure as water gushes out of me.

'That's it?'

Apparently so. Kind of anti-climactic really, especially when you're lying down. Nothing like the movies.

Next the midwife asks if I'd like to have a shower to ease the contractions.

I consider this for a millisecond. 'Do you have any shower caps?' I ask.

'Sorry, love,' she replies, again clearly puzzled by my question. Probably because no one's ever asked her that before due to the fact most women in labour are not vain twits worried about frizzy hair.

'I'll pass on the shower then, thanks,' I manage to get out before another contraction pummels me. It's now close to 4 pm and I've been in labour for years. I'm undulating between adrenaline and exhaustion but my hair's still straight. That's a win.

Jason comes back from parking the car and we're shown to a delivery room. The first thing I see is a bassinet on wheels in the corner of the room, and wham. It hits me. The realisation that we're not leaving here until there's a baby in there.

In my head, this was the part where we'd carefully unpack our labour bag. While I was pregnant, someone had given me a photocopied list called 'Things You Need'. Some of the things it dictated for the labour bag were honey (for a quick energy burst during labour), music (Sade, anyone? Enya?), Rescue Remedy, massage oil (for partners to massage into sore backs) and lip balm (for dry lips due to panting).

But just like millions of women before me, agonising pain derails my plans and suddenly I don't care if there are live chickens in that bag. The bag can get stuffed. And so can that Collette Dinnigan dress I packed to wear during labour.

Yes, I know this sounds ridiculous and it was only a smidge less ridiculous than it sounds. The dress was more like a slip, it was loose and comfortable and it wasn't sequinned or beaded or anything like that. But I was appalled by the thought of ugly hospital gowns and wanted something a bit nicer to wear during the most important moment of my life. And, you know, for the photos immediately afterwards.

It seems I was still having some trouble distinguishing between going to a nice restaurant and giving birth. But I'm not so deluded as to confuse the labour ward with a black-tie function. That is reserved for my obstetrician, Dr Bob, who I learn is at a formal banquet at Government House.

I am unexpectedly calm about this. It's a bit like a movie. Pain is beginning to carry me away from reality.

A few contractions later and a new midwife comes to check on me. She, too, suggests a shower. Clearly, there is a conspiracy against my hair. The difference is that I'm now that much further along in my labour and suddenly I'm all, 'Hell, why not? Fuck my hair.' Pain has finally wrestled my vanity to the mat. Jason helps me down the corridor to the shower room and I'm soon standing naked under the water.

Drugs have always been the plan and I've been clear about this all along. I see no shame in it, no failure. I've never bought into the idea of 'she who suffers the most wins'. Not in any aspect of my life.

But now, when the midwife asks me about an epidural, I demur. I feel almost a bit embarrassed. Like I'm wimping out.

Before I can think too much about this, my concentration is vacuumed up by another contraction. I'm vaguely aware that I'm hanging from the showerhead, but really, it is my mind hovering somewhere near the ceiling.

At one point, I become dimly aware that Jason goes somewhere — where does he go? And then he returns with a midwife.

'Now, Mia, do you want an epidural, love?'

'Ummmmmmm, owwwwww ...' I can barely talk.

'The thing is, if you say yes now, the anaesthetist is still twenty minutes away.'

I'm finding it hard to convert her words to meaning.

'Uhhhh …'

'There's no need to be a hero.'

'Yes!' I blurt.

'All right, pet. I'll let the anaesthetist know. Here are some towels. Come back into the room in fifteen minutes.'

Time is a slippery thing and I'm struggling to have any sense of it. The pain is blowing my mind. A hundred years later, Jason wraps me in a towel and helps me back to the room, my hair plastered to my head and my care factor out the window.

The anaesthetist arrives and I'm rolled onto my side like a sick whale. He starts asking me questions and I can't speak. I think they're talking about my medical history but I'm lost in pain. 'Jason!' I manage to hiss. 'Bloody answer!' This is really fucking hideous. I wasn't prepared. Worse than I expected.

A sharp pain in my back distracts me. 'Oh,' I think absently. 'That's a different sort of pain from a contraction. How novel.' The momentary variation in pain sensation from the grinding agony of contractions to the sharp pushing of the needle into my back is almost a relief.

'In one or two more contractions the pain should be gone,' says the anaesthetist and I want to marry him and have his babies straight after I've had this one. The next contraction is not nearly as bad, and within a few minutes we're all watching the contractions on a monitor but I can't feel them. It's a miracle.

The next hour or two is low-key and I'm in a tiptop mood. 'It could still be a while yet,' cautions the midwife.

And then, at my next check, it's all systems go. Suddenly, in walks Dr Bob, wearing white tie and tails, looking like something out of a Cary Grant movie.

People appear from everywhere, including my mum, who is taking photos. And something about a student and is it okay if she watches. Frankly, a class of work-experience boys could walk in right now and I would not care. Whatever.

I'm awkwardly propped into a more upright position with blue hospital scrubs placed over my legs and underneath me. The scrubs make me scared. At this point, it's looking fairly certain I'm not going to be sent home with a diagnosis of false labour.

Dr Bob is back, in a surgical gown and it's time to push. In just a few minutes, the head is out. And with one more push, my slippery baby is pulled out of my body and placed on my tummy. 'It's a boy!' declares Dr Bob. I slide my son onto my chest in disbelief, looking at his scrunched-up little face and waiting to feel an avalanche of motherly love. He's warm and covered in blood and vernix and he is bald. The moment is so intense and overwhelming it drowns out everything and, strangely, I feel almost nothing. Quickly, he's taken from me by the midwives.

This is okay. I'm pretty out of it. Pretty numb emotionally and from the waist down. He's having a little trouble breathing and the paediatrician is called in to check him. I'm oddly unconcerned. Jason is with him.

Many weeks afterwards, I look back at the photos Mum took in those moments after the birth. There is Luca, being weighed and measured. You can see me in the background, not even looking in Luca's direction but peering intently into a metal dish containing my placenta with a midwife pointing to various parts of it and explaining how it worked.

It's the most incredible moment of my life, so incredible that I'm almost floating above it like I was during labour. I expect to cry or feel a crushing rush of love but neither happens. Not straight away. The tears and the rush will come shortly. Right now, I need something to eat.

AND THEN WE WERE THREE

Voicemail to everyone from Jason:

'Hey guys, I just wanted to let you know that Mia's had a little boy, Luca. We can't wait for you to meet him.'

Toast. I wanted toast. My baby was wrapped up like a babushka with only a few square centimetres of face visible under the swaddling.

His breathing was fine now and his little face seemed serene, unbothered by all the fuss going on around him.

Our parents were in the delivery room now that I'd had a couple of stitches and had my epidural removed. The post-birth endorphins had begun flowing and I was elated.

Luca was being passed around admiringly, the first grandchild on both sides of the family. Flashbulbs were going as I munched merrily on chewy white hospital toast with jam and sipped a cup of tea. It was possibly the best meal I'd ever tasted.

Adrenaline had been replaced by hunger. I hadn't eaten since the Japanese takeaway we'd dined on more than twenty-four hours ago, and having taken a backseat to my uterus for so long, my stomach was now loudly protesting against the injustice.

It was 11 pm and Luca was one and a half hours old. The proud grandparents reluctantly put down their plastic cups of champagne and left to go home and then it was just the three of us in the delivery room. Our family.

Despite my endorphins, I felt surprisingly clingy and needy after Jason finally left for the night, once I'd been safely ensconced with Luca in my hospital room. I'd feel like this for days, presumably programmed to want my baby's father around to provide for us and protect us from predators.

I kept looking at our baby sleeping next to my bed and replaying over and over in my head how he'd got here. Every so often I'd reach out and stroke his head. Did I love him yet? It was hard to determine what I felt, although I was definitely happy. I certainly felt protective of him and very interested in him, and very responsible for his welfare.

I didn't dare reach into his bassinet to pick him up. Was I even allowed? It still hadn't registered that he was my baby and I could do whatever I wanted. Hell, I could even bring him into bed with me! But that would be the beginning of the end, wouldn't it? I'd heard it was important to get them used to sleeping in their own bed and I was terrified to fuck everything up mere hours after he was born. Was that even possible? I'm sure it was.

The midwife had assured me that most babies slept very soundly in the hours after they were born. 'Birth is exhausting,' she'd explained. 'He'll need to sleep just to recover his strength.' Strength for what was unclear. Crying and eating, it would turn out.

Also, much strength was required to produce the giant dark green poo that appeared in his nappy early the next morning. That wasn't in the books … or had I missed it? Small problem: I'd never changed a nappy. Ever in my life.

And since I was starting with hospital-provided cloth ones, this was probably a good thing because I had nothing to compare it to. No easy disposable nappy benchmark.

It never occurred to me to ask if I could bring in my own nappies or clothes for Luca to wear. I was happy — delighted in fact — to be a compliant and obedient sheep and do exactly what I was told. I simply hopped on the hospital treadmill and let it carry me where everyone else was going. With no clue what I was doing, I had little choice.

Jason arrived early the next morning and our family reunion was magic. I took the opportunity to shower and wash my hair and use my travel blow-dryer. Lucky my vanity was still AWOL because this was about as effective as having a small dog pant on my head.

My milk still hadn't come in but my breasts were certainly growing and I was instructed to put Luca on to feed every two hours. He had other ideas for ways to spend his time, though.

'He keeps falling asleep while he's feeding,' I told one of the procession of midwives who came into my room, along with all manner of hospital staff and visitors. It was a bit like living in a nightclub toilet.

'Oh, that won't do; we have to wake him up,' she said briskly. 'He needs to eat.' She showed me how to stroke his cheek or lightly pinch his toes to interrupt his snooze and focus him on the task at hand (or boob), but it made little difference. He was zonked.

She decided we needed to be more proactive. 'It's very important for him to feed. We'll try to express some colostrum and feed him with a dropper. Sometimes that's easier for them than sucking from a nipple.'

So began the fascinating experience of being milked by a robust German midwife called Veronika. How fortunate I had checked my inhibitions at the door, oh, probably when I was begging for an enema. Because this was up there with my least dignified moments.

I was unsure as to the protocol in such a situation. Should we chat while she tugged, tweaked and squeezed my giant nipple? What should we chat about, exactly? I gave it my best shot, asking all manner of questions about breastfeeding and Germany and trying through the fog of my post-birth brain to take in the odd grain of instruction.

It wasn't a huge success. 'Baby's mouths are better at this than hands,' she noted in her Germanic, no-nonsense way, holding up a plastic cup with about a centimetre of yellow colostrum sitting pitifully in the bottom.

I wasn't too bothered thanks to those happy hormones that made me love everyone I saw, even the slightly dodgy man who brought my breakfast and walked into my room while I had my top off.

There was always someone coming in to ask me a question or offer me something. A pad. New sheets. Some lunch. Advice. Panadol.

A lady who may have been a physiotherapist (I wasn't listening when she introduced herself) popped in at one point and gave me a very scary lecture about incontinence. 'Have you been doing your pelvic floor exercises?' she demanded. 'Did you know the majority of old people in nursing homes are admitted due to incontinence? It's vital you do those pelvic-floor squeezes as early and often as possible throughout your life!' Um, sure, yes, Okay. Are we really talking about me being old and incontinent when my stitches are still fresh? Just give me a moment to catch up …

Jason spent most of his time with me at the hospital and went home at night to sleep. On the second night, reality began to dawn. Jason was about to leave, it was 9 pm and Luca was almost twenty-four hours old. We were getting ready for bed and the midwife on duty was instructing me about what I must do during the night. 'You've just fed him so he'll need his next feed in no more than four hours,' she explained.

But wait, I thought, blinking. That can't be right. Four hours is … 1 am. And that's the MIDDLE OF THE NIGHT! Ohhhhhh. This is really it. And it was. I always smile when new parents brag in those first couple of days '… and she's already such a good sleeper!' Sure she is. Until she wakes up from her post-birth snooze-a-thon and starts demanding all manner of things you don't understand at a volume you can't ignore.

Luca never did quite manage the four-hourly thing. He opted for every two hours instead, although in his first few months, every time he opened his mouth to squawk, I stuck a nipple in it so he may not have technically been hungry on each occasion. 'It will be better when your milk comes in, love,' a midwife assured me at 3 a.m. when I couldn't get him to stop screaming. 'He's just a bit hungry.'

Sure enough, on day three, I woke up with one hundred bricks on my chest. Ahhh, milk's here. I could not believe how huge and hard my already enormous breasts had become overnight.

Along with the milk came the tears. I'd been warned about day three and the associated hormone-related weepiness but it still managed to ambush me. Jason was at a meeting and I couldn't calm Luca or myself for what seemed like hours. When eventually Luca fell asleep, I realised, just like the cliché of a new mother, that I hadn't even managed to have a shower yet. I had a desperate, primal need for Jason but I didn't want to be needy. I've never been terrific at saying, 'Help me, I'm not coping,' even to those I love most in the world.

So I stood in the shower and cried for a bit until I started getting wrinkly. When I walked back into the room, there was Jason, like a vision, sitting on the bed holding Luca. Magic.

TRAINING WHEELS

Voicemail to me from my PA:

'Hi Mia. Listen, I have a message here from a journalist who wants to know about Luca and if you'd agree to a photograph for the paper. Call me back and tell me what you want me to say.'

It turns out I needn't have stressed quite so much about my mothering inadequacies. Lord knows there were enough of them — and they'd become glaringly apparent in the next few months — but there were a couple of things that worked in my favour.

First of all, when I told my mum how much I was freaked out by not knowing what to do, she wisely pointed out that Luca hadn't done this before either. 'He has no one to compare you to,' she said. Ah. This was instantly comforting.

Second, I used my time in hospital to take lessons. Actual, practical lessons. On the first morning, one of the seven hundred people passing through my room gave me a timetable of baby classes for new parents. I was thrilled to see all the basics covered — from breastfeeding to settling and sleeping. An hour a day, just down the hall. 'You just wheel your baby along with you in the bassinet,' advised a midwife.

Surrounded by other slightly dazed and confused new mums in slippers and dressing gowns, all of us looking at least six months pregnant still (they don't tell you that in the books, do they?), I was able to absorb some practical tips about caring for a newborn — all the stuff I couldn't get my head around when said newborn was just a bulge in my stomach and a bunch of kicks.

Clearly, I wasn't the only clueless new mother who had ever given birth and miraculously, with pregnancy and birth behind me, a rather large space opened up for new knowledge.

The brain is a wonderful thing. Realising it no longer needed to access the ridiculous amount of information I'd acquired about pregnancy and birth, it hired a storage facility in the far back corner and dumped all that info in there, freeing up the front part for new tricks.

On my last day in hospital, I decided to venture out of my womb-room and across the road to the newsagent to buy a newspaper and begin reconnecting with the world. I nervously left Luca with the midwives and waddled downstairs, feeling a lot like Dorothy when she arrives in Oz. Except it was dirty and raining and there were no Oompa Loompas. And my shoes were ugg boots, not sparkly ruby slippers.

As I stood in front of the news-stand, the front page of the paper assaulted me with a huge headline: 'A NATION OF BASTARDS!' The accompanying photo showed a row of newborns in a hospital. Some study had just been published showing that more Australian couples in the nineties were unmarried when they had children than in the seventies. Gee, what groundbreaking news.

The phone call I'd had several days ago from my PA suddenly made sense. The same newspaper had called my office right after hearing I'd had a baby. They'd wanted to do a quick interview and take a photo of me with Luca in the hospital. This had seemed slightly over-the-top given that my level of celebrity was decidedly C-list. If that. I was just a newish editor of a magazine with a pretty low profile.

My answer had been 'forget it'. This was a no-brainer because I was fiercely private about being pregnant and having a baby and frankly could think of nothing worse than having a camera shoved in my face at this moment. There was nothing to be gained from it.

But now that I'd seen the front page, I understood. New baby. Not married. They'd wanted to use my family as a real-life example of the 'nation of bastards'. I started to cry just thinking about it. Imagine if I'd naïvely agreed, expecting some fluffy item on the gossip page, only to find my beautiful baby boy branded a bastard. Those bastards!

A decade later, I opened the paper to see a big picture of a tired but happy-looking mother photographed in the hospital with her newborn twins. The headline screamed 'BABIES MORE LIKELY TO DIE AFTER CAESAREANS'. The caption stated: *Emma Brown with her twins who were born by caesarean section*. My mind flashed back to my own experience and I immediately knew how she'd been sucked into posing proudly with her beautiful babies for what she'd thought would be a harmless medical story.

Back in my room, I chugged down some Rescue Remedy and prepared to go home. Later that day, Jason arrived and we dressed Luca in a little going-home outfit. It was a lot like trying to dress a small, uncooperative octopus and it took us the best part of an hour. I was going to have to get better at this. Wasn't I?

HOME ALONE

Voicemail to Jo from me:

'Hi, it's me. You are so gorgeous to drop over those flowers yesterday. I can't believe it was my birthday. With all the flowers I got after Luca, I already feel totally spoilt and that was only ... wait, how long ago was he born? What day is it? Two weeks or something? I don't know. I'm tired. Have I mentioned that? Jason gave me this beautiful dress and I put it on because we were all going out to lunch at a café, and just before we left Luca did this giant vomit all over me. I nearly died. Not because of the dress because who cares but because of how much vomit came out of that teeny little body! Where was he storing all that — in his legs? Anyway, we had a lovely day. I was so exhausted by the end of it, we opened a tin of baked beans and collapsed in front of the TV, but I was so tired I couldn't process all the information coming at me so I asked Jason to mute it. We sat there with our baked beans watching the news with no sound. Still, it's been the best birthday of my life and I'm not even joking.'

It was quite a shock when we were allowed to take Luca home, five days after he was born. I mean, didn't these people realise we were unlicensed?

Before we left I borrowed — okay, stole — one of the hospital baby nightgowns that tied up at the back. It was the only item of clothing Luca had worn since birth, and unlike the outfit we'd dressed him in for his homecoming, it could be put on and taken off in less than an hour. Those little suits with the arms and legs and all the press-studs? Oh man, intimidation factor: HIGH.

I sat in the back with Luca on the very slow drive home. The idea of abandoning him alone in the scary backseat was absurd. Suddenly the world seemed huge and threatening and full of danger. It was also very loud. When did it get so loud?

Having been cocooned in a small room for days, my senses were barely coping with the onslaught. Every noise made me jump — and the number of things to look at! I kept blinking as I gazed dumbly out the window, trying to filter the amount of information flying towards my brain through my eyes.

As Jason pulled the car into our driveway, I quickly got my first taste of my changed status. After nine months of being a pregnant princess, not having to open a single door for myself or lift anything heavier than a sandwich, I looked up to see Jason halfway inside carefully carrying Luca in his capsule as I struggled awkwardly from the car. 'What about my bag?' I called out to Jason. 'Oh, can't you carry it?' he called back. Right. That would be the sound of me being evicted from my ivory tower.

The next few months were wonderful. Confusing, exhausting and wonderful. Luca didn't have his own room, so he slept next to us. There was no nursery. Our second bedroom was used as a study for Jason and had my treadmill in it so we set up the change table in an alcove in our hallway and stored Luca's clothes on the shelf underneath.

I've never been a proper girl like that. I've never been interested in interiors or furniture. I can appreciate other people's beautiful homes but I don't speak decorating. So I just kind of give up and make do. Sometimes, Jason picks up the slack but neither of us had considered creating a nursery. I was too busy reading pregnancy books and freaking out.

Having Luca sleep in our room worked perfectly well until he was about six or seven months old. That's when it became clear it would be quite challenging to, ahem, make a sibling for him in the future because he'd begun to sit up in his cot and wave a sock at us during private moments. So we decided it might be time for him to have a room of his own. It was still nothing like a proper nursery. More like a spare room with a couple of bits of baby furniture shoved in it. But we were happy and Luca voiced no complaints.

The sleeping thing was never great though. From birth Luca had been feeding every couple of hours around the clock, and at about four months he started to cry for long stretches through the day. This was new.

Baffled and exhausted, I made my first phone call to the Karitane mothers' helpline and explained my problem to the nice lady on the other end of the phone.

Her: 'And when was the last time you put him down in his cot?'
Me: 'Um, well, last night.'
Her: 'But it's five o'clock in the afternoon now. You mean you don't put him down during the day at all?'
Me: 'No. Um, not really. Should I?'
Her: 'A baby of that age should only be awake for ninety minutes to two hours at a time, maximum.'
Me: 'Oh.'
Her: 'Then he needs to go back to bed.'
Me: 'Oh.'
Her: 'That's why he's crying. Because he's exhausted. He's been up for eleven hours.'
Me: 'Oh.'

I knew the midwives shouldn't have let us go home unsupervised. Despite the fact Jason and I were grown-up, well-educated, intelligent people who had read an absurd number of books, there was a gap in our baby knowledge about the size of the Northern Territory.

Somewhere in one of the books, Jason had read that a baby should associate long sleeps with his cot so you should only put him in there at night. This meant during the day we played with him until he passed out wherever he happened to be lying, no doubt dreaming of parents who knew what they were doing.

And yet we all muddled through, able to see the humour in most situations. The day Luca had his four-month injections he reacted quite badly and was impossible to settle. We tried everything — rocking, patting, driving around the block, baths, the BabyBjörn. Nothing worked.

'I know!' I declared at about 7 pm as we neared the four-hour crying mark. 'Let's introduce solids!' Hell, I figured, things can't get much worse and it might be a good distraction.

Like so many milestones, it was a bit of an anticlimax. A bit of rice cereal that sort of fell out of his mouth. The End.

About a month later, Jason became sick. He'd been to the US for work and had come home with the flu. Nothing major and it passed after a week but afterwards he was exhausted and not himself. His health rapidly deteriorated.

The next few months were spent in a haze of doctors' appointments, alternative therapies and increasing frustration. The eventual diagnosis was chronic fatigue syndrome (CFS), an umbrella description for a post-viral state of fatigue that lasts longer than six months.

There's still a lot of misunderstanding about CFS. Many people mistakenly assume it just means you're really tired and want to sleep. But one of the ironies of CFS is that sleep is often impossible.

Symptoms vary from person to person, but for Jason it manifested itself in severe physical exhaustion, insomnia, joint pain and extreme sensory sensitivity. His concentration was obliterated. He couldn't tolerate loud noises or even music. He found it hard to have conversations because his mind was so foggy. He felt like an old man.

In some ways, the symptoms were similar to extreme sleep deprivation — which I was also experiencing — but worse. Some days he could barely get up the stairs. He couldn't work. The simplest task — like driving to the shops to buy milk — would leave him unable to do anything else for days.

We tried everything in search of a cure. It was 1998 and, like most people, we didn't yet have the internet at home so researching a little-understood illness with no known cure was a nightmare. It was virtually impossible to find information and support and it didn't help that there was a widely held suspicion among Joe Public that CFS was all in the mind. Equally insulting was the idea that Jason was just tired. I wanted to slap stupid people who said things to us like, 'Yeah, I'm tired all the time. Maybe I've got chronic fatigue too!'

Any social isolation we may have experienced by being the only new parents in our circle of friends was amplified a thousand per cent by Jason's illness. The sexy, energetic, positive, enthusiastic man I loved slowly dissolved. He used every ounce of strength and energy to do what he could to help around the house and with Luca, but most of the time he was utterly spent.

By the time Luca was about five months old, I'd returned to work two days a week. Even before Jason's illness, I'd been feeling reluctant about going back. All my pre-birth bravado about only needing four months of maternity leave evaporated in the face of the overwhelming love I had for Luca.

Hadn't factored that into my career plans, had I? I was utterly besotted with my baby son, and the thought of leaving him to go and create a sealed section made me feel physically ill.

Fortunately, my perceptive boss sensed my anguish and initiated a conversation while I was trying to work out how to bring it up. Rather than let me slip away and have to find another editor, she suggested I work two days a week in the office for a few months and three days from home. Her offer provided massive relief and I grabbed it with both hands.

On the days I was at *Cosmo*, my mother and Jason's mum each had a day looking after Luca. I expressed milk in my office, closing my door and sitting at my desk with my boobs out, pumping, while I proofread stories about dating and sex positions. I was blessed to have family to help with childcare and an office with a door so I wasn't forced to express in a stinky toilet cubicle (like so many working mums have to), but things at home were otherwise quite bleak.

Jason showed no signs of getting better. We learned that if the symptoms didn't improve within a few months from onset, sufferers could be stuck with CFS for years, even decades. We were devastated by this slippery prognosis and by the fact no one could pinpoint a cure.

Jason was incapable of being among groups of people or even having a drink with a mate. He just wasn't strong enough physically or clear enough mentally. Our very small social life shrivelled to nothing.

Watching me sink slowly into despair over the situation, my three closest girlfriends, Jo, Jen and Karen, decided to stage an intervention of sorts. It took the form of a girls' weekend in

Melbourne and it was possibly the most I've ever laughed in one forty-eight-hour period.

Luca had turned one and I wasn't breastfeeding any more so my parents took him for the weekend. Jason wasn't yet well enough to look after him on his own.

The four of us girls flew down one Friday afternoon and checked into a hotel before heading to St Kilda for drinks. To call me a suppressed control freak is a little like calling Osama bin Laden somewhat unreasonable. Jen always says the main difference between her and me is that if we're invited to a party, she'll say, 'Great!' and I'll say, 'What time will it end?' Followed immediately by 'And where will I park?' There's a time and a place for spontaneity, I say.

My girlfriends had some potent antidotes to the funk I was in, most notably eating and shopping, distilled with tequila shots. We began the evening with cocktails before breaking for dinner and then we started walking through St Kilda looking for a taxi.

As we ambled past an apartment block with music blaring out a window and a party very obviously in full swing, Jen decided it would be a good idea to crash it. 'Come on, we're going in,' she announced, grabbing my hand and pulling me across the garden and up some stairs with Karen and Jo right behind us. 'Hi, we're looking for John!' Jen said brightly to anyone who looked our way.

That's how I found myself sitting on a beanbag on the floor of a stranger's house chatting to a bunch of uni students bemused by the four older women who had parachuted into their party and were drinking their beer. And then we were dancing in the lounge room while Jen accosted the DJ. 'Have you got any Kylie? We're from Sydney!' she shouted over the music.

These two statements, while seemingly unrelated, would become a theme over the course of the next eight hours as we trekked from the party to half a dozen nightclubs and bars. It was big fun. The kind of fun when you laugh so hard you think you might wee in your pants and, if you've ever given birth, sometimes do.

Because I am not made of strong stuff, I decided I wanted to go home after about three or four bars and four thousand tequila shots. It was 1 am and my friends would not hear of it. 'I want to go hoooome,' I'd whine as they shoved yet another shot glass into my hand. 'No you don't!' Jo would insist. 'You want to go to the MIDDLE OF THE DANCE FLOOR!' and there she'd drag me. Wherever we went, while Karen was at the bar buying us yet another round, I'd look up to see Jen in the DJ booth. In the end, I came up with a cunning plan to halt my alcohol intake in the face of unrelenting peer pressure. As we lined up yet another bit of salt and lemon to 'lick, sip, suck' the tequila slammers, I'd do the lick and the suck but throw the shot over my shoulder instead of down my throat. This bought me time and allowed me to remain standing upright. Mostly. Eventually, at some appalling hour like 5 am, my friends agreed we could go back to our hotel, where we all passed out.

The next morning I thought I was going to die. With no room service and a pre-arranged plan to shop the crap out of Chapel Street, we wobbled gingerly, painfully, down to the lobby in search of a cab that could take us to buy Panadol and then to South Yarra.

In one of those moments in your life when you know with certainty that God is punishing you, the marble lobby of the hotel was being jackhammered. I was not imagining this. It was actually happening. The only reason I didn't burst into tears was that it would have required me to engage facial muscles that were way too close to my throbbing head, which would then fall off.

Jen, adept at hangover management, high-tailed us all to a greasy café and ordered bacon and eggs for everyone. I sipped water and tried not to vomit into my handbag.

After the Panadol kicked in and we were away from the nauseating smell of food, I brightened a little and we spent a restorative day shopping for ridiculous things we would never wear, like puffer vests and complicated trainers. Then we went to a Napoleon make-up store and bought absurd amounts of sparkly eye dust in different colours. Unable to back up for another night out, we spent the Saturday evening watching an in-house movie, eating chocolate and laughing ourselves senseless.

The weekend was a revelation. My girlfriends had pulled me out of my dark place and reminded me of the twenty-six-year-old side of myself. The one without responsibilities as a partner and mother and boss and employee. It was the greatest gift they could have given me. And I've never been as drunk since.

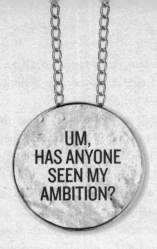

UM, HAS ANYONE SEEN MY AMBITION?

Answering machine message for me from *Cosmo* deputy editor:

'Hi Mia, we need to send a courier around with the cover. The art department needs to get started urgently. Will you be there in the next few hours? Call me! Thanks.'

As soon as Luca was born, I seemed to misplace my ambition and it took quite some time to locate. This was a huge surprise, as was the fact I barely noticed its disappearance. I was a career girl, wasn't I? I know I used to be. Would I ever be again? Frankly, I was unperturbed. Those happy hormones had kicked in and I was blissfully enveloped in motherhood.

When I'd been preparing to go on maternity leave, I'd wondered how I'd ever be able to exist without my job. More importantly, how would it exist without me? How would my magazine survive and flourish when I wasn't there to micro-manage every decision? Perfectly well, it turned out. Which is lucky because moments after Luca was born my attitude was pretty much: 'What magazine?'

Graciously, Pat stepped in to take up much of the slack during those first few months, which must have been a drag for her since she had only just escaped from the day-to-day running of *Cosmo* after appointing me to replace her. She never complained. Combined with all my pre-planning for the issues I'd be missing and the support of my capable staff, I was able to disconnect entirely from the office for at least six weeks. It was a special time.

And then, insidiously, work began to seep back into my baby bubble.

At first, it felt like the worst kind of intrusion. In the days before email, it was all very primitive — faxes and phone calls and couriers. It's not like I could choose to consolidate work into the times Luca was catnapping on the floor or after he'd gone to sleep at night, as I might have been able to in a more technologically advanced time. I was at the mercy of my staff, who needed me to make decisions when it suited *them*. And this could be as often as ten times a day. Each time they phoned or faxed or sent me something, it felt like I was literally being yanked away from Luca. The dislocation was jarring because my brain was not yet accustomed to doing two things at once. Sleep deprivation didn't help my inability to multitask. Luca was still feeding every couple of hours through the night.

One day, I was particularly frazzled and lost it. Jason's mother had just left after dropping over some wonderful home cooking and having a play with Luca. Now my mum had dropped around to see him and the office kept calling. Two different staff members were ringing me about the same thing because they hadn't spoken to each other first. This was infuriating. A courier arrived to drop off magazines and some possibilities for the next cover. The fax was whirring with a features list for my approval. While Mum goo-gooed with Luca, I was running from the front door to the phone to the fax in my maternity bra and pyjama pants, halfway towards having a shower at 3 pm. Suddenly I burst into tears. 'I feel like everyone gets to play with

Luca except me,' I sobbed, feeling desperately frustrated. It was a watershed moment, my first tangible experience of the tug-of-war between my two lives. The first in a million. Would I ever get used to it? Yes. If something happens enough times, you eventually become used to it. That doesn't make it easier, necessarily, just more familiar.

In a heartbeat, it was time to go back to work two days a week, as Pat had suggested. This was hard and not. Hard because I was passionately in love with my baby and enjoying motherhood far more than I thought I would. But also not, because caring for a baby was so much harder and more monotonous than I'd expected. The struggle to try to do both simultaneously at home was also far tougher than sitting in an office with a door, and staff who I didn't have to take with me every time I wanted to go to the loo. In that first week, as I stood waiting for my morning latte, I became aware that I was rhythmically jiggling the pile of magazines I was carrying in one arm. Like a baby. It was the perfect physical manifestation of where my head was at. At home with Luca.

For a long time after dragging myself away from my four-month-old love obsession and returning to the office, I struggled to regain my interest in *Cosmo*. Or anything other than my baby. I begged Pat to let me quit *Cosmo* and launch a parenting magazine for ACP instead. Fortunately, she just smiled indulgently and ignored my fanciful pleas. This was a good thing, because after about a year my complete immersion in all things baby gradually lifted. Like the dissipation of a happy fog.

I still adored Luca, but I gradually became ready to talk and think about other things too. For a long time, it had felt like there was no room in my head or my heart for anything other than my baby. I was full. Sated. But eventually I found the key to the door marked 'Former Life' and discovered there was stuff behind it which was just as interesting as the contents of his nappies. Who knew?

It was a lot like rediscovering all the pre-maternity clothes I'd stored in a forgotten cupboard. They never did fit in quite the same way as they used to because my body was irrevocably changed. But they were a refreshing change from elasticised waists and oversized T-shirts. And so it was with my job. Shortly after Luca's first birthday, I returned to work four days a week and slowly, slowly, I began to love it again.

Jason's CFS was not improving. He was still sapped of strength and struggling. He remained unshakably supportive of every decision I made and did his utmost to keep his spirits up for the sake of his family.

I'd expected to feel a massive pang for Luca while I was at work but this wasn't really how it played out. This was also surprising, yet another piece in the complicated puzzle of the working mother's brain. I found I could easily become immersed in *Cosmo* when I was at the office. I was happy at work and I could focus quite well on what I was doing because I was secure in the knowledge Luca was being lovingly cared for. My mother and Jason's mother each had him one day a week, I worked from home one day and we'd hired a nanny to cover the other two days.

Finding her had been staggeringly easy. I happened to be chatting with our close friend Pete and the subject came up. Pete mentioned a guy we both knew whose girlfriend was a nanny. Her name was Anna and she was a part-time model. Funnily enough, I never considered this to be a problem although many other people thought I was certifiably insane to hire a hot nanny. But I didn't care in the slightest. She was a known quantity. Anchored in my universe to people I knew and trusted. Which, I find, is always preferable to any number of references from strangers.

Even more importantly, Anna was warm and lovely and had an instant connection with Luca. And with me. She became a bit like my little sister even though she was a head taller than me. I ended up taking her under my wing and kick-starting her modelling career, finding her a new agent and encouraging her to stop doing editorial modelling and move into more lucrative advertising work. She was the Elle Macpherson type. Tall, healthy, big smile, great body. She belonged in KFC commercials and ads for Toyota, which is exactly what ended up happening. Once I cast her in a lingerie fashion shoot for *Cosmo*. She was also on the packaging for a hair removal cream and to this day I still see her smiling face on the boxes when I go to the chemist.

Anna lasted about a year with us until her interest in nannying was eclipsed by her interest in modelling. In the end, she was taking Luca with her to castings that fell on days she looked after him. I wasn't thrilled about this but I allowed it because I had to. Like so many working mothers, my childcare arrangements were a precarious hodge-podge of family and paid care, and I lived in mortal fear of my house of cards collapsing in a screaming heap.

That's how my two-year-old son came to spend so much time hanging out with hot models. He'll thank me when he's twenty.

Eventually, I became aware that the power balance had shifted as it invariably does with anyone as soon as you come to depend on them too much. The thought of Anna leaving and the disruption it would cause was so overwhelming I had bent over backwards, sideways and upside down to accommodate her. Her happiness was integral to my work and home life. Before I knew it, it felt like I was working for her.

We agreed it was time to say goodbye when Luca was about two and a half and I sent him to day care a few days a week. We lost touch with Anna soon after when she moved to overseas.

But I always did love casually dropping 'my son's nanny, the lingerie model' into conversations and watching people totally freak out. All that ever mattered to me was that she adored Luca and he adored her.

In the year Anna was with us, I became aware of an acute failing I had as a mother. Unlike Anna, I didn't like to play. I was incapable of singing nursery rhymes or building block towers for long stretches of time. This was a very bad thing, I was sure of it, and it made me secretly ashamed. It still does. I somehow expected to become entranced with playing with my baby when I became a mother but it never happened. I always imagine other parents enjoy this stuff and that I'm somehow deficient. A pretender. I love hanging out with them and chatting and doing stuff but playing games? Going to parks? Ugh.

I'd known almost from the beginning that I'd be a better mother if I wasn't at home 24/7. It was a difficult, confronting, pill to swallow. Surely if I was a proper mother I would be one hundred per cent fulfilled by puzzles and nappies and 'Incy Wincy Spider' and mashing organic sweet potato? Or is the real definition of a proper mother that you're not fulfilled but you do it anyway because it's in the best interests of your child? Should I be parking my ambition and my genuine love of work for the benefit of my child? Those were the questions that haunted me until Luca went to school. Then, it was no longer an issue. Even if I had been at home, he wasn't.

It's strange that I held this expectation of what it means to be a mother because my own mother always had a job, working part time when I was small and then full time once I was in primary school. I had no alternative model.

What she did was quite pioneering because the 1970s was a time when far fewer mothers worked outside the home than they do now. The idea of a career for a woman with kids —

especially small kids — was unusual. Even frowned upon. Of course I didn't realise this at the time. Sure, I was aware most of my friends' mothers were at home when they returned from school each afternoon but this inspired no envy in me. I had something better, I thought. I had freedom. Independence. From the age of about nine or ten, I'd let myself in with my key, call Mum at work to let her know I was home safe, make myself a snack and then head out to play with my neighbourhood friends in the street until dark.

So when I became a mother, it was never a question of 'Should I keep working?' It was a given that I would. But then? Hello guilt. It's taken me a decade but I think I've finally come to understand and accept that it's the things I do outside motherhood that make me a better, more present, mother. Whether it's writing or going for a run or going to dinner with my girlfriends, motherhood is integral to my identity, but it isn't my entire identity. And that's okay. Back when Luca was small, it was a matter of managing my ambition, my guilt and, most importantly, the mechanics of how to be a working mother.

If I could share the daily grind with grandmothers and other people who loved Luca and who could give him full and fun attention during the times I was working, surely that was the balance I was searching for.

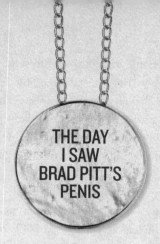

THE DAY I SAW BRAD PITT'S PENIS

Voicemail to Jason from me:

'Quick! If you haven't already left, I need you to bring me Panadeine and Naprogesic. They're in the bathroom, second drawer down. I'll meet you out the front of the hotel. God, I hope you get this before you leave! Call me!'

'Oh shit. I can't see.' This is the thought that ran through my head as I sat at my second International *Cosmo* Editors' Conference, this time in downtown Sydney. I was sitting between my best *Cosmo* friends, Ms South Africa and Ms Hungary, watching the editor of Thailand *Cosmo* give a hilarious presentation on the challenges of producing sex articles in her country where there are no words in the dictionary for 'penis' or 'vagina'. 'So we write things like "man-sword" or "love-pocket",' she deadpanned as the rest of us fell about in hysterics.

As I looked up at the accompanying PowerPoint slide of a sex-story layout, a big splotch of white light suddenly obscured my vision. I knew what this meant. A migraine. Oh dear, I was fucked. In a few hours' time I was due to host a lavish sit-down black-tie dinner and party for 500 people including all fifty-eight international editors, Helen Gurley Brown, assorted media players, celebrities and the Packers. I had to give the main speech. And if I didn't get the right pills into me in the next twenty minutes, I would be unable to do anything other than lie in a very dark room and whimper into a pillow for twenty-four hours.

This was very bad. I grabbed my handbag, scrambled out of my seat and tried to inconspicuously slip out of the conference room. 'Bathroom,' I mouthed to Helen as I crept past. Once outside, I grabbed my phone out of my bag and quickly dialled Jason. Fortunately, he was just leaving home to come and collect the breast milk I'd expressed for Luca in my last break.

I knew if I took the pills while my vision was still obscured I had a chance to circumvent the worst of my migraine and I'd just be left with a whopping hangover feeling. But if my vision cleared, it was too late. Within minutes the migraine would hit and I'd be in the foetal position until tomorrow.

I waited for Jason at the hotel's entrance, the bottle of breast milk clutched in my hand. As I saw his car approach, I ran over and he wound down the window to hand me the pills. 'Do you have water?' he asked. 'No!' I yelped. 'Shit! SHIT!'

I quickly considered my options. I was running out of time. I calculated that getting to a shop or even back inside the hotel to find water would take too long. I didn't have a second to lose. There was only one thing to do. With one hand I tossed the pills into my mouth and with the other I undid the lid of the bottle and washed them down with two big gulps of my breast milk. It was still warm. Clearly, this is known as having it all, I thought. I quickly handed Jason the rest of the milk to take home and feed Luca who was sleeping in his capsule. I gave Luca a quick kiss on his warm fuzzy head before running back into the hotel.

I suffered from migraines only occasionally and they were always stress related. It would be safe to say I was stressed. Hearst had decided to hold the biennial *Cosmo* conference in Sydney to coincide with the twenty-fifth birthday of Australian *Cosmo*. This was handy because it meant I could attend even though Luca was only a few months old. Flying overseas would have been impossible.

Convenience aside, it was stressful being the host country because I felt totally responsible for everyone having a great time. Like a proud parent, I wanted to show off my country and have everyone be dreadfully impressed by it.

Unfortunately, my country was being difficult by bunging on the worst weather I could remember. It was raining torrentially and freezing and horrible. Venturing outside was a lot like standing under a waterfall.

We'd already cancelled the harbour cruise and the surfing lessons at Bondi. After three days, the polite, 'When do you think the rain will stop?' queries I'd been fielding from seventy-five foreigners were threatening to turn hostile.

Having brightly babbled, 'It usually never rains in Sydney!' to everyone at every available opportunity, I sought refuge in small talk with Ms Russia, a fabulous gravel-voiced woman who chain-smoked heavy tar cigarettes at all times. 'Oh well, at least the temperature must be a nice change from Moscow,' I said. 'Actually no,' she shot back drily, lighting her next cigarette from her last one. 'Right now it's a sunny twenty-six degrees.'

Not helping matters, the hotel was a disorganised shambles to the point where one day at lunch when yet something else went wrong, Ms Germany rolled her eyes and said loudly, 'Now I understand why Michael Hutchence killed himself in this hotel.'

In a desperate attempt to divert attention somewhere positive, I kept bringing up the subject of our big twenty-fifty birthday party. It's amazing how language barriers and negativity disappear when fifty-eight women are discussing what they're going to wear.

Two years into my job, I was now a wee bit less starry-eyed about being a *Cosmo* editor and part of such a big global brand. I'd come to realise that these conferences had a more serious purpose than just girly fun and bonding.

Gathering us together for an intense few days of presentations and discussions every two years was a valuable opportunity for Hearst to keep us all in line. The unspoken purpose of the conference was to reinforce the *Cosmo* formula to all the editors and reiterate the advantages of following it.

Because not everyone did. At any one time, roughly sixty per cent of the editors stuck religiously to Helen's *Cosmopolitan* blueprint. Thirty per cent of editors deviated a little (including me) and perhaps ten per cent produced a magazine that was — for Hearst — uncomfortably different from the mother brand. Occasionally, I would slip into this ten per cent.

There were 'good' girls and 'bad' girls among the editors who swelled by around a dozen every conference as Hearst launched *Cosmo* into more and more countries. Helen, while charming to everyone, certainly had her favourites.

Those who deviated from the formula were castigated, privately in Helen's monthly hand-typed critiques and publicly at conferences. Helen would begin every conference with a presentation on what was considered *Cosmo* and what wasn't. To illustrate her points, she used layouts from all our magazines, creating a hall of fame and a hall of shame on the PowerPoint screen. Like naughty schoolgirls, we all sat expectantly, waiting to see if one of our layouts made the shame section.

At the first conference in Amsterdam, much of this went over my head. By the time Sydney rolled around, I too, made it into the hall of shame several times with stories or layouts that didn't adhere to the way Helen felt *Cosmo* should look or read.

One of these stories was a sealed section featuring 'BRAD PITT NAKED'. In my attempts to generate new buzz around *Cosmo*, I'd decided it would be a good idea to publish photographs of Brad Pitt's penis. These were not new photos and they had been published before, but — oddly — only in a men's magazine — the very trashy but often hilarious *Picture*.

As part of the ACP stable, *Picture* and its older brother *People* landed on my desk every week and I often flicked through them for a laugh. Mainstream men's magazines and the internet weren't yet around and these tabloid male weeklies were unique in the way they combined witty humour with bad taste and shock-value pictures. They particularly loved a nude celebrity and if they couldn't find one, they might just print pictures of famous women's heads on nude models' bodies.

At some point during Brad Pitt's relationship with Gwyneth Paltrow, the couple had holidayed in a Spanish villa. A paparazzi photographer had scaled a cliff and hidden under a bush for two days to capture images of Brad and Gwyneth sunbaking and frolicking nude around their private pool. Well, they thought it was private. Had they known there was a photographer watching, they clearly wouldn't have been in the nude, nor would Brad have hidden his penis backwards between his legs and pretended he had a vagina to amuse his girlfriend.

It was gold and I was looking for a gimmick. Something to shake things up a little. I remembered the shots and since no women's magazine had ever published them and few women had seen them in *Picture*, I decided they'd make a terrific sealed section for *Cosmo*.

To pad out the eight pages required to create a sealed section, I came up with the idea of doing a 'Bye-Bye Brad' special. He had just announced his engagement to Gwyneth so I used that as a hook to justify running so much coverage. The fact the pictures had already appeared in print worked to my advantage because it meant I only had to pay for second-run Australian rights. I bought the whole set of nude shots for around a grand and a bunch of other clothed Brad pictures — Brad's movies! Brad's girlfriends! Brad's hairstyles! — to use around the nude ones.

In my editor's letter, I wrote:

BRAD PITT NAKED. There's not a woman I know who hasn't fantasised about using those three words in the same sentence, preferably prefaced by, 'This morning I woke up with …'

Well, as his impending marriage beckons Brad into a life of monogamy, it's becoming less and less likely that any of us will ever fulfil that happy fantasy. So this month, Cosmo is giving you the next best thing: a photographic tribute to what could have been yours if only you'd been born with the name Gwyneth Paltrow … Brad's bits.

Goodbye, farewell and amen to Brad's bachelorhood. We'll miss it.

It was a tortured justification for running old, gratuitous shots but hey, I was editing *Cosmo*, not *Time*. And it worked. Oh how it worked.

Sales took off into the stratosphere but Hearst was appalled. *Cosmo* may have been a pusher of sexual boundaries but naked penises were altogether a different thing. Even worse was the nature of the shots. They'd been taken illegally because Brad and Gwyneth had been on private property. It was also a gross invasion of their privacy. Compounding Hearst's embarrassment, the couple had not long before been guests of the company on a promotional visit to Moscow for the launch of the Russian *Harper's Bazaar*.

Also, coming so soon after the death of Princess Diana, with public anger towards paparazzi and the magazines that published those kinds of unauthorised photos still intense, Hearst felt running the pics was a major error in editorial judgement. In hindsight, I could kinda see their point. But crikey, those shots — and sales figures — were good and that sealed section became infamous among the other *Cosmo* editors who couldn't ever publish such flagrant raunchiness in their own countries.

Brad wasn't happy either. Thrillingly, I received a stern letter from his lawyers threatening to sue. Our own lawyers negotiated a grovelling apology instead and I published it with pleasure. It would be the closest I'd ever come to Brad Pitt, or his penis.

ACP management defended me loyally and Hearst was eventually mollified by my promise not to do it again. In theory, they could take away ACP's franchise or licensing agreement, but it was very rare that a partnership was broken this way and more likely to be a financial decision rather than an editorial one. Brad's penis wasn't enough to cost me my job.

Editors were sacked sometimes, though, if Hearst was particularly unhappy with the way the magazine was heading over a period of time. At each conference there would always be a few new faces and a few hushed stories about editors who had been removed since we last came together.

As the youngest of the *Cosmo* editors and with my circulation figures climbing, I was able to get away with rather a lot. Hearst looked on me indulgently, like a slightly naughty child. I traded on their goodwill at every opportunity. I knew I needed to make *Cosmo* provocative and a little outrageous again if it was going to remain relevant to an audience of Australian women who had more magazines to choose from than ever before.

Stories like 'Learn to be a Penis Genius in 10 Minutes' and 'Genital Makeovers: The OH–MY–GOD Sealed Section!' could never run in US *Cosmo* or most other countries in which *Cosmo* was published, but because Australians had a relaxed attitude to sex and censorship, we could push boundaries with our content in a way other *Cosmos* just couldn't.

Back at the hotel, the only thing I was interested in pushing was my head into a pillow. I wasn't up to returning to my colleague's session so I went upstairs to a room that had been booked for the conference and slept for an hour while I waited for the pills to kick in. When I woke to the sound of a hair and make-up artist knocking on the door, my blinding migraine had been diverted into a dull thud. It was far from ideal but it was manageable. Cinderella, you will go to the ball. Whether you like it or not.

As my post-baby short haircut was smoothed into place and make-up was slapped generously onto my face, I gritted my teeth. Having my hair and make-up done by a pro before hosting a *Cosmo* party was a perk but one I loathed. All that sitting still and being fussed over bored me stupid. I tried to practise the party speech I was due to give in two hours' time, but the words were still a little blurry on the page due to my migraine hangover. I gave up. I'd have to wing it.

The rain didn't let up but the party was a success. I felt extremely out of it in the way you do after a migraine, and mixed with adrenaline, nerves and one glass of champagne, the night was a bit of a surreal blur. I recall watching all the editors on the dance floor in a circle with Helen dancing wildly in the middle — she loved a good boogie — and my speech going off okay, thanks to a well-placed autocue.

I also remember being in the bathroom late in the evening and bumping into Kerri-Anne Kennerley, Australia's queen of daytime TV, who had some sound advice. 'When you have to give a speech, you must plant your feet either side of the lectern like this,' she instructed, demonstrating the correct position in front of the mirror. 'The way you had one leg wrapped around the other made it look like you needed to go to the toilet. And stand up straight.'

She was right.

MY SECRET LIFE AS A MOTHER

SMS to all my girlfriends from me:

'We're engaged!'

Even though Jason was still sick, I needed my fix of forward momentum. Next on my list of Big Things to Do was marriage.

Back when I'd fallen pregnant with Luca, we'd agreed it could wait. We'd already bought a house together after six months and three months after that I was pregnant. On the night of our first anniversary we went out to dinner to celebrate and I had to keep excusing myself to go to the bathroom to vomit because my morning sickness was peaking, oddly, in the evenings. I was editing *Cosmo*, he was busy at work and renovating our new house and we hadn't even had time to go on a holiday together.

By having Luca before we got married, I loved that we'd done things in a non-conventional order. Given that the rest of my life was full of responsibility — my job, our mortgage, Luca — it was the one thing that made me feel a bit reckless and groovy. Woohooo.

I made a decision early on not to write about Luca in my editor's letter or speak about him in the media.

Mostly this was because I wanted readers to relate to me. If they knew I was a mother, I reasoned, it would immediately jar with their idea of me as a *Cosmo* girl. They wouldn't imagine being me and they couldn't imagine me being like them. While I sometimes mentioned Jason, it was only in the vaguest of terms. I think, too, there was a part of me that enjoyed the fantasy, or perhaps felt the pressure to be young and cool and out there — things I was never really good at.

There was my *Cosmo* life and my real life, and they were eons apart.

As Jason's illness entered its second year, we got engaged, although I never wrote about that either. We put the actual wedding on hold because Jason wasn't well enough, but we had an impromptu engagement party combined with Luca's first birthday. It was enough to satisfy me temporarily.

The cure for Jason's CFS, when it came six months later, was dramatic. Conventional medicine had little to suggest beyond 'time', which frankly wasn't good enough. So we'd turned to alternative medicine, trying everything from reiki to vitamin C injections, Chinese medicine, acupuncture … Jason gave it all a shot. Each time he embarked on a new treatment we tried to manage our expectations after having our hopes napalmed so many times. But it was difficult not to hope that each one might just be the cure.

Perhaps the most gruelling thing Jason tried was daily ice-cold baths. I think the theory was that the extreme temperature would shock the body's systems into kick-starting themselves again. Or something. I didn't really care about how; I just wanted it to work.

It didn't. Then Jason's mother called one night with news of a South African doctor who had apparently helped a friend of a neighbour of a friend. I watched Jason carefully write down the details, gritting his teeth at the thought of chasing shadows yet again.

The endless trek down dead ends was debilitating, I knew, but he didn't give himself the luxury of giving up. And it was lucky he didn't because this one proved to be the answer.

There are many triggers for CFS — any number of viruses can do it and not every person is affected in the same way — but this particular doctor had discovered that in some cases CFS is caused by an organism called rickettsia, very common in third-world rural areas, but not so common in Australia. She also discovered that several courses of extremely high-dosage antibiotics would kill the organism and cure the patient of CFS.

Trying not to get his hopes up, Jason contacted the doctor, who asked him to send a blood sample to her in South Africa so she could determine whether he was a good candidate for her treatment.

Bingo. The doctor faxed through the simple instructions for Jason to take to his GP, who then wrote him a script for the antibiotics.

We saw the effects in less than a fortnight. Jason's head began to clear, his sleeping improved, and the oppressive crush of exhaustion that had been suffocating him for almost eighteen months began to slowly lift. Within two months he was pretty much cured.

Next stop? Our wedding. A few months after Jason was back at work, we stood in front of our family and friends and said our vows. It was a wonderful, crazy day, pouring with rain and unseasonably freezing. Jo was my matron of honour and she carried Luca down the aisle.

Before Jason and I had a chance to take a breath, I fell pregnant again.

We hadn't really been trying for another baby. With a hefty mortgage and Jason having just scrambled back into life, the timing was ludicrous. We'd never discussed our future baby plans in detail, except to agree we should wait a while after Luca. Secretly, though, I was thrilled, and soon enough so was Jason. I was totally ready for another baby.

NINETEEN WEEKS

Voicemail to Jo from Jason:

'Hi, it's Jason. Can you give me a call back when you get this? It's about Mia ...'

I wake up in the middle of the night with stomach pains. It feels nothing like labour — the pains are too high — but anything that hurts in the growing expanse between boob and crotch is alarming when you're pregnant. So I call the hospital at 2 am for reassurance.

'How many weeks are you?' the midwife asks, all business.

'Nineteen weeks,' I reply hesitantly, wishing as always it was more.

Her tone changes instantly. 'Well, there's no point coming to the maternity ward at nineteen weeks. You should go to casualty at your nearest hospital or see your obstetrician in the morning.'

I am dismissed.

The subtext of her tone is that at nineteen weeks, my baby isn't yet viable. In medical terms, it isn't even a baby, it's a foetus. And thus not her problem.

I'm stung but there's nothing I can do. The pain isn't bad

enough to turn up at casualty and I'm not bleeding. I've been through labour and this is nothing like it. It feels more like food poisoning.

Somehow I fall back to sleep, and by the morning the pain is gone. Clearly it's some kind of stomach bug working its way through my system.

My nineteen-week ultrasound is booked for three days' time, so once the pain disappears I figure there's no need to call my doctor. I'll just wait until then. Still, I'm looking forward to this ultrasound. I have a small niggle in the back of my mind about the fact I'm not putting on weight and I want reassurance that the baby is growing at the right rate.

I can feel the baby moving occasionally so I'm not unduly worried. It's probably just the stress of work that has kept my weight down. I'll have to eat more yum cha.

Our appointment is for 11.30 am and Jason picks me up from the office at eleven. The plan is to see my obstetrician for my regular appointment after the ultrasound and then grab a quick bite of lunch together. 'I'll be back by one-thirty,' I call to my assistant, grabbing my handbag and jumping into the lift.

'Your afternoon is fully booked,' she calls after me. 'You're in management meetings from two until six.'

'No worries!' I shout back as the lift doors close.

As Jason and I sit in the waiting room, we giggle about a TV show we'd watched the night before. I've put my concerns about my weight out of my mind. 'You know what's great about pregnancy the second time?' I say to Jason. 'I'm so much less paranoid and so much more relaxed about the whole thing than I was with Luca.'

'Mia?' calls the sonographer and we head into the small dark room. 'Hi, I'm Shannon,' she says and we introduce ourselves in high spirits.

'Is this your first baby?' Shannon asks as I clamber up onto the table and hitch up my dress.

'Second,' I say. 'Oh, and we don't want to know the sex.'

Shannon busies herself preparing the machine and squeezing the gel onto my tummy as Jason and I keep talking to each other.

She puts the ultrasound on my stomach and immediately an image of our baby comes up on the screen. We stop talking and look at it, smiling at each other. Jason squeezes my hand. I feel a soft little kick.

'How many weeks are you, Mia?'

'Nineteen.'

'And when is your due date?'

'First of May.'

In my first pregnancy, I used to read far too much into the tone and manner of the sonographers. I'd eventually realised they often go quiet when they're concentrating and it was nothing to worry about.

'When did you last see your doctor?' Shannon asks evenly.

'Um, almost four weeks ago I think. I'm due to see him straight after this.'

Silence. Shannon is peering intently at the screen and suddenly I'm uneasy.

I wait but she doesn't say anything, she just keeps clicking away on the machine. An eternity.

'Is something wrong?' I ask tensely.

I'm aware that Shannon is looking at me but I can't take my eyes off the monitor. 'Mia,' she says slowly, 'it seems your baby has not developed past the fifteen- or sixteen-week mark.'

I feel an instant flash of relief. I speak quickly. 'Oh yes, I know I'm a bit small but maybe my dates could be wrong. I'm not exactly sure when the first day of my last period was —' and then I stop suddenly. Something occurs to me.

'Is there a heartbeat?'

Shannon touches me on the arm in that way you do when you want to make sure someone is paying attention to what you're about to say.

'No, Mia,' she says quietly. 'There's no heartbeat.'

The sensation in that moment is like being dumped by a powerful, suffocating wave. Slowly.

I look immediately back at the monitor. There's our baby, in profile. I hadn't noticed before that the flickering light over the heart, isn't flickering. No heartbeat. No heartbeat. No heartbeat.

I think Jason lets out a small moan. Or is that me?

Shannon says something about getting the doctor and quietly leaves the room.

Jason and I are left to stare up at the TV screen where our baby is floating. Frozen, lifeless. And still, still I can't understand. Didn't I just feel a kick? Didn't I?

I look down at my protruding stomach that suddenly seems shamefully small and inadequate.

I am crying, but very quietly. Jason's face is crumpled in disbelief and he has his arms awkwardly around me as I lie there, trying to comfort me.

We don't speak.

A doctor walks into the room with Shannon behind him. 'Hello Mia, I'm John Beaumont. I'm so very sorry about this terrible news, it must be a shock.'

I've stopped crying. I still can't speak but it seems I don't need to. Things are happening anyway. I've lost control.

'Let me have a look here; is that okay?' he asks gently and I nod. He turns the ultrasound back on and slowly slides the probe around my stomach as the tears roll silently down the side of my face into my ears.

I try not to cry out loud. I don't feel hysterical. Just shocked. Numb. It seems important that I not distract the doctor from looking at the baby, because, if I lie really still and I'm really quiet, maybe he will find a heartbeat after all.

He clears his throat. 'So, you're nineteen weeks according to your dates but the baby has only developed to about sixteen weeks.'

Silence.

'Do you mean that's when its heart stopped?' I whisper.

'Yes, it seems to be that way,' he says.

'Do you know why? Can you tell?' asks Jason. His voice sounds strange, strangled.

'Well, there's some swelling around the baby's brain area but I can't tell if that's post-mortem or a causal factor. I've looked at your medical notes and everything was fine at the twelve-week ultrasound, is that right?'

'Yes.' My own voice is soft and far away. I can't think of any questions. I can't think. I can't feel.

The doctor is speaking again. I must concentrate. 'Sometimes these things just happen. I know that's an awfully unsatisfactory answer when something as devastating as this has occurred but we might not be able to ever give you an exact reason for it, although there are certainly some tests we can do.'

Silently, we try to take in everything he says, all of us crowded into this tiny room, looking up at the image of our baby on the screen. It seems like there's no oxygen in the room. Just horror.

'Mia, I'm going to call your doctor now to tell him what's happened. You're going downstairs to see him after this, aren't you, so he can talk with you both about what happens next. I'm so sorry. Please stay in here as long as you like.'

And then the doctor and Shannon are gone and it's just us again. Us and our floating baby.

When I look at Jason, his face is twisted with concern and I can tell he's waiting for me to collapse. But I can't.

I pull my dress down roughly, feeling suddenly ridiculous in my high heels, wanting to disappear, feeling like I'm already gone, retracting further and further into myself.

We stumble out of the dark room and into the fluorescently lit corridor, blinking. Jason has his arms around me, holding me up and I lean heavily on him in the lift on our way down to Dr Bob's waiting room.

'I'm so sorry,' says his receptionist quietly, squeezing my arm. I feel like I might collapse if anyone is too nice to me and I dimly become aware that I have to go to the toilet. My bladder had to be full for the ultrasound and I haven't emptied it yet.

My doctor is with another patient so I use the opportunity to go to the loo. Jason walks with me to the door but he can't come in. It's only when I'm inside, alone for the first time, that the wave breaks over my head again and I'm suddenly gasping, sobbing, gulping for air.

I sit on the toilet and instinctively hold my hands over my stomach while the cries come from somewhere deep in my heart.

And then it subsides. I revert to shock and pull myself together enough to splash water on my face and walk back into the waiting room.

Somehow, I'm in the doctor's office and Jason is asking questions while I sit there blankly. This isn't happening, I decide at one point. But it is. It is happening.

Through the fog, I struggle to understand what Dr Bob is saying. He is kind and compassionate and he's being very gentle. Something about tests on me, on the baby, to try to find out what happened. I squint, trying to focus my eyes and my attention.

Suddenly, a question bursts to the surface, wrapped in a sob. 'Is it my fault?' I ask.

'No, it's not your fault. Sometimes this just happens because the baby isn't viable.'

I need more specific absolution.

'Could it have been the fake tan I used a few times?'

'No.'

'Hair dye?'

'No.'

'That glass of champagne I had?'

'No.'

'Exercise?'

'No.'

I'm sure there are more sins I need to confess but those ones are top of mind and the effort of asking questions and listening to answers has exhausted me mentally. My awareness recedes into the fog as Dr Bob continues talking.

Something about what happens next. Something about having options. Something about inducing labour and delivering the baby vaginally.

Now I'm more alert. This is important.

'No,' I say firmly. Even though I'm reeling, I know that to go through labour and give birth to a tiny stillborn baby would be too traumatic. It would scar me forever. Well, scar me more. And forever pollute the idea of giving birth. Retrospectively it would taint the beautiful birth I had with Luca.

'No,' I repeat. 'What's the other option?'

An operation. Under general anaesthetic. Dilation and curette. A specialised procedure because of the size of the baby. My doctor doesn't perform it but he knows the best person who does and he picks up the phone to call him as we sit there, flattened beyond all imagining.

I assume we'll be going straight to the hospital from here. An operation today. My mind flits distractedly, alighting on one thought, trying to process it and then darting to the next.

I'm pregnant but I'm not. Everyone knows. So many people to tell. Meant to be in budget meetings at work all afternoon. Luca. What to tell Luca? What happens to the baby now? All the thoughts are horrible. I don't want any of them. I push them away instead.

I watch Dr Bob speak on the phone. Jason holds my hand and it feels dead. I feel dead.

'Dr Peters can do it on Friday. He's the best.'

Friday. Friday? But today is Monday. How is that possible?

Dr Bob reads my mind. 'It's the earliest it can be done by Dr Peters and I wouldn't recommend anyone else,' he says, gently answering my unspoken question.

Some more things are said. Consoling words. I can't recall any of them. And then we're back in the car. I'm not ready to go home. Luca is there, with the nanny who comes two days a week. I can't possibly face anyone.

Jason drives us a few streets away and pulls over near a park. I watch joggers go past. City workers having lunch on the grass or walking to get sandwiches.

The tears have gone. I can't cry. I can barely breathe.

I look at my mobile and notice three missed calls. One is from Mum — she knew I was having the ultrasound this morning and she's calling to find out how it went.

When she can't reach me, she tries Jason. His phone rings and he answers it.

I hear him murmuring something to her. The phone call is over quickly.

Good. I'm saved from having to break the news. She'll tell my dad and call Jason's mum. Our families will know. Word of our tragedy will spread like a fungus.

Suddenly something occurs to me.

'I want to know if it's a boy or a girl,' I say to Jason.

He winces. I can tell he's parked his own feelings about the baby behind his acute concern for me. He's treating me like an unexploded bomb, which I guess I am.

'Okay, why don't I call the ultrasound place and ask.'

I look out the window as he makes the phone call, not seeing anything.

'Yes, hi, we came in for an ultrasound a little while ago and … and there was no heartbeat…yes, the patient's name is Mia Freedman. Yes. Thanks. Oh hi, Shannon. Yes, thanks. Listen, we were wondering if you could tell whether the baby was a boy or a girl.' Pause. 'Right, okay. Hold on a second, I'll just check what Mia wants to do.'

He reaches for my hand while he covers the phone. 'She thinks it was a girl but she can't be positive because she wasn't looking closely after everything happened. She said if we wanted to we could come in again now and she might be able to give us a more definite answer.'

'Yes, I want to.'

A girl. A girl. I'm back in the wild surf being dumped by grief again. It's not just a baby we've lost but a baby girl.

Our waking nightmare takes us back to the ultrasound office. We're met at reception by Shannon who shows us straight into the same room. The one with no oxygen.

I clamber back onto the bed and with arms made of lead I lift up my dress. My stomach seems to apologise to me for how small it is, how pathetic it looks. I am ashamed.

Our baby appears back on the screen and my tears begin to

fall instantly and silently. I know it's the last time I'll see her. My stomach bounces gently with my quiet sobs. The pain and the horror of this moment are unbearable.

'Yes, I'm almost certain it's a girl,' says Shannon gently. 'I'm going to print you out some images so you have them to keep.'

She presses them into my hand. I can't take my eyes off the screen. 'I'm so sorry for your loss; please stay as long as you like,' she says, leaving us alone.

We cry together quietly for a few minutes until I feel ready to go. I say a silent goodbye to my baby girl floating on the screen. In the car on the way home, Jason calls our nanny to tell her what's happened so she can take Luca out to the park for a while.

I tune out most of the conversation until three words leap into my ears: 'the baby's dead'. I physically recoil as though they're gunshots. Even though they were said gently and quietly, it's a sentence too brutal to comprehend and it jolts me to a level of awareness that's far too painful.

I say nothing. I have already begun to pull away from Jason and from the world. I'm falling down further into darkness and I don't fight it.

When we arrive home, I'm not sure what to do. Instinctively, I get into bed even though I feel neither sick nor tired. My eyes are dry and I'm sort of detached, wondering absently why I'm not weeping and wailing.

Isn't that how I should behave? Isn't that the appropriate reaction of someone who has just been told their baby daughter died inside them three weeks ago?

Three weeks ago. How could I not have noticed? What sort of terrible mother am I to have let my baby die inside me and not have even felt it, not even sensed it? I torture myself thinking about the moment I missed. The moment she slipped away from me forever. And all the moments after that when I'd foolishly thought I'd felt her moving.

Not only had I failed my baby physically by not keeping her alive inside me, I'd also failed her emotionally and spiritually by not noticing when she had died.

Wendy and Jo ring. My mother comes over. Her face is lined with distress and she hugs me but I feel nothing. My eyes stay dry. I just want everyone to go away and leave me alone. No one can reach me in this place. Not even me.

When Luca comes back from the park, the nanny hugs me and starts crying. I'm stiff. Later that day, Jason and I speak to Luca about the baby.

'You know the baby in Mummy's tummy?' Jason ventures.

'Yeah,' says Luca distractedly.

'Well, we have some sad news. The baby got sick and it went away.'

'Okay,' says Luca and wanders off to look for his gumboots.

I'm happy with this. He doesn't need tortured explanations. He's never been particularly interested in the subject of my pregnancy or the new baby and we don't need to burden him with information or grief.

I still haven't cried since we left the ultrasound room the second time. I feel in a place beyond tears.

Jason takes Luca out to pick up some takeaway for dinner and I run myself a bath. My grief is locked away and I want to be with it but first I need to open the door. Maybe music will help me.

I find a classical CD and scroll through until I find the saddest track. I climb into the bath, cradle my stomach and let the music and the water envelop me. Quickly, my body is heaving violently with sobs. The sound of my crying echoes around the bathroom, and after a while I make out some words: 'Why? Why did you leave me? Why did you go?'

It's a plea to my baby from the depths of my despair. And hearing it breaks my heart a little bit more.

My own anguish comforts me in a strange way. This is the way I should be reacting. This feels right.

By the time Jason and Luca return, the grief has receded in what will become a familiar pattern. Like a tide. Without warning it will come from nowhere to crash over me, toss me around brutally and then slowly pull back, depositing me on the shore, shaken and gutted.

For months and years afterwards, the piece of music I found that day would become the key to unlocking my grief because sometimes I'd want it to wash over me. Sometimes, I felt that was the only way I could truly connect with my lost baby.

I get out of the bath and look at myself in the mirror. From the outside, I'm still pregnant. My baby is still here, still tucked away, floating inside me. But she's not really. Really, she's gone.

The next day, there are details to sort out, none of which I'm capable of dealing with. Jason calls Pat, who gathers my staff together to tell them. Word begins to spread among our friends.

I am adamant that no one find out that the baby died three weeks ago. I am ashamed that I didn't know.

The phone begins to ring with sympathy calls. 'I don't want anyone to send flowers,' I growl at one point, but then someone does and they're beautiful and welcome. So are the cards that a few people send. I treasure them as proof that our baby existed, that she'd meant something.

Mostly, people don't know how to react. I don't blame them but I notice. Death is an awkward, unpleasant business. And death before birth? There's no ritual for that in our culture.

In the weeks that follow, as painful and uncomfortable as it often is to have a conversation about our baby's death, it is infinitely preferable to silence. People who say nothing leave me feeling angry.

My world has stopped turning; how can that possibly be glossed over without comment?

The few days between learning our baby has died and going to the hospital are in some ways horrific and certainly surreal. I am carrying my dead baby inside me. But in many more ways, they are a gift. A chance to come to terms with what has happened. A chance to make the jarring transition from pregnant to bereaved. From excitement and anticipation to anguish and sorrow.

Still, there are some unbearable moments.

The day before I'm due to go to hospital, Jason and I seek some respite from the oppressive atmosphere at home and walk to a nearby café for lunch. Two tables away are some people we haven't seen for a while and they come over to say hi. I'm dressed in very baggy clothes to try to disguise my stomach, but I'm still visibly pregnant. They say congratulations and want to know when the baby's due. Jason looks at me, stricken, and I quickly plaster a frozen smile on my face. 'May next year — still a while to go yet!' I say and then we quickly make an excuse to leave.

I struggle to re-draw my life in the short and long term, deleting this baby from my imagined plans. I remember an older relative who discovered her baby had died at a similar stage and had to carry it for several weeks until she went into labour. I'd always imagined it would be horrific and somehow repulsive to carry a dead baby inside you, but I'm surprised to find neither is the case.

Devastating, absolutely. Excruciatingly upsetting at times, yes. But also strangely comforting. Your own body cannot disgust you and neither can something you created and carry inside it. I still feel protective of my baby. I still feel like I am her mother.

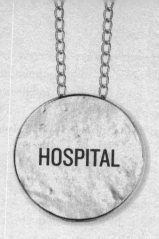

HOSPITAL

Answering machine message to White Lady Funerals from me:

'Hello, I want to ask about a cremation for a baby. Well, a pre-term baby. Do you do that kind of thing? If someone could give me a call, that would be great. Thanks.'

In a million years and the blink of an eye it was Friday. We dropped Luca at my mum's on the way to the hospital, the same hospital in which Luca had been born.

After doing the paperwork, we were shown to a room and a nurse came to ask me some questions. For a moment, I wondered if she thought I was having a late-term abortion. Imagine that. I wanted to scream how much I'd wanted this baby, how devastated I was by what had happened and what was about to happen.

She glanced at my chart and I detected an immediate softening. She reached out to pat my hand and I began to feel wobbly again.

Dr Peters came in to introduce himself and explain the procedure. He was surprisingly chirpy, which was disconcerting while at the same time welcome. The heaviness and misery of the situation were oppressive enough already.

'We're going to put some gel on your cervix to soften it up,' he explained matter-of-factly. 'You'll have some mild contractions but nothing too bad and then we'll take you down to theatre and put you to sleep. Then we'll remove the foetus and you'll wake up a bit crampy but able to go home in a few hours. How does that sound?'

I wasn't sure of the correct answer. Terrific? Shocking? Devastating?

'Um, I wanted to ask you something,' I ventured by way of response. 'Would it be possible to … keep the remains of the baby?'

He cocked his head to the side and thought for a moment.

'Yes, I don't see why not. We could organise something, although you understand that during the removal process, the foetus can be … well, it might not come out intact. And we'll want to do some tissue tests to see if we can determine … factors —'

I rushed to interrupt him. 'Oh, I don't mean we want to take it home with us today or anything. Just more that if we wanted to organise for a cremation or something later on …'

'I see,' he said, nodding his head vigorously in agreement, visibly relieved. 'Yes of course! I see no problem with that at all.' And he made a note on my chart.

As soon as he left, I looked at Jason and burst out laughing. It was utterly macabre but the idea that he'd thought we wanted to take home a doggy bag with our baby's remains in it was so completely horrifying that it struck me as funny.

I hadn't laughed in days and the sound was unfamiliar. It was over almost immediately and the heavy atmosphere returned. I felt faintly desperate about what was about to happen. I knew my baby was dead but I wasn't ready to give her up.

As Jason read the paper and I flicked through magazines, a nurse came to apply the gel to my cervix and the contractions began slowly, like period pains.

Two hours later, I was wheeled down to be prepped for surgery. My hands were still protectively held over my stomach, not from pain but from love. I desperately wanted this to be over and I desperately didn't.

Usually, I don't mind a general anaesthetic; I like the physical sensation of slipping so quickly into unconsciousness — but this time, when it was the final chapter in the long goodbye to my baby, I drifted off reluctantly.

I woke in the recovery room, crampy and disoriented. Dr Bob was the first face I saw. I didn't even know he'd been at the hospital, but he'd come to be in the operating room and to be there when I woke up. What a kind, wonderful man … I was lucky to have him see me through this.

He was saying something to me about the procedure having gone well, but it was all foggy. Just seeing him made me start crying and then I couldn't stop.

It was over, really over. She was gone.

The physical and emotional sensations of the next few days are difficult to describe. I felt gutted, quite literally. My womb was empty, my baby was gone.

And then one morning, two days after the operation, I stood in the shower and watched milk leak from my breasts. Oh my God. My milk had come in. I sank to the floor and sobbed violently, barely able to breathe. Why had no one warned me about this? About any of it? I'd been sent home from the hospital with instructions about not driving and Panadeine for the cramping. But no one warned me about the milk.

As I watched it swirl into the drain and disappear, I wanted to dive down after it into the darkness. It was just too painful, this disconnect between my body and my mind. Nature was telling me I had a baby to take care of and my breasts were merrily making milk to feed her. My arms felt so shockingly empty without the weight of a newborn in them. They ached.

Emotionally, I continued to pull away from everyone who loved me. From my family, my friends and even Jason. It wasn't a choice, I was simply unreachable.

Except when I listened to my music, to her song. Then I could allow myself to fully dwell on the horror of my baby lying in pieces in a hospital morgue, her tissue samples being taken for testing.

Yet another strike in my heart of failure. Not only had I let her die inside me but now I'd abandoned her in a cold, impersonal hospital lab.

Frantic with grief and guilt, I decided to call a funeral home to ask about cremation. I didn't want anything formal like a funeral but I wanted some ashes for some kind of private ceremony. I wanted to reclaim her. Just for us.

The lady I spoke to was lovely and said they could organise to collect the remains from the hospital, transport them to the crematorium and then I could collect the ashes afterwards.

When I told him about it, I could instantly see Jason was uncomfortable with the idea. But he knew to tread carefully around me and wanted to facilitate whatever I felt I needed to do. He unquestioningly made all the necessary arrangements.

Within a few days, I returned to work. It had been just over a week since I'd gaily walked out of my office for the ultrasound, promising to be right back. I wasn't sure I was ready to return but I didn't know what else to do. I had a hole in my heart and my life and I had to fill it with something. I wasn't physically ill, so lying in bed all day was unthinkable. It was time to start putting one foot in front of the other even though the ground beneath them felt like quicksand.

For the first time in a long time I didn't care about my appearance, although in a way I did. Specifically, I wanted to look as dreadful as I felt. I wore drab clothes and no make-up. I didn't blow-dry my hair. I wanted my grief and my loss to be written on my face. I felt so irrevocably, drastically and fundamentally altered, I wanted the proof of it to be visible to the world.

Deep in grief, I found myself back at my desk, surrounded by a subdued and protective team of women who didn't know what to say but were silently supportive. I was physically weak, mentally fragile and emotionally shattered but I was glad for the distraction of work.

A week or so later, I received a call.

'Mia, it's Judy here from White Lady Funerals. I'm afraid with the cremation of your little one there wasn't enough physical matter to leave any ashes.'

'You mean the baby was too small?'

'Yes, I'm so sorry. I know you wanted something.'

'So … what happened …? Do you mean she just sort of evaporated into the atmosphere?'

'Yes, that's right.'

Her voice was full of compassion, but it was yet another breathtaking punch. How many more times would I have to lose this baby?

Jason was relieved — I could tell — although he tried to hide it and be sympathetic. By now though, I was looking for any reason to snap at him because being angry hurt less than being devastated. So I lashed out.

I wanted to name the baby; he didn't. I wanted to have some kind of ceremony; he didn't. While he was trying to be supportive, he was also grieving in his own private way, untangling the complex knot of his own emotions. I should have respected that, but instead I exploded at him for not following my path, not reading my mind, not feeling the same way I did about everything.

In the Disney version of this story — if Disney ever made a movie about neo-natal death — losing our baby would have brought Jason and me closer, forging an unbreakable bond between us in the immediate aftermath.

But in real life, in our life, it did the opposite. The grieving process, which we undertook so differently and so separately, put us under incredible strain and pushed us further apart.

TWO AHA! MOMENTS

Voicemail to Jason from me (sobbing):

'Hi, it's me and ... and ... I've missed my flight and ... and ... and ... I ... have ... to ... wait ... nine hours for ... the ... next one and ... and ... I'm freaking out. Where are you? You can't even call ... me ... back 'cause I'm ... I'm calling from a public phone at LA airport ... and I'm running out of credit and — [click]'

There was a lot of wreckage to sift through in the aftermath of losing our baby. Physically, there were tests to be done on me and the baby to try and determine a cause of death.

Was there something in my system that had caused her to die? It seemed not. Was she severely retarded or deformed? No. The chromosomal and structural tests and the ultrasounds we had before she died hadn't waved any red flags and neither did the tests done on her remains.

I was shocked by the fallibility of medicine. I've always been one of those people who like to think doctors and science have all the answers. When they don't, I'm indignant.

How could no one give me an explanation for why such a terrible thing had happened to me? Why couldn't anyone tell me why my baby had died? They couldn't, and I had to make some kind of peace with that. I had to let her go. I knew this intellectually, but my heart was smashed into pulp and intellect didn't come into it.

The hunger I had for a baby was visceral. Catching sight of pregnant women — who had suddenly fallen from the sky in a downpour by the thousands and were everywhere I turned — was like a kick to the stomach. My empty stomach.

Emotionally, it was clearly too early for us to be trying again. I was a mess. But physically? The medical opinion was mixed. One school of thought was that you should wait at least three months after a miscarriage before conceiving again so your body could recover and give you a better chance of carrying the next pregnancy to term. Another theory was that as soon as you ovulated, nature was saying your body was ready. And this could be within weeks of miscarrying. I was torn.

Part of me was way too fragile to contemplate another miscarriage and thought I should wait three months. But another part, the primal part that was screaming out for another baby every waking second, couldn't bear to wait even another day. This is the part that had an iron grip around my heart and my head. The need to be pregnant again immediately was so overwhelming that I became quite batty.

It was Luca who kept me anchored to daily life. I had to get out of bed each morning and take care of him and deal with his needs, so as much as I wanted to pull the covers over my head and disappear, I couldn't.

This distraction was a blessing. He was a blessing too, of course, but I wanted to slap people when they tried to console me with platitudes like, 'Oh well, at least you have Luca.' Yes, he was the light of my life but in no way did that lessen the grief I felt. In the same way that had our daughter been born, I wouldn't have loved him any less. I walked through work like a zombie, detached and desolate.

As the months passed and the growing pile of pregnancy tests cruelly refused to show two lines, I became deranged with disappointment. Every failed test felt like losing my baby again. My grief and anger and frustration intermingled with a bucket of other emotions I couldn't even articulate.

The date our baby was meant to be born was looming like a nightmare. On the actual day, bizarrely enough, I was in the Bahamas. It was *Cosmo* conference time again, and if the universe wasn't already testing me enough, it decided to really mess with my head by forcing me to confront my fear of flying. I had to endure three flights there and three back, including a return trip on a very light plane from Miami to the Bahamas.

By the time I had to fly to LA for the first leg of the trip, I was emaciated by grief and beyond fragile. The flying triggered panic attacks and by the time I arrived at my hotel, I was a shaking wreck.

In LA for two days, I threw myself into shopping with the dedication of a lunatic. I went to Barneys and bought expensive jeans and beaded tops. I went to boutiques and bought leather jackets, dresses and shoes. So consumed was I by the urge to buy things and block my anxiety, I arrived late at LA airport on the day I was meant to fly to the conference and missed my flight.

I was so brittle that when I discovered the next flight was nine hours away, I fell into a heap — almost literally. When I couldn't get hold of Jason on his mobile, I did what any self-respecting adult would do in such a situation: I called my mum and dad and cried down the phone.

I'm not sure why it never occurred to me to put my bags in a locker and go back to the centre of LA to shop more or just wander around. My fear of flying makes me nutty and I become easily institutionalised at airports. I get trapped and lose my mind. So instead of doing something fun or constructive, I spent the next nine hours wandering around LAX and sitting in Starbucks. I ate a lot of cardboard muffins. And each time I thought my anxiety levels couldn't possibly get any higher, they surprised me and did.

Eventually, I made it to the Bahamas and checked into the hotel, a massive structure on the beach with multiple giant pools and waterslides. I collected my conference pack from the *Cosmo* hospitality suite, hugged a few familiar *Cosmo* people and collapsed in my room.

The following days were difficult. I was not coping well. Usually, I loved these conferences and adored seeing my sister editors. They were a sensational bunch of women and I'd made some fast friends over the years. But my anxiety overwhelmed me. I insisted on working out in the hotel gym every morning before conference sessions began, despite being weak and thin. I couldn't control my fertility, but dammit I could control my exercise and my weight. And I craved the endorphins. They were the only thing able to alleviate my anxiety, however briefly.

One afternoon, after a manicure in the spa — a gift to all the editors from Hearst — I became convinced I'd been infected with HIV because the therapist hadn't sterilised the cuticle cutter. Or had she? This triggered more anxiety, to the point of panic attacks. My clothes hung off me. I couldn't sleep. In the sanctuary of my room I cried and cried. I was falling apart and I knew it. Worst of all, the timing meant I was overseas when I ovulated. Another month lost. It was unbearable.

Fortunately, a couple of enormously significant and wonderful things happened at the conference, one that impacted my professional life and one with far more personal meaning.

The guest speaker at this conference was Eve Ensler, the feminist and author of *The Vagina Monologues*. She was working on a new book about body image and had accepted Hearst's invitation to the conference so she could interview some of the foreign editors on the subject.

There's something about Eve, an X-factor that makes her utterly compelling to listen to and completely inspiring to be around. She's warm and funny and extraordinarily perceptive. When my turn came to be interviewed about body image, I quickly dissolved in sobs as I told her about losing my baby. I couldn't really speak about anything else. 'I feel like just when I was making peace with my body as a woman and a mother and feeling proud of what it could do, it's gone and failed me,' I stammered, through tears.

She passed me a tissue and held my hand. 'What do you mean, "failed"?'

'I couldn't keep my baby alive inside me,' I sobbed quietly. 'I failed her.'

Squeezing my hand, she told me about her own miscarriages. And then she said something I've never forgotten. 'Mia, the fact your baby died was not about you. It was about her. If you make this about you, you're dishonouring her soul and her journey. She didn't stick around for whatever reason, but it wasn't because of you and you didn't fail. Honour her by knowing that.'

Eve's words cut through my grief and gave me some clarity for the first time in months. It was a defining moment in my healing process. What she said to me that day, about how this wasn't about me and how I needed to honour my baby's journey, has stayed with me ever since. And it helped. I still remind myself of that conversation sometimes.

The other aha! moment of the conference was far less personally profound but would have lasting consequences for my magazine. Since I'd begun editing *Cosmo* three years earlier, I'd tried all sorts of different cover treatments. While US *Cosmo* and most other editions around the world used the signature *Cosmo* cover pose every month — a three-quarter shot of a model or celebrity on a plain-coloured background — I took a different approach. I liked to think of it as creative. You could also call it inconsistent.

Shunning the predictable *Cosmo* formula, shot in a studio, I decided to be a maverick. I had no rules, and no formula for choosing my cover image. One month, I had a tight headshot of a model. The next, a shot of Jennifer Aniston in cut-off denim shorts and a bikini top standing in a cornfield. My most memorable cover was of Kylie and Dannii Minogue, lying next to each other in a spoon pose on a bed. Hearst hated that one — 'Why are there lesbians on your cover?' they railed — but it sold well. And good sales were the justification I always had for my wildly fluctuating cover treatments.

But at this conference, sitting there looking at the other editors' presentations and all the covers of the US and foreign editions that applied the *Cosmo* cover formula to their magazines, I suddenly realised I was being a goose. By producing a totally different-looking cover every month, I may have had success with individual issues but I was doing nothing to build my brand. In fact, I was harming it.

One month *Cosmo* looked like a beauty magazine. The next month? A men's mag. This was partly due to the fact I was sourcing my cover material from everywhere — beauty mags and men's mags included. Gone were the days when a local cover shoot with a model in a studio was possible. You grabbed whatever you could from overseas magazines for the price you could afford to pay.

Perhaps the purpose of these conferences was to brainwash the editors into submission. Perhaps it worked. When I returned home, I immediately met with my art director and told her we were going to follow the formula. We narrowed our cover-image searches to shots that were three-quarter crop and shot in a studio on a plain-coloured background. It greatly reduced the pool of shots we could buy but the consistency had the desired effect on readership and circulation, which continued to rise.

It was a valuable lesson for me. Sometimes, there is no need to reinvent the wheel.

DOING TIME IN THE HALL OF MIRRORS

SMS to Jason from me:

'I won.'

'And the winner is ... Mia Freedman!' It was the highest point in my career at the lowest point in my life. The annual Magazine Publishers Association of Australia awards are the Oscars night for the magazine industry. A panel of former and current magazine editors and publishers judge a couple of dozen categories including best magazine, cover, editor, feature writer, art director and marketing initiative.

I'd just been announced Editor of the Year and my table of *Cosmo* staff was going nuts. I rose from my chair and I must have walked from our table at the back of the room up to the stage although I barely remember it. I do remember several people touching me on the arm as I passed their tables and seeing the smiling faces of judges and publishing legends Richard Walsh and Nene King, but it's mostly a surreal memory.

By the time I arrived at the podium, accepted my award and turned around to face the audience, I was spectacularly nervous. Somehow I managed to get out the one sentence I had in my mind: 'I'd like to thank the incredible *Cosmo* team because without them I would be editing a magazine of blank pages,' and then I think I started to waffle. I wrapped it up and went back down the stairs and through the audience to my seat.

Wine was poured, toasts were made. I was numb. Awards are meaningless rubbish until you win one and then they're suddenly very important and you are humbled. In some remote part of my brain, I exhaled. Even though I genuinely felt I didn't deserve the award, by one small measure at least, I'd proven myself as an editor. But my heart was still heavy. In photos from the night, I look like a lollipop. I was extremely thin and my eyes were dead.

I was still deep in grief for the loss of my baby. I should have been nursing a newborn, not a glass of champagne. I should have been on maternity leave not in a ballroom. So while everyone around me began to kick back and party, I waited until the official proceedings were over and then I pretended to go to the bathroom and kept walking to the car park.

I drove home happy about my win but unable to shake my sadness. As I climbed out of the car, the heavy rectangular silver trophy fell out of my hand and bounced onto the road. I crouched down to pick it up and saw it was dented and scratched. How apt. The emotions of the past few months instantly bubbled to the surface. I sat in the gutter and wept.

The next couple of years would be so many things. Lonely, liberating, distressing, angry, depressing, exciting, confusing, happy, unhappy, disappointing, regretful, bitter, intense, devastating, frustrating, sad, bewildering, rewarding, empowering, wistful, frightening, jealous, hurtful, cruel, accusatory, proud. After more than three years of doing things at breakneck speed, everything in my life would grind to a halt.

I would start to see a counsellor every week. Jason and I would stop trying to get pregnant. We would spend some time apart. Therapy was a crucial aspect of that time and the way I eventually found my way out of the mire.

A friend once described therapy as 'spending time in the hall of mirrors' and that sums it up perfectly. It's difficult, unpleasant and confronting to see the less attractive parts of yourself reflected back. But for me, it was vital.

I had so much emotional baggage to unpack. About losing the baby, about the whirlwind of the past few years … there was a lifetime to cover, issues big and small.

Despite how tempted I was to just rent a garage, dump all my suitcases in there and march merrily, blindly forwards, I knew this wouldn't work for long. Because those damn bags hunt you down. Until they're unpacked and put away, you have to schlep them through your life.

My weekly therapy sessions were the best thing I've ever done and the best money I've ever spent. They were also the hardest. It's a bit like renovating. You know you're doing something good, something of value, something that will benefit your life in the long term. HOWEVER. In the short term? In the short term it sucks hard.

It's neither easy nor pleasant to reach inside yourself, pull out your darkest, dingiest bits and hold them up to the sunlight for close examination.

I knew that therapy was the right thing and the best thing and the only thing. But some weeks? I would have preferred to drink soup made entirely of fingernails.

A couple of months in, at the beginning of an appointment, my counsellor gently said to me, 'Mia, let's talk about your resistance to this process.'

'What do you mean?'

'You've "forgotten" two of our appointments in the past four weeks and you've been fifteen minutes late for the other two.'

'Um, well, yes but that's because, you know, well, I've been really busy at work and …'

'This isn't uncommon, but it's no accident either. What it usually means is that we're coming up to some issues you don't want to confront. So subconsciously, you forget your appointments or "accidentally" come late.'

'Oh.'

'You know, in therapy, the times you want to come the least are always the times you need to come the most.'

'…'

She was right, of course. From that point on, I dutifully ploughed through these difficult, confronting sessions, treating them like a job I wasn't allowed to quit. And every single time it was worth it. Every week, I felt such relief as I walked back to my car afterwards and it was rare not to have at least one 'ka-ching' moment in the hour we spent talking, moments of clarity and understanding why I'd done a certain thing or felt a certain way.

I began to wonder how anyone got through difficult times without the impartial help of a counsellor. 'I've got lots of friends I can talk to,' I often hear people say when the idea of seeing a professional comes up, but the two things could not be more different.

When someone you love is in pain, it can be hard to watch and impossible to be impartial. Mostly, my friends and family tried to cheer me up. Without meaning to, they all brought their own baggage to my situation. They couldn't help it. And as much as they all reached out to support me, I found myself unconsciously withdrawing from them.

The people who love you are also much less likely to force you to confront the more unpleasant aspects of your personality. They're much less likely to point out your failings because it's confronting and difficult for everyone. Difficult, but necessary if you want to better understand yourself and untangle your emotions from a crisis.

It was a revelation to finally understand some of the patterns I'd repeated through my life, particularly my driving need to race from one big moment to the next, never able to stay still and process anything — let alone appreciate it.

I also started to deal constructively with my grief over the death of the baby. On every significant anniversary — the day she was due to be born, the day we found out she'd died, the day she was ripped from my body — I had created a ritual.

I compiled a box of all the tangible evidence that she'd existed — ultrasound pictures, sympathy cards, the pregnancy test that first told me she was coming, medical records — and I made a little shrine around it with picked flowers and a candle three times a year, on each anniversary.

Once, on what would have been her birthday, I even bought a tiny little cupcake. It took all my strength not to buy her a teddy bear. She was my baby and I'd never got to nurture her, to mother her, and it kept breaking my heart.

To jolt myself out of my comfort zone and kick myself off my goat track during the long-term aftermath of my miscarriage, I did new things. I took up yoga. I taught myself how to cook — an activity Luca and I got into together. We started with fun stuff — Nigella Lawson's *How to be a Domestic Goddess* was our bible and for a while it replaced bedtime stories. We sat together with a pile of post-it notes and marked all the treats we wanted to cook together. And then we did.

My friendships with my closest girlfriends deepened. I learned how to be vulnerable and ask them for help and support when I needed it. I was approached to write a Sunday newspaper column and rediscovered my love of writing, which I hadn't done much of since I began editing. I drew strength from my staff and poured a lot of my nurturing into them. Work continued to fire me up in a good way.

AN UNLIKELY COVERGIRL

SMS to my deputy editor from me:

'Never seen so many bunny ears. Sara-Marie mania peaking. We have to do something on this.'

In the two weeks before September 11, 2001, I was feeling pissed off. I'd done what I thought was a great thing. A brave thing. An inspired thing. And it had blown up in my face.

A few months before, the first season of 'Big Brother' had ended and the whole country was now on a first-name basis with a large, cheery girl called Sara-Marie.

I was a huge fan. Of the show and of Sara-Marie. I'd begun watching 'Big Brother' out of a sense of pop-culture duty. For work. Editing *Cosmo* meant I had to keep current with whatever the zeitgeist hurled at my readers, even if it didn't float my boat personally.

It was instantly obvious that 'Big Brother' was going to be a big deal for the demographic who read *Cosmo*, so I couldn't afford to be sitting in editorial meetings looking blank and saying, 'Huh? What's a bum dance?'

Since my personality tends towards the addictive, it didn't take long for my professional interest to turn to personal obsession. I loved that first season of 'Big Brother' like a crackhead loves her pipe. I didn't care that it was bad for me; I was hooked. And, like a crackhead, this addiction obscured my better judgement in certain areas. Jason certainly thought so. 'I can't believe you're letting Luca watch this shit,' he grumbled when he came home night after night to find me and my three-year-old sitting together on the couch watching Sara-Marie, Ben, Blair, Peter, Christina Ballerina, Gemma and the other housemates.

But I saw no harm in it. The rude stuff was quarantined to a separate late-night show and anything remotely adult went straight over Luca's head. Because it was the first season, there was an innocence about the whole thing — the housemates were wide-eyed and there to have fun. And it was fun to watch with Luca — a bit like a Wiggles video but without the skivvies and with a bum dance instead of 'Rock-A-Bye Your Bear'. It was all quite harmless and cartoony, I thought, and Luca loved it as much as Jason loathed it.

Naturally, when Channel Ten offered to fly me up to Queensland for the final couple of nights of the show and a private tour of the house, I couldn't say yes fast enough. Luca stayed at home with Jason. Even in the grip of an unhealthy reality-TV obsession, I knew where to draw the line for my child.

Sitting in the audience the night of Sara-Marie's surprise eviction, I was astonished by what I saw. Around me were girls of all ages, shapes and sizes dressed like Sara-Marie in pyjama bottoms and bunny ears, with little singlet tops, their rounded bellies wobbling merrily as they bounced with excitement. I'd never seen anything like it. Their body confidence — like Sara-Marie's — was astonishing. I was inspired.

Back at the office, I couldn't stop thinking about it and immediately organised to shoot Sara-Marie for an eight-page fashion story. I recognised this was a zeitgeist moment and I wanted *Cosmo* to be part of it.

As an editor, I rarely went on shoots any more. Not because I didn't have time, but because I found them excruciatingly boring. On any kind of shoot, there is more mindless waiting around than you could possibly imagine and even when the action gets going and the photographer is shooting, the novelty wears off in two minutes and it's dull again.

But on the day we shot Sara-Marie, I was so there. I even took Luca, who wore the bunny ears I'd brought back from the 'Big Brother' finale. He had a lovely time and couldn't quite believe he was meeting Sara-Marie, who was, at that moment, the most famous person in Australia.

Like all the shoots we did with 'real' girls and bigger models, I had no intention of hiding Sara-Marie's curves. The clothes brought along by the fashion editor were sexy and fun, evening wear mostly and also a blue bikini. Sara-Marie was a delight to work with and her body confidence was no act. She was utterly uninhibited in front of the camera and I watched her chow down on a big lunch before the bikini shot — something a skinny model would rarely do.

When the pictures came back from the photographer a few days later, I excitedly pored over them with my art director. Impulsively, I decided to do something radical.

Britney Spears had already been locked in for the October cover and the shot we had was pretty standard. She was wearing hipster jeans and a white bra with a fuchsia lace wrap top, exposing acres of flat brown tummy and a diamond stud in her belly button. Her hair looked great, her outfit and accessories were strong, her make-up was beautiful, the pose was sexy. Tick, tick, tick, tick. Very *Cosmo*.

We'd run Britney on the cover several times before and she

was always a great seller. This cover would tie in with her tour of Australia — the ideal situation for circulation, readership and publicity — the publishing trifecta.

But I loved the Sara-Marie shots and wanted to do something more special than just run them inside the magazine. I wanted to make a statement about body image by putting someone who wasn't size eight or even size twelve on the cover.

So I decided to do a 'flip' cover — have the shot of Britney on one side of the magazine and a shot of Sara-Marie on the reverse side. There would be no 'back' cover, just alternate fronts. Newsagents could decide which of the two equally gorgeous images — with the same coverlines and text — to display. I also decided to build an entire special Body Love issue around the shots and phenomenon of Sara-Marie. I asked her to guest-edit the issue, which is something that magazines do from time to time with a celebrity who resonates with their readers. *Vogue* did it several years ago with Karl Lagerfeld.

Does the celebrity actually come into the office and sit around having meetings, brainstorming coverlines, reading copy and choosing pictures? Uh, no. Not even close. Usually it's a chat with the editor and a couple of emails. But it sounds impressive and it's PR gold.

In practice, guest-editing means that the issue is themed around the celebrity and the content slanted to reflect their signature area of fame and expertise. Sara-Marie had plenty of fame but no expertise. What made her so appealing was her authentic surprise that she'd somehow become famous. To me, it was all about her bubbly confidence, particularly her body confidence. What was her secret? How could she be so uninhibited, letting it all hang out and happily slapping her own bum, even though it was quite big? That's what women — even those far thinner than her — wanted to know.

I put all the Body Love content for that special issue — about twenty-four pages — behind the Sara-Marie cover to justify doing the flip and make each side feel like a 'proper' magazine. We went to print and I felt satisfied that I'd done something really positive for women. I knew the issue would be a talking point and I was looking forward to the reaction from readers — I was sure they'd adore it.

The reaction built quickly. But not in a good way. If I'd been expecting a ticker-tape parade in my honour for Services For The Advancement Of Positive Female Body Image In The Media, I'd have been brutally disappointed.

It started with a trickle of letters saying how much they loved the shots of Sara-Marie and Sara-Marie herself. So far so good. I waited for more to come. But then, one newspaper printed a small, snarky piece about how appalling it was that *Cosmo* had put Sara-Marie on the 'back' cover and size-eight Britney on the front.

It wasn't a big story but it was a slow news week and so it ignited a firestorm, one I was totally unprepared for. Overnight, media around the country were calling me for interviews to explain my 'shoddy treatment of Sara-Marie'. Readers' letters began to pour in, protesting against her relegation to 'second-class citizen' on the 'back' cover. 'Shame, *Cosmo*, shame,' they jeered.

I was called a hypocrite. A traitor. A sell-out. A coward. Definitely no ticker-tape parade for me, then.

The media coverage snowballed. Everything I said was twisted and used against me as yet more proof that *Cosmo* was insulting Sara-Marie and dissing all women larger than size eight. The story got bigger and uglier and refused to go away. The

Women's Electoral Lobby even issued a statement condemning *Cosmopolitan* and me.

At first I was shocked and bewildered by the reaction. Then angry. And finally, dismayed. Dismayed that my intentions had been so drastically misinterpreted and that I was being accused of the very thing I had always railed against — promoting body insecurity among women.

The interviews I did went something like this.

Them: 'You put Sara-Marie on the back cover because she's fat, didn't you? Britney was the real cover because she's skinny.'
Me: [trying not to sound upset or defensive and failing miserably]. 'Not true! Britney was always going to be on the cover of the October issue. Sara-Marie was a late and controversial inclusion, not because she wasn't skinny but because she was famous for coming third on a reality TV show — not the usual criteria for a Cosmopolitan *covergirl.'*
Them: 'Why did newsagents have the Britney cover face-up instead of Sara-Marie?'
Me: 'We treated the two covers exactly the same way from a design point of view and explicitly asked newsagents and supermarkets to display half Britney and half Sara-Marie. But apart from visiting newsagents personally, we have no control over how they display the magazine.'
Them: 'It was all just a gimmick to sell magazines, wasn't it? You don't care about body image at all.'
Me: 'That's absolutely not true. I won't pretend my job as an editor is not to sell magazines. Of course it is. But Cosmo is not new to the issue of body image. And this could never be described as a cynical or token gesture. We're the only women's magazine to feature women up to size sixteen every single month.

*'And we built an entire issue around Sara-Marie. Not only
was she the guest-editor, inside the magazine she had ten pages
of coverage compared to Britney's four. Doesn't that count for
anything?'*
Them: *'Not when larger women feel you've insulted them.
Because you have.'*

It was a feeding frenzy and I was being mauled by pissed-off
sharks. Ironically, by trying to buck the typical magazine trend
towards skinny girls, I'd made the ultimate mistake: I did
something, but not enough.

Not for the first or last time, I had become the whipping girl
for everything that was wrong with the fashion and magazine
industries in their portrayal of women. And the more I tried to
explain myself, the angrier people seemed to become and the
bigger the story became.

In the end, I did dozens of interviews with hostile journalists
and replied personally to hundreds of readers' letters. In the next
issue, I printed a Q&A, answering all the questions I'd been asked
and refuting the accusations made against *Cosmo*.

Meanwhile, Hearst was horrified that Sara-Marie was
anywhere near the cover at all. They were by now familiar with
my body image obsession and while they weren't thrilled about
the bigger models I used inside the magazine, they indulged me
because sales were very good. But by putting Sara-Marie on the
cover — back, front, flip, whatever you wanted to call it — I'd
pushed them too far.

I received a terse lecture from Helen about the bad example I
was setting for other *Cosmo* editors. What if Poland wanted to
put a rotund housewife on the cover? It just wasn't *Cosmo*.

Through it all, Pat was a calming voice. 'With all this media
attention, sales should be good,' she reassured me. 'Just watch.'

And they were. Fantastic, despite the ongoing press frenzy that was entering its third week.

And then it was September 11 and Sara-Marie and *Cosmo* suddenly weren't important at all any more.

FEAR OF FLYING

SMS to Jen from me:

'Cosmo *conference not in Paris any more. I think they're trying to kill me ...'*

From a human point of view, September 11 was tragic beyond all imagining. From a business point of view, circulation was instantly affected. Sales of magazines froze completely as everyone bought newspapers and compulsively watched TV instead. But after about a week, things changed. Like many, I made the decision to turn off the TV and look away. It felt like the coverage had gone from reporting the news to ghoulishly chronicling people's private pain. It felt like voyeurism. Grief porn. And I desperately wanted to avert my gaze. The crisis was over — in immediate terms — and the personal stories of the victims and their families were just too distressing and too vast to digest. Collectively, we seemed to make the same decision: Enough. I need distraction. I need trivia. I need something superficial to take my mind off the deeply shocking things I've seen and read.

And with that, people went back to the movies, started watching sitcoms and began buying magazines again. Sara-Marie seemed like a lifetime ago. It had only been ten days.

As I'd watched the planes hit those buildings, again and again during that week, I remember thinking to myself, 'I will never be able to go to New York again.' I was already a terribly nervous flier, and now I had images that transcended my worst fears by a million per cent. I knew with complete certainty that I would never again have the courage to board a plane to the US. I wondered if I'd ever be able to board a plane again period.

And then, in an act of spontaneous patriotism and parochial largesse, Hearst decided to support its local economy by cancelling plans to hold the forthcoming *Cosmo* conference in Paris and instead flying all its editors from around the world to … New York. Specifically, downtown New York, mere blocks from the still smouldering ruins of Ground Zero. It was less than six months after September 11 and attendance was compulsory. Clearly, the universe was trying to tell me something. Possibly, Harden the Fuck Up.

Before giving birth, I quite enjoyed flying. I'm not certain how I went from 'This is fun!' to 'We're all going to die!' but I'd been stuck there for several years.

When you're not scared of something, it's hard to understand the headspace of someone who is. If you told me you were scared of, say, walking down the street because a lion might eat you, I would want to slap you about the face and shout, 'Pull yourself together, silly twit! Lions don't roam free in the street!' But for you, the fear would be real and paralysing and my no-efforts to snap you out of it with logic would be futile.

So here's what you need to know if you meet someone with aerophobia: save the 'More-people-die-in-car-accidents-than-plane-crashes' speech because it will not — I repeat not — cut the mustard. All we will hear is '… people die in … plane crashes.' And we knew that already.

For a long time, my hopeless solution to this inconvenient fear was to avoid flying. Genius. And when I absolutely couldn't avoid it? Prescription drugs.

And just when I thought I couldn't be any more terrified of flying? Terrorism. Overnight, I could now panic not just about accidental plane crashes but deliberate ones too. Previously I'd been able to hold it together for essential domestic flights and took sleeping pills for overseas ones to block out as much of the experience as possible. But now I was being forced to face down my fear by flying to New York.

Clearly, sleeping pills weren't going to be nearly enough. When I went to my GP on the verge of tears at the mere thought of getting on that plane, she prescribed a lovely little anti-anxiety tablet called Xanax. It's also used to treat panic attacks and is one of the most commonly prescribed medications for aerophobia. She gave me sleeping pills for the flight itself as well, but I could start taking Xanax a few days before departure in order to make it to the airport without a straitjacket.

Well, let me tell you, Xanax was a hoot. God, how I loved those little blue guys. I was so utterly chilled during that flight to New York, I even managed a jaunty spot of duty-free shopping while in transit at LA airport. Not until I checked my Visa statement the following month did I notice I'd spent $345 — on lip gloss. Three hundred and forty-five American dollars. That's a whole lot of happily whacked.

Unhappily, Visa-abuse wasn't my only Xanax side effect. When its beautifully calming effects wore off, I awoke that first New York morning in absolute blind terror. It didn't help that, mere months after 9/11, New Yorkers were still jumping every time a plane flew overhead, a siren sounded or a car backfired.

I remember virtually nothing of that conference except Woody Allen and Kim Cattrall being guest speakers and a Hearst executive sussing me out at a group dinner about the prospect of my moving to New York to edit a magazine for them over there. I believe the words 'Are you fucking kidding me?' may have escaped my lips. The sensation that I was going to die was so strong and my need to get back to Jason and Luca so primal, I was almost out of my mind. This raw panic barely eased for the five days of my trip and only subsided when I popped another happy blue pill for my return flight.

If only that was the end of it. Shortly after I arrived home, the panic returned for another forty-eight hours. This made no sense because I was back with my family and away from any perceived danger. I put the whole experience down to my aerophobia reaching new post-9/11 extremes, but my GP disagreed. 'Rebound anxiety,' she concluded. 'It's not uncommon with Xanax. The drug holds your anxiety at bay but as soon as the effects wear off, your anxiety returns even more intensely.' So, no fear of flying while in the air but a paralysing fear of being on the ground for several days afterwards! Superb! Bye-bye beautiful Xanax; I'll miss you like the deserts miss the rain.

I don't like taking drugs in my regular life and I don't have a lot of luck taking them while up in the sky. On one trip to Europe a few years ago with Jason, I was making do with sleeping pills alone. This was mostly effective until the final leg of a million-hour trip home. After a torturous transit day in Tokyo airport, we boarded the plane along with a tourist group of about a hundred excitable Japanese students. 'Goodness, it's a bit like being at a Spice Girls concert, isn't it?' I cracked to the male flight attendant, who giggled with me conspiratorially.

Accepting his offer of a glass of champagne, I knocked it back with a Stilnox sleeping pill, eagerly awaiting the sleepy wave I knew would break over my head within a few minutes. I politely refused the offer of dinner and happily, sleepily, reclined my seat. Ahhhhhhh.

The next thing I knew, breakfast was being served and, according to my watch, seven hours had passed. I felt well rested although I was slightly puzzled by the odd looks coming from the flight attendants. The guy I'd joked with wouldn't look me in the eye. And why were my hands covered in chicken?

Jason helpfully filled in the blanks. Apparently, soon after going to sleep, I woke up again and decided that I did, in fact want dinner. Immediately. So I sat up in my reclined seat, started to groggily eat the chicken cacciatore I was brought and then began to sob hysterically. In silence.

Concerned, but not surprised (he's been travelling with me for years, poor man), Jason calmly inquired what the problem might be. This is apparently when I started shouting at him. Again, in silence. My mouth was moving — a lot — and tears were streaming down my face while I waved my arms about, but no noise was coming out of my mouth. Which is a good thing really because it was full of chicken.

Ignoring all this, he gently tried to adjust my seat so it was upright while I ate and cried, but, perturbed by his actions, I attempted to stab his fingers with my fork, which I then dropped before continuing to eat with my hands. The flight attendants made a few attempts to see if everything was okay, but when it became clear I was certifiably cuckoo, they vanished discreetly to leave my husband to deal with his nutbag alone.

Eventually, I passed out with a piece of chicken clutched in each fist and slept solidly for seven hours. Dreaming of train travel, no doubt.

This little incident would have forever been consigned to the family file marked 'Mia's Eccentric Flying Episodes' were it not for the publicity that later surrounded Stilnox. It turns out I wasn't the only one to have a strange reaction to the drug, although perhaps I'm the only one who's done so on a plane with a chicken.

I WANT TO BE FAMOUS, DON'T I?

SMS to me from my mum:

'Darling, you were fabulous this morning! And I'm not just saying that because I'm your mum. Dad thought so too!'

'First, we have to get you some voice coaching,' the TV executive announced immediately after suggesting I become a regular on Channel Nine's 'Today'. And with those mortifying words, my stint on breakfast TV began.

I still adored my job but there was a repetition and rhythm about magazine production that made me feel secure and comfortable and also a little … bored.

After more than a decade working for *Cleo* and *Cosmo*, I wanted some new challenges. I was already writing a column each week in a Sunday newspaper. And then 'Today' approached me about becoming their lifestyle reporter. They wanted to introduce a bit more magazine-style content and needed someone to do stories on fashion, trends and 'women's issues'.

I was flattered and anxious.

And that's before the TV executive told me I had a rubbish voice. The massive insecurity inherent in being in front of the camera had begun. Welcome to TV! Check your self-confidence at the door! Until that day, I'd thought my voice was perfectly acceptable. Pah! Stupid girl. To work on television, you need a particular type of voice. One different to mine, apparently.

This is how I came to find myself several weeks later marching around a Channel Nine boardroom table in bare feet loudly humming 'Jingle Bells' in an attempt to sound less 'nasal'. It was my voice coach's suggestion. My. Voice. Coach. How did this happen? And more importantly, was I on crack?

Like most people who watch TV, I thought being on it would be easy peasy. You turn up. You be yourself. Not too tricky, surely?

Over the next year or so, I would be taught many things. How to talk was merely one of them. I also learned how to sit on an interview couch, how to walk and talk simultaneously, how to stop slouching and how to wear a bra to prevent VBD (visible boob droop).

In my first appearance on 'Today', a riveting segment about buying jeans, I did all of the above incorrectly and was given a stern talking-to from the woman at Nine whose job it was to notice such things. After making me watch the video tape of my segment, I had to admit she was right, even though it was hard to concentrate when all I wanted to do was reach through the TV and slap myself across the face.

From that first week on air, I was on the back foot. Voice lessons were stepped up. Bra straps were tightened. Couch sitting was practised. Seriously. I was so busy trying not to slouch, droop or mumble during my weekly six-minute segment, it's a damn miracle I had time to hold down my day job.

Even with all the coaching, I had some corkers. One week, I did a segment on people hiring private investigators to trail cheating spouses. As part of my chat with then host Steve Liebmann in the studio, I was given a few props to discuss.

Most of them were innocuous, like handbags with hidden inbuilt cameras. But there was also a kit for detecting semen on underwear. The nauseating idea being you retrieve your partner's knickers, squirt this stuff onto the crotch and wait for the fabric to change colour if semen present, indicating that the wearer of the undies had seen some action.

Steve, understandably, wasn't keen to mention the semen detection kit and tried to ignore it, but I hauled him back from his journalistic integrity with the following display of TV Tourette syndrome: 'Now Steve, the kit says it can be used to detect infidelity in both men and women and that's got me a bit baffled.'

Steve had gone slightly grey under his make-up but I ploughed on, unable to stop myself. 'Like, I understand how it would work on women's undies — but men? I mean, what if some semen just fell out during the day?'

Across the studio, I heard Steve's co-host Tracy Grimshaw spit out her coffee. Possibly through her nose. The crew similarly began convulsing with laughter.

Back on the couch, Steve's face turned to stone before he quickly wrapped up the segment and threw to a commercial. As soon as we were off air, he gently hit me over the head with his script and stalked off.

To my surprise, he didn't have me summarily fired, or even killed. In fact he never mentioned it again and was always supportive and encouraging. Sadly, it was also poor Steve who bore the brunt of my next debacle.

It was Melbourne Cup day and I was set to do my first live cross at 8.10 am. We were at a posh garden party where some ladies in hats had been wrangled to stand around and look glamorous. Then there was me. And a horse. A big horse that had some claim to Cup fame I was meant to mention and instantly forgot.

Before I could check with the producer what I should say about the horse, a microphone was shoved in my hand and we went live. I stumbled awkwardly through for the first thirty seconds or so of the segment, babbling away to Steve, mispronouncing the name of the champagne sponsor, forgetting the name of the park we were in and stammering like an idiot. Then the big scary horse lunged towards me and tried to eat my microphone.

In my panic, I threw back to Steve in the studio, but since I'd been supposed to talk a fair bit longer, Steve had taken the opportunity to duck out and refill his coffee. Sorry again, Steve.

No doubt, hundreds of thousands of people were at that moment looking at their TVs and saying, 'Who is the idiot with the horse?' One senior executive at Nine who was watching TV at that moment happened to be married to a friend of mine. Later she told me he'd looked pityingly at the screen and said, 'She's really not a natural, is she?'

There were other problems too. Being an editor and a control freak, I hated having other people involved in deciding what my segment would be about and how it would work. Not that I wasn't willing to take direction — I knew nothing about TV and I wanted to learn — but no one had time to explain anything to me and every week I was assigned a different producer.

The other challenge was discovering how insecure TV made me feel. It took a while, but I eventually realised that if anyone said, 'You were great,' it simply meant they liked what I was wearing. Not once could anyone remember a thing I'd said.

In this way it was so different to writing where it's all about the content. For a print journalist, it doesn't matter if you have three heads and hairy palms. You can sit on a couch backwards and still write a good story. On TV, appearances are everything. And when you're sitting in hair and make-up at 6 am with your eyes glued shut because your child woke three times in the night with a bad dream, appearances are not your strongest suit.

I always felt a bit dirty after being on TV. Exposed. Vulnerable. In need of reassurance that I had indeed been great because I never had a clue if I was, and usually I wasn't.

This was all horribly tiresome, so it was almost a relief when a new executive producer decided to axe my segment. I never missed being on TV for a moment. Unfortunately, TV wasn't quite done with me yet.

ONCE UPON A TIME THERE WAS A BANANA

I met the real Kylie Minogue once. Back in the day, a year or so after I first started at *Cleo*, I was filling in at the front desk one time for the editorial coordinator, who was at lunch.

The role of 'editorial coordinator' sounds hugely important and in many ways it is, although receptionist would be an equally accurate title. You could be forgiven for assuming the coordinator was deeply integrated in the editorial process, regulating the flow of words and pictures that goes into the magazine. In truth, it is a purely administrative role.

Still, it's an important one because the editorial coordinator is the gatekeeper for the magazine, the first voice you hear when you call, the first face you see when you visit. And she knows where the biscuits are kept.

For someone keen to break into magazines, editorial coordinator is the most common entry point and one that almost always leads somewhere if you're smart, hard-working and disciplined.

There is, however, a trap that frequently thwarts the chances of promotion of the editorial coordinators. In fact, it applies to every level of the career ladder if you're interested in climbing it. Usually, around the time you become sick of your job and yearn to climb higher, you start doing it badly. Consciously or unconsciously, it can be difficult to disguise your boredom and frustration. Your standards slip. Your boss notices. So when you finally summon the courage to walk into her office and ask for a promotion, there's every chance she'll refuse since it appears you can barely handle your current, more menial job. Why should she trust you and reward you with a better one?

This happened to me a few times at significant points in my career and it was a lesson I was slow to learn: the less you like your job, the better you have to do it in order to land a better one.

Anyway, on this particular day when the real editorial coordinator went to lunch, she asked me to cover for her. I was beauty writer at the time and as a relatively new and very junior member of staff, the task of minding the front desk sometimes fell to me.

I didn't mind at all. I loved answering the phone and doing admin. Possibly because it wasn't my real job and it felt like a novelty. Like babysitting someone else's child for an hour or so. In fact, working at *Cleo* in the first place still felt like such an extraordinary dream I was continually surprised every fortnight when I received my pay slip. All this and money too?

At first I didn't recognise the small, pale, skinny girl who wandered up to the front desk alone. Her hair was cropped boy-short and she was wearing jeans, a jacket, flats and no visible make-up. 'Hi, I'm looking for Nicole Bonython,' she said in a small voice with an upwards inflection and I began replying automatically before it registered who I was talking to.

Nicole was *Cleo*'s fashion director and had known Kylie Minogue since early in her career when she had styled her for some photo shoots and music videos. They'd been friends for years, and even though Kylie now lived in London, they always caught up when she came home.

I tried to stop the flash of recognition before it showed on my face, partly so Kylie wouldn't feel awkward but more to suggest that I was completely used to chatting with celebrities in the course of my workday. Which, of course, I wasn't.

Kylie thanked me politely and disappeared into the cramped rabbit warren of our office, following my directions to Nicole's desk.

Meeting Kylie Minogue — if you can call our fifteen-second exchange 'meeting' — was not just another day at the office for me. Such exciting things rarely happen at a magazine. The reality is far more mundane and even the aspects of mag life that appear glamorous from the outside quickly become background noise.

Editors and magazine staff don't mean to become jaded but, yes, it happens. I won't pretend there aren't some tremendously fun, indulgent, bizarre and impossibly fabulous things about working on a magazine. There are exotic location shoots and film premieres and celebrity interviews and travel and fashion shows and mountains of free stuff. But like anything, if you do it often enough, the wow factor eventually fades. It's just What You Do Every Day At Work.

I'm so used to rattling off a stern lecture entitled 'A Magazine Career is not Glamorous' to wide-eyed girls desperate to break into the industry, I'm quite capable of making it sound about as appealing as working in an abattoir.

This is something all magazine editors do regularly — for several reasons. First, it's to justify our own existence as something more than caricatures. According to 'Absolutely Fabulous', 'Ugly

Betty' and *The Devil Wears Prada*, there are really only two types of women who work in magazines: the ambitious bitch and the vacuous bimbo, neither of whom does much actual work.

These stereotypes are annoying for most of us who are neither bitch nor bimbo. That's why we're sometimes defensive and trumpet the lack of glamour a little too loudly.

But mainly, we do it to deter the thousands of girls who've watched those TV shows and read those books and seen those movies and are gagging to wangle their way into an industry that looks like a cross between 'Australia's Next Top Model' and the MTV awards. Girls who assume working at a magazine will be the same glossy, glamorous experience as reading it.

I was one of those girls and the realisation that the pages of the magazine bore little resemblance to what goes on behind the scenes hit me fast. It began as I walked into Lisa's office that first day and tripped over the masking tape holding down the frayed carpet. It was completed a few weeks later when a cockroach fell from the air-conditioning vent into my coffee cup perched on my tiny work-experience desk.

Frankly, I couldn't have cared less about my surroundings. The business of making magazines was more exciting to me than anything I'd ever experienced. I was not a princess. My broken chair didn't faze me and neither did my crappy desk shoved against a wall in the windowless features room. Pathetic gratitude was the overwhelming emotion I felt during my weeks and months of work experience.

Which was why when I became an editor myself, the very different attitude of some work-experience girls was a rude shock.

One Sunday morning, soon after I'd left *Cosmo*, I was sitting peacefully on my couch, sipping tea and reading the papers. I was flicking fairly mindlessly, my brain preoccupied by the pressing question: 'How early is too early for yum cha?' and the related dilemma: 'Can I feasibly eat prawn gow gees before 10 am?' Just when I'd decided 'Yes I can!', my focus was drawn back to the newspaper by the unwelcome sight of my own face staring up at me. It took a moment before I processed what I was looking at.

Oh dear. I detest looking at pictures of myself in any context, let alone the news section of the paper. That always meant trouble.

The gist of the story was that the magazine industry was apparently in a 'tizz' about some anonymous rumours on a website. One of them tut-tutted that 'Mia Freedman once sent a work-experience person out to buy her son a banana.' A banana. Wow. Lucky I was sitting down when I read that jaw-dropping revelation.

Here's a brief snapshot of the thoughts that flashed through my mind at that point:

1. Did I do that? Possibly. But more likely banana was for self. Son not partial to bananas.
2. Even if true about son, banana is fruit. Good Mother points there.
3. At least no mention of the time I sent art director to buy my son McDonald's. That definitely happened. Look, she was going there anyway.
4. Why is this ridiculous thing in newspaper? Has world gone mad?

As my friends and family woke up and read the story, my phone began to beep.

'At least it wasn't a Mars Bar!' texted my mum.

'You are a selfish cow,' texted an editor friend. 'Why didn't you let work-experience girl choose the cover and send her to a fashion show in Paris?'

For the next few days, I thought a lot about work-experience students and how their expectations had changed since I'd been one. In short: a lot. When Lisa gave me my break, I was genuinely grateful for the chance to fetch her coffee or her mail. I would have gladly washed her car — or her feet — had I been asked. Heck, I would have blow-dried her dog. (I do know someone who was asked to do this for the editor when she did work experience at a fashion magazine.) During the time I did work experience at *Cleo*, I believe I was also regularly sent out to buy assorted muffins and sandwiches for various members of staff. And one time? Some sushi. I know. But it's true.

I was stoked just to be in the office, breathing magazine air. Certainly, I was ambitious and knew from day one I wanted to be an editor, but even with the arrogance of youth, I understood it would take a little time before I got to do the fun and important stuff.

Since I'd started my own career as one, I'd always had a soft spot for work-experience girls and most of them were fantastic. As *Cosmo* editor, I insisted we have a structured program to give them a well-rounded understanding of how a magazine worked. Inevitably, this included some boring tasks because — GUESS WHAT, KIDS? — there are many boring tasks to be done in every workplace. By everyone, including the editor.

Over the years, I began to notice a change in attitude from some of the girls who passed through the office. Gratitude and ambition were being replaced with a sense of entitlement and absurd expectations.

I'm guessing that Banana Girl was one of those: a sixteen-year-old who rocked up for her week at *Cosmo* expecting to interview Madonna and sit front row at fashion week. That's the kind of experience she was after, thanks. And she wasn't the only one. It was starting to drive my already overworked staff nuts.

Accommodating work experience kids takes a lot of extra time and energy for whoever is managing them — usually the very busy, poorly paid editorial coordinator.

So all the talk about work-experience students doing 'unpaid labour', as some of them put it, needs to be put in the context of the 'unpaid labour' done by whoever is responsible for looking after them, answering their questions, setting them tasks, supervising the completion of these tasks (and often having to redo them) and trying to ensure they have a pleasant, educational experience.

The other expectation I noticed among work-experience girls was that they would be — should be — spending quality time with me. When I was an editor, the truth was that I didn't have much to do with work-experience girls. Not because I was superior or a snob or a bitch but because I was just too busy. I had to prioritise the needs of my boss, my staff and my own family above those of work-experience girls. There were simply not enough hours in the day to sit down and have long or even short chats with the hundreds of girls who came through our work-experience program every year.

Often, this was my loss, and I knew it.

Whenever it was possible, I'd try to talk to the girls or answer their questions, but the demands of my job meant this rarely happened. I always tried, though, because I knew the work-experience girls were not just readers, but likely to be passionate and loyal readers. I always valued hearing their thoughts on my magazines and magazines in general.

When I was at *Cosmo*, I designed a questionnaire for all work-experience girls to fill out, and whenever possible I'd call them into my office and ask them to pick their most and least favourite covers from my wall. I was never so arrogant to think I couldn't learn from them. My success depended on listening to their opinions.

As far as menial tasks go, I can't remember ever asking a work-experience student to do anything personally. I didn't have that kind of involvement with them, and anyway, that's why I had an assistant. That's not to say they weren't asked to do things for me by other people. Because sometimes, when she was exceptionally busy, I'm sure my assistant passed on some of her more menial tasks to the work-experience students. Like banana retrieval. It's called time management and delegation, two crucial skills in any workplace.

It got to the point where before 'workies' came in, we informed them in writing that 'You will be required to do administrative tasks and whatever else is required to help around the office, including trips to the mail room, coffee runs, filing etc.'

Most were fine with that and grateful for the opportunity, but some decided this wasn't, like, acceptable and never showed up. Others showed up and then sulked. Or disappeared mid-week. There were some real standouts over the years.

Like the girl who emailed me directly with a story idea and signed off with, 'Get back to me ASAP.'

Or the one who refused to help the fashion assistant take clothes down to the courier dock, insisting, 'I have a degree; I'm not a Sherpa.'

Or the one who announced to my deputy editor, 'I'd really like to interview a celebrity while I'm here. Can you arrange it?'

Of course, many work-experience students were wonderful young women and, occasionally, young men, bless their brave souls. As my features editor once observed, 'It would be a fifty–fifty split: the little creatures who slump and sigh at being asked to get the mail, and those who have already gone down and brought it back before you can ask.'

Guess who gets invited back and is ultimately offered a job?

SEX AT THE CHECKOUT

SMS to Mia from Alice:

'In car listening to Triple J today after school. Heard you on radio. Jimmy's been telling everyone, "I heard Luca's mummy say sex on the radio!" Hilarious. A xx'

Sometimes big moments in your life don't happen the way you expect them to. I always thought my decision to quit *Cosmo* would be an agonising one. But after seven years and one hundred issues, it all came down to two simple moments, a few hours apart. They would suddenly crystallise a murky mix of thoughts, emotions, doubts and suspicions that had been brewing for more than a year.

My moment of clarity came while I was in the eye of a media storm that had taken me completely by surprise, just like the Sara-Marie cover incident. Even after seven years, I still couldn't always pick what would spark publicity. Sometimes I'd think we had a killer story, get all excited, and then be utterly deflated when it died, ignored by the media.

Other times, like this one, I was blind-sided by a PR disaster I never saw coming.

A couple of months earlier, I knew exactly what I was doing when I commissioned yet another sealed section, a how-to oral-sex story that ran over six pages. I was trying to sell magazines in the same way editors of *Cosmo*, *Cleo* and others had done for decades. With sex.

The September 2004 issue of *Cosmo* was unremarkable, as far as I was concerned. I was lukewarm about the cover image of Kirsten Dunst that had come from US *Cosmo*. She was wearing a truly atrocious purple beaded mini-dress with midriff cut-outs, but it was the best I had that month.

Inside there were some nice stories but nothing stop-the-cab★. Still, we'd managed to massage the coverlines into something reasonably compelling. Among them were:

a funny, naughty one:

> ### *Bent*
> ### *Huge*
> ### *Pierced*
> ### *Uncut*
> ### *How to deal with a surprise penis*

a relationship one:

> ### *8 LOVE TRUTHS*
> ### *YOU NEED TO KNOW*
> #### *(Babe, if he hasn't called by day 7, he never will)*

a body-love one:

> ### *HAPPY WEIGHT*
> #### *Ditch the diets & depression*
> #### + Cosmo *girls tell how they beat obesity, bulimia & anorexia*

★ 'Stop-the-cab' is short for 'stop-the-cab-I-need-to-jump-out-and-buy-that-clever-magazine-immediately'. It's a term that was coined by Wendy to refer to an irresistible coverline that will boost sales.

and a sex one:

Oral sex lessons
Blow-by-blow tips for you & for him

The 'oral sex lessons' coverline was the largest and occupied the prime real estate, on the top left-hand side of the cover, just under the *Cosmopolitan* logo. This is where you always put your strongest coverline because it's where the reader's eye naturally goes first.

This story was an oldie but a goodie. Classic *Cosmo* content. Evidently there are a lot of women who aren't confident with their technique or who want to improve it, because whenever *Cosmo* ran a how-to oral-sex story, sales spiked. So following the golden rule of publishing — 'If you find something that works, flog it to death until it doesn't' — we did one every year. At least.

Around this time other magazines were sticking lipsticks and mascaras and bags and thongs and sarongs on the cover. As bribes, plain and simple. And because I didn't want to do that, I had to make sure our editorial offering was compelling enough to compete with the freebies being flung about by our competitors.

Since I'd published far more sexually explicit content in the past, it never occurred to me that anyone would have a problem with yet another oral-sex story. If anything, I worried that the subject had lost its, ahem, potency and might fall flat.

Ha. Once again, just as with Sara-Marie, I didn't see the controversy coming until it punched me in the face.

About a week after we went on sale, I received a call from the circulation department. The news was dire. Woolworths had pulled the current issue of *Cosmo* from sale after complaints about the oral-sex coverline. This had never happened before

I quickly went through my usual emotional spectrum in a work crisis: shock, bewilderment, alarm, anger, frustration.

At first, I was shocked that Woolworths had taken such an extreme measure — we usually had some warning if they were displeased.

Then, I was bewildered that this particular coverline was deemed so offensive. And I'd seen other mags do much worse. Why had everyone suddenly gone all prudish?

Next, I was alarmed by how fast things escalated. The media quickly picked up on the story and Coles followed Woolworths' lead, yanking *Cosmo* from the checkout magazine-stands in all its stores too. Gulp. I felt sick. This would be disastrous for sales and management would not be pleased.

As the situation escalated, I became angry that the complaints of a few people could have such a dramatic effect, and that the supermarkets could essentially censor content they didn't think appropriate — even though oral-sex stories had been touted on the covers of magazines for more than a decade without a problem.

Ultimately, I felt frustrated that we couldn't even fight back. The two supermarket giants represented almost half of our sales every month and, after newsagents, were our biggest distribution channel. They were hugely powerful and had the ability to affect not just sales of *Cosmo*, but of all the other ACP titles. We couldn't afford to piss them off permanently. Or even temporarily. Cue: massive back-pedal.

Since we were only a few days into the four-week on-sale period, it was vital we get back on the stands as soon as possible, so the circulation department, in consultation with the supermarkets, printed tens of thousands of stickers to go over the offending coverline. They said something twee and cheesy like 'Bedroom Secrets Inside' and it cost us a fortune, not just to print the stickers but for them to be applied to every issue by hand.

We also had to foot the bill for the removal of the magazines and their replacement. The whole debacle cost more than $100,000.

While I worked through the logistics privately with various ACP departments, publicly I had to do media interviews and tread a delicate line between defending *Cosmo* and placating the supermarkets. A lovey-dovey relationship had to be maintained regardless of how pissed off I was.

This is how I found myself one Wednesday doing an interview on the ABC's youth radio station Triple J, about the 'supermarket oral–sex scandal' with the afternoon presenters who, understandably, found the situation hilarious.

In a forty-eight-hour period, I must have done a couple of dozen interviews with media outlets that delighted in being able to report such a salacious story in the guise of news. Some of the AM radio interviewers seemed hostile, with some presenters accusing me of peddling porn to unsuspecting kiddies in the supermarket under their parents' noses.

In hindsight, I think the word 'lessons' in the coverline somehow gave the impression that we were targeting the information to schoolchildren. Clearly we weren't, but the ambiguity of the wording didn't help my cause. No matter how aggressive the tone of the interviews, I had to calmly address concerns and validate the actions of the supermarkets while trying to justify having such a story in my magazine. 'I understand where the concern is coming from,' I said through gritted teeth. 'But the content is sealed and unless you buy the magazine you can't read it, so no children were at risk at the supermarket checkout.'

Although I was incensed by the censorship and was a passionate advocate for sex advice in magazines like *Cosmo*, I could also understand my critics. And for the first time in my career, I wasn't relishing my public role as *Cosmo* editor, defender of sex stories. In fact, I was starting to feel downright uncomfortable.

Luca was almost seven, and I was beginning to understand the concerns of parents who didn't want their children to be seeing sexually explicit words on a magazine cover while they stood in line to buy milk. Yes, the content may have been sealed but the words on the cover weren't and there are few places more mortifying to have to answer your child's innocent questions about sex than in a supermarket queue.

As I tried to play it straight in my conversation with the Triple J announcers, who were making all kinds of smutty jokes at my expense, I suddenly felt the conflict between my role as *Cosmo* editor and my role as mother more strongly than ever before. I couldn't shake the overwhelming feeling that I didn't want to be there; I didn't want to be doing this any more.

And then I got the text from my friend Alice, the mother of Luca's best friend. She thought it was funny but inwardly I cringed. And with that, I knew for sure I was no longer the right person to be editing *Cosmo*. To stay relevant and successful, the magazine needed an editor whose life was anchored firmly in the lifestyle of its readers: mostly single, girls in their late teens and early twenties. *Cosmo* needed someone who could be fearless in her promotion of everything the magazine stood for, including — especially — the sex.

Even though I'd never really been that girl during my editorship, I was able to effectively channel her, quarantining my private life and feelings from my professional ones. But I couldn't fake it so well any more. More importantly, I didn't want to. It was time to grow up.

START YOUR ENGINES

SMS to Jo from me:

'Um, do you have any idea where exactly I'm meant to put my ovulation thermometer?'

Finally Jason and I were ready to start trying for another baby. It had been a few years since the miscarriage, and our life was back on track. I was wary, nervous and excited. Mostly though, I was terrified it wouldn't work. I'd lost all confidence in my body's ability to sustain a pregnancy and keep a baby alive. And I knew the emotional ride would be a rocky one. Still, we decided to take a deep breath and give it a whirl.

The first step was to go off the pill. I'd gone on a pill called 'Diane' a couple of years earlier to clear up my skin. The hormonal avalanche after the miscarriage and the stress of the aftermath had manifested itself physically in two ways. I lost a lot of weight and my face turned into a pizza.

The crappy state of my skin back then — the worst it had been since puberty — was another nail in the coffin of my self-esteem when I was already miserable. I finally fled to my dermatologist in despair.

'I'm a gargoyle,' I wailed.

She was too polite to agree outright, but she did write me a script for Diane. I sprinted out the door to fill it, guzzling my first pill while the chemist was still putting my money in her cash register.

I hadn't been on the pill for years because it turned me into a nutbag. Literally within days of taking it, my personality would change. Since my late teens, I've tried a bunch of different pills and they've all been hugely effective in preventing pregnancy because they all turned me into a stark raving loon who was so hideous, no guy wanted to be near me.

But after I lost the baby and then my mind for a while there, I became so desperate to control something in my life that my skin seemed the most simple problem to fix. And I was so emotionally all over the place anyway, I figured I'd barely notice any lunatic side effects.

Diane and I became fast friends. I loved her with every pore on my face. There didn't seem to be any adverse mental effects but who could say for sure. In the murky soup of my headspace, Diane barely registered as an ingredient.

I took her faithfully every day for the next few years and my skin was better than it had ever been. I almost looked airbrushed.

However, since it's a little tricky to fall pregnant on the pill, breaking up with Diane was an inevitable first step on my road to conception.

About a week after I'd binned my pills and replaced them with folic-acid supplements, complete hell broke loose from my neck up. All the oil production Diane had switched off for two years suddenly got the message to return to work. It was like the taps got turned on full blast in order to clear two years of backlog.

My face was an oil slick and so was my hair. Pimples followed immediately. And the whole oily mess lasted for months. I had to wash my hair every day, but even that wouldn't lift it off my head. I was desperate to get pregnant but I wasn't thrilled about becoming a human oil refinery.

Even apart from the superficial stuff, I was not feeling great. There are few things unsexier than a woman who is completely desperate to get pregnant.

Early on, we went back to see Dr Bob. Even walking into that building was incredibly difficult for me. All the memories of having sat in his waiting room within minutes of having learned our baby had died reached into my throat immediately and made it hard to breathe. I could feel the tears behind my eyes and fought to keep them there. I'm not a public crier. I prefer to bottle it up even if it makes me feel like I'm being strangled by sadness and my own inhibitions.

Jason took my hand, squeezing it for support and we were soon ushered into Dr Bob's office. I hadn't seen him for a few years and he looked mildly surprised but visibly happy to see us.

'Well, hello you two,' he greeted us warmly and his voice made me feel like I was losing a grip on my tears. Deep breath.

'Well, hi. We're back.' I tried to laugh. My voice caught in my throat. Keep breathing.

In front of him was my file. It was very thick.

'We're um, well, we're ready to have another go at getting pregnant,' I started haltingly, trying not to cry as Jason kept squeezing my hand supportively. 'But … I'm really scared.'

Dr Bob nodded. 'Let's have a look at where we left off,' he suggested gently, looking through the pile of papers. There were reams of pathology results but they didn't reveal much. The facts were simply that my last pregnancy had ended unexpectedly and without symptom, at fifteen or sixteen weeks. Death In Utero. No explanation was ever found.

'You've had one successful pregnancy with Luca so that's a fantastic indicator that you'll be able to do it again,' he pointed out encouragingly. 'The best indicator we could hope for.'

I sniffled. 'Okay,' I said in a very small voice.

Then Dr Bob gave us some basic instructions in baby-making.

'To find out when you're ovulating, you can take your temperature every day and chart it here on this ovulation graph. Your most fertile days are the ones directly on either side of your temperature going up. Ideally, that's when you should have sex.'

My head was spinning with the effort of trying to stay in the present moment and not cry. It felt like I was drowning in my memories of being here when we'd lost the baby. I couldn't snap out of it. I nodded absently at Dr Bob and took the chart while Jason asked some questions.

In the car, I clutched the empty chart and looked out the window, blinking back silent tears and clenching my teeth. Years later, I still had my guard up and I found it almost impossible to let it down, even with Jason. I couldn't talk about it and I couldn't cry. My grief was so tightly sealed I could only access it in private.

But at this stage, apart from my emotional baggage, I had no reason to seriously think getting pregnant would be that hard. Formative teenage years filled with scary warnings about how easy it is to get knocked up and ruin your life are a stubborn legacy to shake.

Even when I was a virgin, I was paranoid about getting pregnant. My boyfriend and I would fool around but I was always petrified. 'Sperm can swim!' I'd insist. 'They told us that in sex education!'

'Not through my jeans,' he'd sigh.

Of course I let my guard down — heck, I sent the guard home — almost as soon as I met Jason. He was the first guy I'd ever seriously imagined having children with. With other boyfriends, sure, I'd momentarily thought about babies. But the fantasy was always about me being a mother, not about them being the father of my baby. And there's a *biiiiig* difference.

Falling pregnant twice with Jason had done nothing to disprove my conviction that getting pregnant was easy. Surely this time, since we also had the right intentions, it would be as simple as throwing my pills in the bin and my legs in the air. Wouldn't it?

TWICE THE SEALED SECTIONS

Voicemail to Jen from me:

'Okay, so I had my meeting with Pat and I have good news and bad news. Need to debrief. Call me.'

'I don't want to edit *Cosmo* any more,' I told my boss over lunch one day, explaining how I'd come to my decision. 'I have sealed-section fatigue.'

Pat understood. She'd been there herself.

And it wasn't just the sealed sections I was sick of. Including my time at *Cleo*, I'd been working in the same 'young women's lifestyle' genre for twelve years. My entire career. In the hundred issues I'd edited, I'd pushed *Cosmo* as far as I could. I'd staved off boredom by launching some extension titles — *Cosmo Hair and Beauty*, *Cosmo Weddings* and *Cosmo Pregnancy* — but they were all established and profitable now. I needed a fresh challenge.

We talked for a long time about what I might like to do next. 'Get pregnant' was the truth, although I didn't say it out loud. Partly because I didn't want to jinx the idea but also because no matter how outwardly supportive I knew Pat would be, having staff go on maternity leave was a managerial headache. And not a particularly helpful context in which to discuss my future career prospects.

I tried hard to be inspired about my next move but I kept coming up blank. Having been hell-bent for so many years on editing *Cleo* and then shifting that dream slightly to edit *Cosmo*, I'd never really thought beyond it.

There was no other title in the company — or any other company — I was busting to edit. The weekly market held no appeal because of the workload. The hours were insane. And while I enjoyed reading gossip magazines, I didn't want to turn a guilty pleasure into a daily job description.

At the other end of the spectrum, I was equally uninterested in editing a fashion magazine like *Vogue* or *Harper's Bazaar*. Sure, I like a frock as much as the next girl but I've never believed fashion is life or death and you have to feel that way to edit a fashion title effectively. My preference has always been to work on the perimeter of the fashion industry so I could holiday there without having to take up citizenship.

What else was there? The *Australian Women's Weekly* has always been the jewel in the crown at ACP and is the most iconic magazine in Australia. At thirty-one, I still felt too young for that. So even if I'd had my pick of every magazine in Australia (which I didn't), there was no title I was busting to get my hands on.

The answer turned out to be more of the same. Much more. It was suggested I take on a newly created umbrella role as Editor-in-Chief of *Cosmo*, *Cleo* and *Dolly*. I agreed. Why not? *Cleo*'s editor was about to leave to launch *Madison*. With me stepping down from *Cosmo*, there would be two new editors requiring guidance. I was already Editor-in-Chief of *Dolly* so it wasn't a big stretch, although it was a big responsibility looking after about two million readers each month.

Staying involved with *Cosmo* meant a smooth transition for the magazine and for me. I wouldn't be walking away from my magazine baby altogether. But it was a different kind of baby I wanted. Desperately. My head and my hormones were consumed with trying to get pregnant and it wasn't going at all well.

AN
EMBARRASSING
ADDICTION

SMS to Karen from me:

'Got my period. Shattered.'

Discovering that getting up the duff was not, in fact, quite so easy, not for me, not this time, was a slow-dawning shock made more acute by the way my last pregnancy had ended. The first month was disappointing. The second month upsetting. The third month devastating.

After a bit of googling to establish exactly where I had to stick the thermometer for my daily temperature check (my mouth), I started charting my graph. It was confusing. My temperature was meant to spike around day fourteen of my cycle, but it didn't. Some months it didn't seem to spike at all. Others it sort of spiked but not convincingly.

Oh, and if one more person told me to just relax and not think about it, I was going to stick a chopstick in their eye and see how relaxing that was for them. Not very, huh? So shut the fuck up.

Sometimes it seems like your chances of conceiving are inversely proportional to how much you want to be pregnant.

Sixteen years old? Dating someone entirely unsuitable? Skipped one day of the Pill when your script ran out? Condom broke during a one-night stand? Bingo. A sperm and egg hook-up is practically guaranteed.

But if you're desperate to conceive after a miscarriage? Battling infertility? Biological clock ticking at deafening volume? That's when sperm will say, 'Look egg, sorry, but I'm just not that into you,' before swimming away. Or egg will decide it can't be bothered venturing into the uterus singles bar to mingle with desperado sperm, and will stay put inside an ovary eating Tim Tams.

Morale deteriorated. We found ourselves muttering words like 'stressful', 'not again' and 'over it'.

There was other sexy conception talk too. I quickly discovered there's nothing guaranteed to put a smile in a man's pants faster than the words 'ovulation' and 'basal body temperature'. Just try to keep his hands off you after that.

Also, forget the lingerie. All you really need to turn on your partner when you're trying to conceive is to wave a thermometer around while he's shaving in the morning and shriek like a fishwife: 'Fucking hurry up, will you! I'm OVULATING!' If he demands proof, you can always pore over your ovulation graph together. Who needs porn when you have a graph!

At conception time, the cliché about men not getting enough sex in long-term relationships is spectacularly turned on its head. Suddenly, it's the blokes who are feigning headaches, pretending to be asleep or trying to hide from demented naked women chasing them around the house while frantically waving a graph.

I had a few friends who were also trying to conceive around this time or who'd been through it in the past. They were invaluable venting buddies.

'It's the only time you'll ever hear a guy say, "You want to what? Tonight? AGAIN? Really? Do we HAVE to?" to a naked woman who wants to have sex with him,' said one.

'Why do my most fertile nights never fall on a weekend or any other time I actually feel like it?' complained another. 'Usually for me it's a Monday or Tuesday, which are my go-to-bed-early-wearing-old-nanna-knickers-nights.'

A friend in Melbourne trying for her second child emailed me this complaint: 'How can I enjoy it when my head is full of clinical thoughts like: "I wonder if this will work … Oh God this is only night one of the fifteen shags in a row I have to have this month … Why didn't I start this ten years ago when I was more fertile? What time does kindy start tomorrow and is it dress-up day?"'

Sadly, the first casualty of conception is romance. Next? Spontaneity. Finally? Dignity. Bye-bye. All gone.

'I've started standing on my head after sex,' emailed my Melbourne friend after trying to get pregnant for eighteen months. 'Maybe gravity will help.' Her husband, bless him, used to hold her feet up against the wall. After six months of headstands she gave up, did IVF and fell pregnant on her third round, four years after she first began trying.

I tried standing on my head too. Until I read that elevating your legs too high can actually cause the sperm to pool behind your cervix and defeat the purpose entirely. That put me the right way up, quick smart.

I didn't tell Dr Bob about the headstands when we went to see him for a follow-up appointment. Couldn't bear it. I felt pathetic enough.

I passed my four graphs to him across the desk. They were crumpled from being held anxiously in my frustrated hands several times each day as I studied them in search of an explanation for why it wasn't working.

'Why isn't it working?' I demanded. 'I can barely work out when I'm ovulating or if I'm ovulating at all. What else can we do? IVF?'

'No, not yet. The average couple takes a year to conceive and you've only been trying for four months. I'm going to send you off for an ultrasound to check your ovaries and some blood tests to see where you are in your cycle and make sure you're ovulating. That will give us more information so we can decide on our next move.'

I was comforted a little bit by the idea that we were all in this together. Me, Jason and Dr Bob.

I dragged my sorry self out of his office and made the ultrasound appointment where a diagnosis was made by the sonographer. 'It looks like Polycystic Ovarian Syndrome,' she said, pointing to the white blob-like shapes on the fuzzy image of my ovaries that appeared on the screen.

Oh, okay. Terrific. I knew from numerous *Cosmo* articles that PCOS was a leading cause of infertility. Fantastic.

Dr Bob prescribed Clomid to stimulate ovulation. I was relieved that we were doing something proactive but I continued my downward emotional spiral and became anxious on top of it. It was hard to tell where my angst began and ended, let alone what it was caused by. My skin was still terrible, which made me feel ugly. My hormones were all over the place due to the Clomid and coming off Diane. My overwhelming feeling during this time of trying to conceive was of failure. Desperation and failure.

This feeling was reinforced every time I took my temperature and it didn't spike on the days it was meant to. Every time I did a pregnancy test and one line came up. Every time I saw a pregnant woman in the street. Every time I heard about yet another friend or acquaintance or even celebrity who was pregnant.

All of this was, of course, a fantastic backdrop to having conception sex.

On we trudged into month five. Then six. Weary is an understatement. 'I think maybe this month we should just try on the days we really have to,' ventured Jason one morning.

'We're already doing that,' I snapped angrily. 'I know it's hideous and you'd rather stab yourself with a fork but it BLOODY WELL HAS TO BE DONE.'

When you're trying to conceive and it's not working, this type of conversation is known as 'foreplay'.

And then I fell pregnant. Two lines. I couldn't believe it. The second line was faint but it was there. I did three more tests in the next twenty-four hours and the lines got a little stronger. I held my breath. I checked my graphs, went online and tentatively entered the date of the first day of my last period so I could calculate my due date.

No. It wasn't possible. I entered the numbers again. And again. Each time the due date came up onto the screen I blinked.

It was the same due date as the baby we'd lost. How on earth was this possible? It seemed surreal. Too obvious. The idea that our baby had come back to be born on the same day she'd been due four years later was just too much to wrap my mind around. Was I really being given the chance to have my baby again?

I was overwhelmed. The pressure felt too much. We told no one. I held my breath. And then, at about the six-week mark, I started to bleed. I'd almost been waiting for it. The grief hit me like a train, full force. Instantly, I withdrew into myself, raw with the emotion of shredded expectation. Again.

I fought the temptation to lash out at Jason, even though I wanted to so badly. With no one to blame, I turned the anger and the bitterness back on to myself. After a few weeks of this, I went back to therapy for a while to sift through my feelings. It helped enormously.

This time, I reached out to Jason and accepted his support, and together we got back to the business of conception.

Another three months of baby-making. Woo hoo.

It was around this time that I realised I had developed an unhealthy and secretive addiction. This addiction was a fleeting oasis of happiness at a time when I was deeply unhappy. It was expensive, and I grew horribly dependent on it. Soon, the length of time I could go between hits became ever shorter. I hid the evidence at the bottom of my bathroom rubbish bin. I was ashamed and I was spending a fortune.

I was addicted to pregnancy tests. In no time, I was buying them weekly. Sometimes I'd splurge on half a dozen a month. Why so many? Well, my twisted thinking went something like this.

1 pm. Buy pregnancy test during lunch hour, a two-pack. Promise self not to use it until a week before period is due.

1.20 pm. Can't stand anticipation. Read back of box for hundredth time to check how early a positive result could show. Box says one week before period due. Already knew this, but had hoped box might somehow have revised its earlier answer to two weeks. Period not due for ten days. Promise self to wait three days.

2 pm. Box burning hole in handbag. Can't wait. Perhaps ovulated early without realising. Perhaps dates wrong. The thought that news of possible pregnancy could be just one wee away too much to bear. Take test out of box and stuff under shirt. Scurry to office bathroom.

2.05 pm. Wee on stick. Can't face sitting in bathroom for two minutes so wrap stick in toilet paper and stuff back under shirt.

2.07 pm. *Back at desk. Sneak furtive glance at stick now sitting in handbag in nest of toilet paper. One line. Maybe needs longer to develop.*

2.08 pm. *Still one line.*

2.09 pm. *Still one fucking line.*

2.10 pm. *Fuck it. One line. Not pregnant.*

2.11 pm. *Wait, might still be pregnant but did test at bad time of day. Decide to repeat test first thing in morning when urine more concentrated.*

Of course the next day, after I've done another test, it's still nine days before my period is due. Technically, it's too early still for any pregnancy to show up on a test. I use this fact as justification for buying another test the following day and beginning the entire process again. And again, every day until my period starts and plunges me and my bin full of discarded wee sticks into fresh despair.

If only I'd had shares in a pregnancy-test company. Or worked in a chemist and been eligible for a discount.

Discover One-Step was my favourite but if that wasn't available, any old thing would do for a fix.

I found it astonishing that a $20.95 stick had such power to change lives, to be the gatekeeper between two such vastly different states: Not Pregnant and Pregnant. Or, for me, Hell and Heaven.

The second month after my Clomid dose had been increased — almost a year after we'd begun trying — Jason and I went to Melbourne. I had to go for work and we decided to make a weekend of it.

On the Saturday night, we had a big boozy dinner with friends and got back to the hotel late and merry. We woke up on the Sunday morning feeling a bit dusty and, as usual, the first thing I did was reach for the ovulation thermometer and shove it grumpily in my mouth.

It was day nineteen and my temperature still hadn't spiked. Which meant the Clomid wasn't working, even at this new higher dose.

I whipped out the thermometer after two minutes and the result was as predictable as it was disappointing. I sat up in bed and angrily threw the thermometer across the room. It hit the wall and smashed.

'This is BULLSHIT,' I cried. 'I haven't ovulated this month AGAIN. I CAN'T STAND THIS.'

Jason tried to comfort me but I didn't want to be comforted. I wanted to be upset.

'I feel like I have this massive marathon to run and I'm not even at the fucking STARTING LINE. I can't even get to the BEGINNING OF THE RACE and I fucking HATE THIS!'

I jumped out of bed and stomped into the bathroom, furious at my body and the world.

I pulled on my sneakers and my sports clothes and stormed down to the gym. The only way I knew to work through my fury was to run.

After half an hour on the treadmill and another twenty minutes on the stepper, I went back to the room, slightly buzzed with post-exercise endorphins. I was still upset but the intense anguish had passed.

The endorphins didn't last and we spent the day driving around with me trying to pick a fight to justify how miserable I felt. The weekend ended with us sitting on the plane home, me crying quietly while looking out the window at the clouds.

Back to Dr Bob. This time, I was highly emotional and not doing a very good job of holding back the tears.

'It's not working. It's. Not. Working. Please can we move on to IVF?' I pleaded.

He looked at me compassionately and I could tell he was choosing his words carefully.

'If we did IVF now, it would be an emotional decision, not a medical one.'

I was crestfallen.

'You're still only thirty-two. Medically, we have some time, even though I understand emotionally it's hard for you. Let's just try Clomid at an increased dose for three more months and if we still have no luck, we'll look at IVF.'

I felt defeated but he was right. Jumping into IVF before we'd given Clomid a proper chance was dumb and reckless. And I was trying hard not to be dumb and reckless any more.

'Let's do a blood test to see where you're at in your cycle so we can be sure before we start the new dose.'

I slunk out of there with a new prescription for Clomid and an irrational desire to slap the happy faces of all the pregnant women in the waiting room as I walked past them.

I jabbed the elevator button to take me up to the pathology collection lab and sat there sullenly, unable even to make small talk while my blood was taken.

Two days later, I rang for my results and the receptionist put me through to Dr Bob.

'Well, it turns out you did ovulate,' he announced.

'But I took my temperature up to day nineteen and it never spiked.'

'According to your results, you ovulated on about day twenty or twenty-one. The higher dosage of Clomid should bring that forward to day fourteen or fifteen. Come and see me in four weeks and we'll go through it.'

It wasn't until an hour later that I remembered Melbourne. Hang on. Late night … feeling merry. That was day nineteen. And if I'd ovulated on day twenty or twenty-one, there was a chance …

Off to the chemist. No, wait. I still had two spare tests in my bathroom drawer at home. I'd begun to store them. Squirrel-like.

With supreme willpower, I got through the next few hours at work without making an emergency dash to the chemist. By the time I arrived home, it was 7 pm and I just had a few minutes to wee on a stick before friends arrived for dinner.

One line. Sigh. Bugger. Knew it. Bugger. Sigh.

I flung the test on the bathroom counter and went to say hi to our friends and try to enjoy the evening.

After everyone left, I went back into the bathroom to take off my make-up and brush my teeth. Out of habit, I picked up the test to check it One More Time.

Two lines.

I sat on the edge of the bath for a few minutes to look at the stick. I held it up to the light to make sure my eyes weren't playing tricks on me. No, still two lines.

I didn't cry. I walked out of the bathroom and into the kitchen to find Jason stacking the dishwasher. I held up the stick. He whooped. We hugged.

Finally, hopefully, tentatively, we were on our way.

TOO MANY WOMEN, NOT ENOUGH PATIENCE

Voicemail to Wendy from me:

'I just had a sub-editor resign because her priest thinks Cosmo is the work of the devil. She's Christian. She's a good sub so I tried to talk her out of it. I told her God created sex so what was the problem? She quoted the bible. It went downhill from there. Do you know any subs who are looking for a job and who aren't morally opposed to stories about being bi-curious? I'm desperate. We're on deadline. Call me. Lots of love.'

In my role as Editor-in-Chief of ACP's young women's lifestyle magazines, I oversaw a staff of around seventy women, the vast majority of them under thirty. Since I'd begun at *Cosmo*, I'd gone from being the youngest in the office to the oldest.

Like most editors, I'd never had any formal training in how to manage staff. Nonetheless, I'd picked up some skills along the way by working with different editors and bosses, and observing some wildly different management styles, both good and bad.

My aim was to be inclusive, kind, supportive, nurturing and encouraging with my staff while maintaining stability and being realistic. A boss cannot afford to be moody or play favourites. I did have favourites, of course, but I tried not to be obvious about it. Sometimes I succeeded.

Mainly, I tried to lead by example, although as the only one on my immediate team with a small child, I was never the first one there in the morning or the last one to leave at night. I turned that into an example of sorts, urging everyone to work shorter, but more efficient, hours. 'Go home!' I'd say as I headed for the lift at 6 pm. I was adamant, too, that the staff go out in the world and garner experiences they could bring to the magazine. We had to stay in touch with our readers and it was impossible to do that when you spent every waking hour in a building full of magazine people under fluorescent light. And also? I wanted to feel less guilty about going home.

Early on, I realised that managing a team is a bit like being one of those variety show entertainers who spin plates on sticks. Just when you think you have all the plates spinning, one wobbles and needs your attention. When that one is spinning again, three more will start to wobble and you'll have to attend to them. And so on until you're so sick of the bloody plates you want to go Greek and smash them all on the floor.

There were some workplace situations so bizarre, they could only have happened on a magazine. Like the time I came to work to be greeted by my fashion director shrieking, 'You're wearing my dress!' I assumed she meant I was wearing a dress similar to one she owned. But no, I was wearing *her dress*. One that she had paid for and that had come from her closet.

This was easier to accomplish than you might think. As with most magazines, *Cosmo* had a fashion 'cupboard' that was actually an entire room, packed with rails full of new-season clothes sent to us for upcoming fashion shoots. I would often spot things I wanted for my own wardrobe and would either buy the sample or a new version when it was ready. One afternoon I popped into the fashion cupboard for fluffy diversion after a particularly unpleasant budget meeting and saw a lovely green dress. I tried it on while a wide-eyed work-experience girl sat quietly in the corner taping the soles of dozens of pairs of shoes for a fashion shoot the next day. I didn't really care who saw me getting changed. Hell, I'd had a baby; flashing my boobs in a fashion closet was no big deal.

The dress fitted perfectly. The fashion department was all out on location so I took the dress home, figuring it had either been shot already or wasn't going to be.

The next morning, I threw on the dress with a belt and some boots and headed into the office, happy in the way you are when you're wearing something new. I hadn't technically bought it yet but I'd already decided I was going to.

My poor fashion director. She'd come into the office before her appointments, hung up her dress — the one she was going to wear on a date that night — then returned late that afternoon to find it gone. To add insult to injury, she discovered her boss wearing it the next day.

That could only happen at a magazine. Or perhaps only happen to me.

Baking was a motivational tool I used to great effect with my staff. I love to bake cakes and biscuits, fudge and brownies. I have since I was a kid. I've never been that interested in savouries, but I've found everyone loves sugar. There are more compliments in sweet than savoury. With only so much we could eat at home, I began to bake for my staff. This made them happy, particularly around deadline time and during PMS week, which — frighteningly — would coincide every few months. Yes, it's true about women working closely together. All our cycles did tend to match up. Hence the need for sugar, and lots of it.

Despite the sugar, there were still casualties. The three parts of management I hated most were interviewing new staff, having staff resign (because it meant I'd have to interview to replace them) and firing people.

I did my fair share of all three, starting mere months after I began at *Cosmo* when I had to fire my PA. She was also the magazine's editorial coordinator and really not great at her job. But her general disorganisation wasn't what got her fired in the end. It was the fact she had been holding 'castings' for firemen in the office before and after work. On weekends, she'd visit fire stations and hand out leaflets with details of open casting calls for a *Cosmo* firemen calendar we were producing. Except we weren't. It was just a way for her to meet firemen.

Working with women wasn't bitchy in my experience — I wouldn't allow it — but it was intense. And the fact most were young women meant the drama was high because, well, they're the high-drama years, aren't they? There were break-ups, breakdowns, drug problems and eating disorders. Never a dull moment.

One girl forged my signature on petty-cash forms to pay off her credit card. When I found out, I could have fired her — should have, probably — but she'd been through a hard time. Her mother had died not long before and she was under extreme stress. So I gave her another chance. She paid back the money and turned out to be one of the best and most hard-working staff I've ever had.

A valuable lesson I learned as a manager is that you will never have one hundred per cent of your team performing at one hundred per cent capacity one hundred per cent of the time. Everyone has off days and off months. Even so, several times over the years I had to pull girls into my office and talk to them about partying too much or tell them to lift their game. Even when someone went completely off the rails, it was sometimes salvageable.

Many tears were shed in my office because women tend to cry when they're angry or stressed, hurt or disappointed. I always had a box of tissues handy and I'd simply pass it across the desk and wait for the tears to stop.

There were many more happy staff than sad ones though. I was always a big believer in internal promotion, possibly because this meant I didn't have to interview new people. I never forgot how I'd been groomed and mentored by some incredible women and I tried to do the same. Seven of my staff would go on to become editors of other magazines. One of those started at *Cosmo* on work experience and two had been my PA.

By the time I became Editor-in-Chief of *Cosmo*, *Cleo* and *Dolly*, Generation Y had infiltrated all three magazines and I found myself having some bizarre conversations.

Y: '*I feel like I've hit a glass ceiling. I have, haven't I?*'
Me: '*Um, didn't I just promote you? I'm sure it was you.*'
Y: '*Yes, but that was three months ago. I'd really like more responsibility, more money, a car spot and a four-day week.*'

Inevitably, even if I acquiesced to all of Gen Y's unreasonable demands, a few weeks later she'd be back in my office announcing she was resigning to travel around Europe indefinitely.

Sometimes, an impatient and ambitious staffer would be placated with a title change. This is a tactic used by all editors when there is no other job and no more money available. There are all sorts of fancy-sounding jobs I don't recognise in the staff list of magazines these days for this exact reason.

When your twenty-three-year-old features writer marches into your office to demand a promotion 'or I'm going to *Marie Claire*', you are forced to invent something fanciful to call her that implies increased status. Like Associate Features Director. It's a meaningless bunch of words and the job stays the same but she gets a new business card and her ambitions are satisfied for, oh, five or six minutes.

Dealing with Gen Y en masse every day, I decided I had to turn my frown upside down and focus on these young women's strengths.

This took some time.

But I realised I could learn from such supreme self-confidence and manifest impatience. I also learned that Gen Ys weren't interested in having it all. They'd watched Gen X trying to do it and wisely decided it looked like punishment. They were right. It was a myth, a form of cruel torture. By trying to do it all, all at once, we'd merely created a different type of limitation for ourselves and a whole other layer of pressure and expectation.

It was a revelation to me to see these women who had very different ideas about what their futures might hold. I came to value the energy and new ways of thinking I learned from my Gen Y staff. And my Lord they were smart. Impatient, demanding and smart.

DIARY OF AN ANXIOUS PREGNANCY

Week 5

Terror and elation. Jason and I have decided to tell no one. I know our friends and family will be worried for me and I want to keep as much positive energy around this pregnancy as possible to help it stick.

Week 6

Our first ultrasound to check my dates. I was weirdly convinced it was twins and I'm oddly disappointed when it isn't. And I'm only six weeks. Bummer. I thought I might be at least eight. Why on earth am I focusing on my disappointment when there is a heartbeat? This baby is such a blessing.

Week 7

Where is my morning sickness? With Luca and my second pregnancy I was nauseous until twelve weeks. This time, I'm starving. I should be delighted that I'm not sick but it's making me nervous. I frantically check books and internet sites which assure me there's no connection between morning sickness and the viability of a pregnancy.

Week 8

Still ravenous. From the minute I wake up to the minute I go to sleep. What happened to the part where your pregnant body is meant to instinctively protect you from risky food by turning you off it? All I want is sushi washed down with cocktails. And coffee. I haven't drunk coffee for eight years.

Week 10

My first weigh-in. I don't have scales at home so I don't know what I weighed pre-pregnancy. But with the amount I've been eating, I'm psyching myself up for a very big number. Worse, my appointment is at 2 pm, after I've eaten breakfast, lunch and snacks. Every woman knows the only time to weigh yourself is naked, after going to the toilet, first thing in the morning. I try to compensate by undressing as much as I can in the waiting room. I even take off my rings. I give myself a stern talking-to about priorities. Weight be damned, I just want this pregnancy to be okay.

Week 11

The new issue of *Cosmo Pregnancy* hits my desk fresh from the printer. Despite having been intimately involved in the magazine's production as Editor-in-Chief, I take it home to actually read from a pregnant perspective. Am immediately drawn to all the stories about weight, food and body image. Somehow it's easier to focus on that than the possibility of miscarriage.

Week 12

We still haven't told anyone. When my friends commented that my boobs are big, I mumbled something about a new bra. I sneak out of the office for my nuchal translucency. My stress levels go ballistic as I walk into the ultrasound room. There's a heartbeat. Thank you God. I'm buzzing with happiness and can't stop smiling. The baby is moving. Afterwards, we have a meeting with a high-risk specialist and he is very positive. We arrange another ultrasound for week fifteen to help me over my anxiety. On the way out I bump into an editor from a rival magazine company — also pregnant. She swears to keep my news secret and confides she fell pregnant on her fifth round of IVF. She's forty-one.

Week 13

I'm feeling confident enough to tell our families and my closest girlfriends. They're thrilled for us but they're surprised and a smidge hurt that I didn't tell them sooner.

It's time to tell Luca. It goes down a treat.

> *Jason:* 'Guess what, little guy? You're going to be a big brother because Mummy is pregnant!'
> *Luca:* 'But I wanted to be an only child.'

Week 14

I'm starting to seriously show. Fortunately, most of my clothes still fit. Between empire-line dresses and loose, bias-cut tops my wardrobe seems to have been preparing for this pregnancy for years without realising it. It's just how I dress.

Week 15

A tough week. This is when our baby died in our second pregnancy. By the time I get to the ultrasound, I'm white and in tears. The technician is lovely and points to reassuring signs like the fact the baby is moving its arms and all the measurements are right for my dates. I'm starting to feel movement — a few weeks earlier than I did with Luca.

I field a call from a gossip columnist who saw me doing 'The Glass House' on TV and noticed a bump. I avoid calling her back and hope she'll hold the story. Still not ready to go public.

Week 16
Time to put away all my clothes that no longer fit. I read this tip in *Cosmo Pregnancy* — apparently it makes it easier to get dressed each morning. For me there's the extra challenge that no one at work knows yet. It's no fun dressing for pregnancy when you're trying to look un-pregnant. I visit a friend who's about the same way along as me but with her first. She's upset that she's not yet showing. My stomach has popped but is far from taut. If I grab it with both hands, I can make a spare tyre. Room to grow, I suppose.

Week 17
I'm craving some interesting things. A few weeks ago I placed a little pile of sea salt next to my keyboard at work and nibbled it during the day. Lately it's been grape-flavoured bubblegum. I'm so paranoid about getting listeria that most foods make me anxious. The lady at the sandwich shop helpfully points out I shouldn't be eating ham. Super. Will add this to the growing list, which now includes seafood, sushi, smoked salmon, processed meat and soft cheese. How soft does it have to be to be dangerous? Feta is apparently bad, but it's not that soft. Ricotta? Cream cheese? Is yoghurt like cheese? I ban them all just in case.

Week 18
A colleague at another magazine who is also eighteen weeks with her second has become my pregnancy email buddy and we swap questions and problems. I ask her what the strange pain in my upper back might be. She has the same pain and we decide it's the weight of our breasts, which have doubled in size.

I also have this hideous zitty rash on my chest. Reading *Cosmo Pregnancy*, I notice a celebrity referring to the same thing. At least I'm not vomiting into garbage bins behind my desk like another friend who is in the early stages and trying to hide her pregnancy from workmates.

Week 19

Jason picks me up for the ultrasound and I pick a fight in the car the same way I have for the last three ultrasounds. I'm tense. He knows it and doesn't take the bait. All clear on the ultrasound, a huge relief. This was the ultrasound where last pregnancy we discovered there was no heartbeat. A huge mental hurdle. The kicks and movement are really regular now. The periods of wake and sleep are quite noticeable too. Nothing for a few hours then some kicks and wriggling and then back to sleep.

Week 20

Popped. My tummy is now officially sticking out further than my boobs, which is saying something. This is the most aesthetically pleasing phase of pregnancy, I think. You look obviously pregnant — not just fat — you're still totally mobile and the bump looks reasonable in clothes. I seem to remember this phase is short-lived. Given that I'm only halfway there, will I be twice the size by the end? I send three pairs of jeans to my alterationist, who turns them into maternity jeans for $36 each.

Week 22

Watching TV one night, I suddenly notice I'm having a Braxton Hicks. Panic. Remembering that I only had them with Luca in the last month of pregnancy, I send Jason rushing for *What To Expect When You're Expecting*, while I quickly hit the internet. The book only mentions it in the seventh month. I grab it to make sure, accidentally open up to the 'Best-Odds Diet', which suggests I don't eat dessert during my pregnancy 'except fresh fruit like watermelon'. Hurl book across room while reaching for more Kit Kat to console myself. Find reassurance on the net on medical Q&A pages that say Braxton Hicks actually happen all through your pregnancy. Unless they become painful or regular it's perfectly fine. Double-check with my doctor on Monday morning and he says the same thing.

Week 23

I'm invited to the DJs fashion parade and swanky dinner so I borrow a new-season Zimmermann dress to wear from their showroom. Bump into Nicky Zimmermann at the parade wearing the same dress and due two weeks before me. With a toddler to run around after, she's tired and I'm reminded how great it is that my first child is old enough to fetch me chocolate biscuits.

A newspaper magazine editor wanders over to chat with us, also pregnant, also wearing the same dress. We are knocked-up fashion triplets.

Week 24

I officially adore being pregnant. I do. I love it. I'm constantly asked how I'm feeling and people seem surprised when I say 'fabulous'. I feel almost guilty. Maybe it's the hormones making me happy. Or deluded. Or maybe I'm just grateful.

I see Dr Bob, and while he's listening for the heartbeat, the baby kicks him in the stethoscope.

Week 25

It's a relief to be in the same life-stage as our friends. Finally. When we had Luca, they were all years away from having babies.

But we seem to have caught the second wave. Several friends with toddlers are now expecting their next baby, and other friends are having their first. Jo and my close friend Karen are both pregnant. It certainly makes a change from the isolation I experienced the first time around.

Week 26

Anxious again. Actually, freaking out. My Braxton Hicks seem to be getting stronger and there's pressure around my cervix. Maybe it's just the baby growing and getting heavier? Call Dr Bob who kindly says 'pop up' and I bolt out of a meeting with fifteen people in it and race to his office. He examines me and says my cervix is closed but seems a little shorter than he would expect at this stage, which can be a sign that the Braxton Hicks might trigger early labour. He bans me from exercise and sends me off for an ultrasound. Turns out cervix is fine. Baby is fine. Ultrasound lady tells me Braxton Hicks are much more noticeable with second pregnancies, and by third pregnancies, some women feel them as early as twelve weeks.

Week 28

I have officially lost contact with my bikini line and my bra options have become drastically limited. I make a reluctant pilgrimage to DJs to get properly fitted for maternity bras. Oh my lord does it change my world. Maternity bras have certainly improved in the past eight years. I pick up some lovely ones and note with bemusement that I am a DD cup. Holy hell, my norks are huge.

Week 29

We're fighting about names. I'm pissed with Jason for his complete lack of interest in tossing names around with me and his refusal to make any suggestions. A typical exchange goes like this:

> **Me:** 'What about Zeke?'
> **Him:** 'What about Freke?'

He says he's sure it's a girl so there's no point in talking about boy names. 'Naming a baby is like going to an auction — all the action happens right at the end,' he insists. I manage to burst into tears to make him feel bad. Happy.

Week 30
Thankfully, Luca takes the naming situation very seriously and is constantly coming up with suggestions, which so far include Reverend, Paralisa, Bomber and Chilli. At least he's trying.

Week 31
It's a bitch getting dressed for a black-tie event when you're the size of a small planet. I have to go to the Magazine Publishers Association awards and I have nothing to wear. I stand in front of my wardrobe with the cab tooting outside, ankle-deep in a sea of utterly inappropriate frocks. Some I can't get over my shoulders. Some are too short once my stomach is shoved in. And some are just a hundred shades of wrong.

In the end, I decide to wear a black Morrissey tuxedo jacket with matching pants that I hold together with a hundred safety pins. Underneath, I'm wearing a black Bonds singlet, which doesn't quite cover my belly, but whatever. *Dolly* wins Magazine of the Year and Bron and I climb up to collect our award. My pants don't fall down. That's two wins right there.

Week 32

The baby is bottom down, head up. My doctor would like it to turn any time now so I don't have to have a caesar. I'm strangely calm at the thought of whatever type of birth I need to have. I remind myself it's about the baby, not the birth experience.

What will I do all day at home with a newborn? I can't believe I've totally forgotten what it's like. I'm in the headspace of someone who's never had a child and thinks she's going to have lots of spare time to take cooking classes and learn French.

Week 33

Now I get it. When second-time mums are asked whether they want a girl or boy and they reply 'I'll be happy with either,' I used to think they were lying. Surely everyone wants one of each, right? Not necessarily. Jo, Karen and I are all slightly unnerved at the idea of having a different sex child. We know how to do the gender we've got. The fear of the unknown is real and the nappy-changing issue is top of mind. I know how to do a boy's nappy, it's easy. The thought of a girl's terrifies me. My friends with girls are the reverse. No idea what to do with a penis. Maybe we'll have to swap babies for nappy changes.

Week 34

Our first trip to Babies Galore. Overwhelmed even though we've been through all this eight years ago. Hugely amused at the sight of the shocked faces of the fathers traipsing around the store several steps behind pregnant women. I feel a bit like them. Jason decides he needs to leave immediately to find a hardware store and re-orient himself. I wander around in a daze. I'd forgotten how much STUFF babies need. I finally lose the plot while standing in front of the breast pumps and abandon my mission in search of a doughnut.

Week 35

I've officially entered 'look at the freaky lady' territory when I'm out in public. Depending on what I'm wearing, I can look five months or ten months pregnant.

Some strangers smile (usually mothers); others gape openly.

Week 36

Baby is head down but now Dr Bob is concerned that my fundal height is a bit smaller than it should be. Sends me for ultrasound to confirm baby is thriving and placenta is okay etc. Jason is away so Mum comes with me. Thankfully all is fine, baby is just really low down, which can make tummy appear smaller.

Low-down baby sometimes feels like it may fall out when I walk. Pubic bone feels like mush.

Week 37

I'm starting to mentally withdraw from the world. And I'm getting more intolerant — at work, at home, in shops. I think it's nature's way of focusing you on the task at hand. All I want to do is watch birth documentaries on the Discovery health channel. This is because they don't show any of the gory stuff and everything always turns out fine. However, am disturbed by how big babies seem when they come out. Jesus.

Week 38

I spend an hour in the chemist standing confused in front of the baby stuff. I call a friend with a six-month-old. 'What do you wash babies with? What do you use when you change their nappies?'

I am a total novice. Again. Stock up on maternity pads and a million different creams for nipples and bottoms.

Week 39

I'm in that weird headspace where it feels like I'll be pregnant forever. I've left work and I'm at home trying to relax, but feeling uncomfortable and impatient. I don't want to leave the house because I keep having to have conversations with strangers. Why do you lose your personal space when you're pregnant? Can't I just buy some bloody ice cream without having to talk to five people about when I'm due, whether I'm having a boy or a girl, blah blah blah? I adore being pregnant but even I'm over it. Bring this baby on.

A BITCH CALLED AMY

SMS to my parents from Jason:

'Bring Luca to the hospital. We're on.'

It's 9.30 on Saturday night and I'm sitting on the couch playing with my nipples. Jason glances at me briefly, rolls his eyes and goes back to watching the stupid DVD he rented, the DVD that caused me to shove both hands down my top. I fume and fiddle silently. But a few minutes later, I'm forced to speak. 'Um, babe?' I venture. 'I think I've fucked up.'

It had seemed like a good idea at the time. I was almost nine months pregnant and over it. I adore being pregnant but not at the end. Those last four weeks are hideous. To say I lose my sense of humour is an understatement.

I was hot, huge, grumpy, puffy, snarky, bloaty, uncomfy ... the seven nightmare dwarves of late pregnancy. Jason had made the grave error of renting a DVD I didn't like and my considered response was to explode like a fat, angry hand grenade.

'I'm pregnant and I'm bored and I'm over it and you can't even rent a decent DVD!' I railed attractively. 'Is it too much to ask to find something in the video store that would be interesting to me and didn't have GUNS in it? Something in which nobody DIED? Where nobody gets their FACE WHACKED IN? Something with JENNIFER ANISTON, maybe? Or Gwyneth bloody PALTROW? Is that too much to ask when I'm carrying your child and I'm SUFFERING?'

From there, it was a logical step to induce my own labour. That's where the nipples came in. I remembered reading somewhere that nipple stimulation can trigger contractions. I thought I'd give it a whirl. What I didn't expect is that it would work.

Within two minutes, I felt a slight twinge which I immediately dismissed as coincidence. With a few more nipple twiddles, the twinge became a contraction. Not massive. Not unbearable. Not even painful really. But a contraction nonetheless. I stopped twiddling and thoughtfully reached for another handful of Smarties. A few minutes later, another unmistakable contraction. Time to confess.

Jason has lived with me for more than ten years and is used to my ability to create unwanted, unnecessary and unpleasant drama out of a perfectly nice evening. 'You're an idiot,' he said mildly, shaking his head as I nodded mutely in agreement.

As impatient as I was to hurry this pregnancy along, late on a Saturday night was not the ideal time to go into labour. Particularly because my beloved obstetrician, Dr Bob, the man who had helped me through an emotional decade of gynaecological triumph and tragedy, did not deliver babies between 10 pm and 6 am.

Not to mention the fact it was bedtime and I wanted to go to sleep. I hadn't slept properly in weeks and I was exhausted. Luca was already asleep, blissfully enjoying his last hours as an only child, a status he'd enjoyed for eight lovely years. Another contraction. And was that another? Yes. Oh dear. This was most definitely not the plan.

★

I've always been baffled by people who talk about 'medical intervention' as if it's a bad thing. The more doctors around me during pregnancy and birth, the better. It makes me feel safe. Bring on all the people in the white coats, I say. And if they can bring with them as much fancy medical equipment as possible? I'd really appreciate it.

If I could have moved into the hospital at thirty weeks to be closer to the white-coated people, I would have been ecstatic. So I have to admit that the only birth plan I'd made was, like last time, 'Get to the Hospital and Get Drugs'.

However, this time is different from when we had Luca, because, well, there's Luca. At eight, he isn't going to be there for the birth itself, so logistical preparations have had to be made. And our son likes a plan. He is an organised Virgo, who's ruminated over every detail and canvassed every possible labour scenario and potential outcome. We've discussed all of them at length many times. We are ready.

There is some added excitement about it all going down at 3 am — Jason and I managed to snatch a few hours of sleep, post-DVD fiasco — and, taking after his mother in so many ways, Luca would have been disappointed with any less dramatic option, except, perhaps, me giving birth on the kitchen floor. That would have been cool. Except for, you know, like, the blood and stuff.

Jason goes to wake him up and, according to the plan, call my parents to come and collect him.

Out of habit, I hit the shower to wash and blow-dry my hair. As if to prepare for a night out. Or a meeting. More control. I'd foolishly forgotten how fast I tossed that out the last time I did labour.

A few days ago, I'd dragged my bits — which I hadn't seen for months — to the waxer for my regular Brazilian, an experience even more undignified than usual due to my size, heft and inability to lie on my back without suffocating.

'Get on all fours,' commanded the waxer before calling for back-up.

'Hi, I'm Angie,' came a perky voice from behind my bottom, which was pointed elegantly at the door.

'Hi, I'm pregnant,' I snapped. I was in no mood for meeting new people.

The experience may have cost me some dignity but compared to what was to come, it was a tea party with scones.

Being December and hot, the weather is on my side wardrobe-wise. So much harder to dress a whale when it's cold. Between contractions, I peruse the very small section of my wardrobe containing things that still fit in search of an outfit to wear to the maternity ward. Something I can hike up to my armpits every time someone new comes into the room to rummage between my legs, which I'm guessing will be often. I find a knee-length silk dress with a sort of Japanese snow-blossom print. Loose, light, comfortable and pretty. Come on down.

Just then, I hear Dad's car pull into the driveway. It's 3.30 am. I give Luca a huge hug with the vague sadness of knowing the next time I see him, our intense only-child bond might be somehow different. Then another contraction comes along to blow away any sentimentality and all I can think is: 'BLOODY OUCH.'

Luca safely away, my dress on, my hair dry and straight — a quick GHD to smooth down those stray fly-aways; did I mention vanity? — and Havaianas on my puffy feet. Time to go.

★

At the hospital, we're ushered into an examination room. This is not the delivery ward; it's a holding pen where it's decided what stage of labour you're at and where you must go next.

My contractions have been getting longer and stronger. I want a bed and some drugs. Drugs first. Gimme. But there are no drugs in sight yet. Jason helps me up onto the bed, where I lie on my side, holding my belly. Every so often, the baby kicks.

A youngish midwife comes in to examine me. 'Hi, I'm Amy,' she says in an English accent. Soon I will hate Amy, but not yet. At this point, our relationship is still a blank page and I want her to like me in the way I always want people to like me. Especially when they are people who control access to drugs.

'How frequent are your contractions?'

'Five minutes apart, started last night about 9.30 but didn't get bad until about 2 am.'

'Let's time one,' she suggests, and we wait. Three minutes later, I say, 'Now,' and ride the pain wave while she looks at the second hand on the watch pinned to her shirt.

'Okay, finished,' I grimace.

'About fifty seconds,' she pronounces. 'Now let's see how dilated you are.'

This is the big moment. Well, one of them. Every woman in labour imagines herself to be more dilated than she actually is because it means you're closer to the end. It's like a tangible measure of the distance you've travelled on the Pain Bus. Are we there yet? Huh? Huh? Are we? Are we? It's also worth noting that the further you journey on the Pain Bus, the faster you lose your dignity and your inhibitions. And sometimes, your mind.

As I hike up my pretty silk dress and wriggle awkwardly out of my knickers, I decide on the spot that I'm done with them. I know Amy will be merely the first in a conga line of strangers to stick their hands in my vagina in the foreseeable future, so, really, what's the point?

The silence stretches as I wait for Amy's verdict. Based on the intensity of the contractions and comparing it to my labour with Luca, I figure I'm a little further gone than I was when I arrived at hospital with him. So I'm guessing at least four centimetres but hoping for more. If it was five or six centimetres I wouldn't be surprised. It hurts that much.

'One and a half centimetres,' Amy announces briskly. My heart falls through the floor. It's not possible. 'Really?!' I manage to spit out as another contraction hits.

'Yes,' Amy replies and I immediately detect a hint of condescension in her attitude. She has decided I'm a drama queen. Which, sometimes, I am. But definitely not at this moment. I begin to hate Amy.

'You know, Mia, you may not even be in labour,' she sing-songs. 'This may be pre-labour. The baby might not come for another few days yet. When's your actual due date?'

My hate for Amy intensifies. 'The seventeenth,' I mumble petulantly. Five days away. She's delighted with this answer. 'You see!' she declares smugly. 'You might not have this baby for a week!'

Just as I'm thinking about how I'd like her to die, she delivers the killer punch. 'So, we can't take you to a delivery suite. In fact, you might want to go home and rest there where you feel more comfortable.'

Comfortable? COMFORTABLE? What part of having the pain equivalent of a rocking chair shoved up your arse might be COMFORTABLE, Amy?

Instead of those exact words, what I say is this: 'Amy, there is no way we can go home. I'm staying here. I'm in too much pain.'

She thinks for a moment. 'Well, you could go outside and walk around the car park.'

The car park? THE CAR PARK?

'Moving around can help get the labour going,' she adds helpfully.

'What about the pain?'

'Well, if you like, I can give you two Panadol.'

It's official. Amy is on fucking crack and I've never hated anyone more.

I resist the temptation to jam the Panadol into her nostrils with my foot and instead ask for a glass of water to wash the pills down. What I really want to ask for is an epidural. But no, I must suffer.

This is how Jason and I come to be staggering slowly around a hospital car park in the inner western suburbs of Sydney at 4.30 am on a warm Sunday morning in December. Thankfully, the two lovely Panadol have taken away all my pain so I'm feeling fantastic. No, wait. The Panadol doesn't even touch the sides because I AM IN GODDAMN LABOUR AND PANADOL IS FOR PISSY LITTLE HEADACHES. Amy may as well have given me Tic Tacs.

Every few minutes, when a contraction comes, I lean forward and brace myself against Jason or a car. And I'm starting to make noise during my contractions, which is a new thing for me. With Luca, I'd been as silent as a Scientologist.

But this time? Tom Cruise would not be impressed. In another inhibition-losing milestone on my road to birth, I care not a hoot about passers-by. Fortunately my shape and proximity to the labour ward tell the back-story pretty effectively, so no one calls the police.

And hey, I bet Amy the Sadist probably sends all her patients to car-park purgatory. A gigantic woman doubled over in pain and wailing among parked cars is probably standard stuff around here.

After about half an hour of this, I can't take it any more. 'We have to go inside,' I pant to Jason. He's gone quiet. Dammit, I'd forgotten to tell him I wanted him to be very bossy and take charge. Since being bossed around is not something that would usually wash with me, he has no way of reading my mind and I have reached that point where I can no longer communicate my wishes in any detail.

He understands enough to help me inside and we head back to the examination room. Surely I must be eight centimetres by now. My nemesis, Amy, returns.

'Amy, Mia can't keep walking around the car park,' Jason says, anger creeping into his voice. 'When can we be admitted?'

'Well, it's only been an hour since I examined her, so it's still too early to go to a delivery suite, but if you like, you can go into the waiting room.'

Fucking great. But I'm in no position to argue. That would have taken words and a functioning brain. 'There's a shower in there she can use,' she adds brightly. 'Sometimes that helps.'

Amy ushers us out of the examination room and a few metres down the hall into a small poo-brown carpeted room with some ugly art posters on the wall and eight Formica chairs around the perimeter. 'The shower's in there,' she says, gesturing to a door inside the room, directly opposite the chairs. And then she walks out.

Through the pain haze, I try to feel grateful for small things. Like the fact there's no one else in the dingy waiting room. And that it's not a car park. 'Shower,' I grunt, my straight hair already forgotten. Jason helps me into the bathroom, which is about the size of a disabled bathroom. There's a sink, a toilet with handrails and a shower nozzle attached to the wall. No actual shower area.

Just a tiled floor under the nozzle where I am soon standing, naked and moaning.

Jason tries to aim the hot water towards my back as I brace myself against the wall. The sounds I'm making mildly surprise me, although in my head I'm already somewhere else. I can feel every wave but my brain is curled up in a little ball in the corner. With my discarded silk dress.

Time falls away. I have no idea how long I've been standing in the shower or if, in fact, I will ever stand anywhere else in my life. Later, Jason tells me we were there for about forty-five minutes. At some stage, I start to notice blood on the tiles. Bright red blood. Had I been in control of my mind, this would have worried me, but I'm detached, just focused on surviving between contractions.

Every so often, Jase says something like, 'I'm going to try and find someone; will you be okay for a minute?' I know he can't help me. He doesn't have an epidural needle in his pocket, so, frankly, I don't care where he is or what he does. Labour is an extraordinarily lonely experience.

Eventually, he drags a midwife back to my shower prison to prove that I am indeed worthy of a delivery suite. The bathroom door is now wide open to the public waiting room. I'm past caring. I look up from under the shower, my hair plastered to my head, my body huge and wet, and the floor red with my blood to see a grey-haired midwife quickly taking in the scene. 'Right, I think we can take you through now.'

You RECKON?!

Jason wraps a towel around me and helps me walk around a corner to a delivery room. Finally. 'Epidural,' I moan. 'I neeeeeeed drugs now.' In the relative comfort of a non-public place, my body decides it's time to kick things up a notch. Or five.

'Hi Mia, my name is Bianca and I'm the midwife who's going to look after you. Let's just hop up here on the bed and we'll check the baby's heart rate. Jason, is it? Jason, why don't you go and run a bath for Mia. The heat might help as those contractions build.'

Build? BUILD?

'And we'll just check how dilated you are, okay, Mia?'

'Okay,' I wail quietly, like a broken child.

The baby's heart rate is good and Bianca waits for my next contraction to subside before checking my cervix.

'Five centimetres, very good.'

My thoughts turn to Amy. 'Amy tried to send me home,' I wail. 'She. Tried. To. Send. Me. HOOOOOOOOME.'

At this moment, more than anything else, maybe even more than drugs, I need everyone to agree that this was a terrible injustice. A grave error of judgement on Amy's part. A travesty.

Bianca pats my arm non-committally. 'Yes, dear, well Amy has been called upstairs for a caesarean, so she won't be looking after you any more.'

It's not nearly enough but it's a start. 'Good! Because she TRIED TO SEND ME HOME!'

Drugs. Back to the drugs. 'I REEEALLLY need an epidural,' I sob-wail. 'Where's the anaesthetist?'

'He's upstairs for the caesarean, too, but I'm sure he'll be here soon, dear.'

'I want to POOO,' is my next thought, which goes straight from my brain and out my mouth with no filter. At full volume.

Dear Lord, what is happening to me? I am not that person. I am not someone who talks about poo. I am not the woman in labour who is out of control. Oh wait, I am. My hair is plastered to my head, my pretty silk dress is scrunched up in a wet ball somewhere — who cares? — and nothing is more important than making everyone understand how much I hate Amy and that I want to poo. I don't think this was in the brochure …

'That's normal, dear. It's just the feeling of the baby pushing down, getting ready to come out.'

'But I want to POOOO,' I shout, sliding myself off the bed and lurching towards the bathroom. As I sit there on the toilet, in agony, watching the stupid bath fill up, I can't actually do anything except moan like a farm animal. This is not cool. Bloody Amy.

A couple of contractions later, I stagger back to the bed in agony and despair. How do all those women do that active birth stuff? All I want to do is lie down and die.

Every so often, Bianca comes and waves the foetal heart monitor over my stomach to check the baby's heart rate. It's always fine. This is a brief and remote comfort. Regularly, new people come into the room. 'Are you the anaesthetist?' I beg every time.

'No dear, but I'm sure he'll be here soon.' Fucking liars.

Jason is conspicuously quiet. I find out later that this is because each time someone promises me that the anaesthetist is coming, the midwife catches Jason's eye and silently shakes her head. They know with near certainty the drugs aren't coming but no one wants to tell me. Bastards.

My waters break. A sudden gush all over the bed. Whatever. The noises are getting louder. At one point, I hear a terrible wailing sound and wonder who the hell that is. Hang on, it's me.

When I do manage to form words instead of barnyard–animal sounds, it's to wail one of the following three sentences:

1. *'Amy tried to send me HOME.' (I am still finding it hard to move past this.)*
2. *'I want to POOOO.' (Having patiently explained to me twenty times that it's not poo, it's just the feeling of*

> *the baby pushing down, everyone just ignores*
> *this now.)*
> 3. *'I want to DIEEEEE. Just take me outside and run me*
>   *over with the CAR.' (Jason ignores this too.)*

The next time I am examined by Bianca, I am eight centimetres dilated. My response to this happy news is naturally to raise the subject of Amy. Jason reacts with slightly less vitriol and ducks outside to summon my parents to the hospital with Luca. At least I think he does because soon after I dimly recall him saying, 'Luca and your parents are here. Just outside.' I don't care. Unless they have brought a big needle to stick in my back.

Now eight o'clock on Sunday morning, we've been at the hospital for what feels like three weeks but is actually three and a half hours.

Suddenly, a new man walks into the delivery room. Even in my out-there state, I can feel the energy in the room change immediately.

'Epidural?' I whimper, forever hopeful.

'Good morning, Mia. I'm Stephen. Remember me?'

It's the obstetrician. Dr Bob doesn't do deliveries during the night or on weekends, so I had known there was a good chance my baby would be delivered by his back-up, Dr Stephen. I'd only met him once, for a meet-and-greet appointment, and I'd been nervous about the prospect of someone other than Dr Bob delivering the baby. Dr Bob made me feel safe and knew my history. But right now? I want to roll off the bed and kiss Dr Stephen's feet. His voice is commanding and confident. Finally, someone with power and influence.

'Hi, Stephen,' I wail pathetically. 'Thanks for coming.' Then it's back to animal noises, punctuated by wailing pleas for an epidural as he examines me.

While I'm still begging, whining and ranting, he comes up to the side of the bed, takes hold of my arm and puts his face quite close to mine to get my attention. 'Mia, there is no epidural. There's no time. We're having this baby right now.'

This takes a moment to sink in but I'm swept up in his confidence. I love to be bossed when I'm feeling out of control. This is good. Had he suggested it, I would have agreed to adjourn to the car park to give birth there. I had that much faith.

'Okaaaay,' I nod in my now signature wail. 'Thanks for coming, Stephen.' This becomes my new refrain. It has finally dawned on me that it's no use mentioning Amy again. And Dr Stephen is the first person to actually do anything constructive like suggest I give birth now. My gratitude must be expressed ever five or six seconds.

As I begin to follow his instructions about pushing and stopping and breathing and panting, it all feels very ... organic. Simple. Unadorned. With Luca, there had been so many people in the room, and I'd been hooked up to so many machines. But now it's just me, naked on the bed, Bianca over one shoulder, Jason over the other and Dr Stephen in a shirt and chinos gently and carefully easing my baby's head out of my body.

Dr Stephen looks up. 'The head's out. Lots of hair!'

'Thanks for coming, Stephen,' I whimper. 'I really appreciate it.'

Another contraction and Dr Stephen asks casually, 'Do you want to pull the baby out?'

Really? Oh, um, okay, sure. I reach forward and he helps me hook my fingers under the baby's armpits. 'Now pull.' And I do. My baby slides out of me, as slippery as a tiny seal and I automatically pull it onto my stomach. Dr Stephen helps to gently turn the baby over.

A girl. My girl. Our girl.

I look at Jason and a sob escapes from me. It holds everything we've been through over the past nine years. As I look down into our little girl's face, it hits me that it's all been for a reason. Losing the baby, the pain and grief, and Jason and I finding our way back to one another — it's all been so she could come into our life. Our daughter. Coco.

FAMILY OF FOUR, PLUS BOOBS

SMS to Karen from me:

'This is it. I never want to work again. I just want to stay home and fold teeny tiny socks. Bliss.'

I'm never happier than the first couple of weeks after I've given birth. God bless those hormones. I do go a little bit strange but in a good way. A self-imposed media blackout is how I approach the post-birth period, which is quite a turnaround for a media junkie.

Before Coco, it was not unusual to find me with my computer on my lap in front of the TV with remotes close by for channel surfing and a pile of magazines for flicking through during those microseconds of mental space while a website loads.

Bombarding myself with pop culture, diving in deep and splashing happily around is my idea of relaxation. It's how I unwind.

But nature speaks loudly to me during the whole pregnancy process and never more so than directly after the birth. I'm highly sensitive to any negativity and it feels a lot like my chest has been cut open and I'm walking around holding my beating heart in my hands. I feel exposed and full of love but my ability to feel emotional pain on behalf of others is unbearably heightened. So dealing with the pain and brutality of life via the news is unthinkable.

In the weeks after having Coco, all I could manage to watch on TV was the Food Channel while I ate fudge. It was as if watching people cook was somehow helping me make milk. That and the fudge.

Unfortunately, no amount of watching Jamie Oliver and Nigella and Bill Granger prepare delicious meals could stop breastfeeding from quickly turning into a disaster.

I'd loved breastfeeding Luca. It went swimmingly. I fed him for about a year and continued even when I went back to work, expressing on the days I wasn't with him.

I'm one of those women who are quite happy to breastfeed in public, probably because when I'm pregnant or feeding I see my breasts as being about as sexual as my elbows. The first time we took Luca out for a walk in the park when he was a week old, we sat down for a cup of tea at a café so I could feed. Various people walked past although I was only dimly aware of it because I was concentrating. 'That was subtle,' Jason remarked mildly at one point.

'What do you mean?' I replied.

'That guy had such a long look, he almost walked into a tree.'

'Oh don't be silly,' I scoffed. 'He was just looking at Luca!'

'Babe, adult males are not that interested in babies but they are very interested in breasts.'

Point.

Another time, a couple of months later, I opened the front door to a courier who was delivering some work from the office. His face was startled, but it was only when I went back inside and ten minutes later walked into the bathroom that I realised why. Looking back at me in the mirror was a dishevelled scarecrow with her shirt open to her waist and the flap of her maternity bra open, exposing one enormous breast. I'd read I should 'air' my boobs as much as possible between feeds to help heal my cracked nipples, and somehow between doing this and answering the door I'd completely forgotten to put them away.

The only problem I ever had with breastfeeding Luca came right at the end when I was trying to wean and got mastitis.

Mastitis is when one of your milk ducts becomes blocked and then infected. Another way to explain it is like this: FUUUUUUUUUUCK.

It starts with pain and sometimes a red or hot patch on your breast. Because my body doesn't like to do anything half-heartedly, for me it escalates within hours to a sky-high fever, an agonisingly sore breast, convulsive chills and generally feeling like I've been hit over the head slowly and repeatedly with a cricket bat.

The books make all sorts of suggestions about massaging the area to clear the blockage under a hot shower, and for some women that perhaps does the trick. More power to you if it does.

But for me, the only thing that worked is an urgent ten-day course of antibiotics and Panadol every four to six hours for forty-eight hours. I also have to get into bed immediately and cover myself with eighteen blankets for when the chills and shakes hit. This all lasts for two to three days. In short, it's a fun fair.

When Coco was about four weeks old, I felt the telltale pain in my boob. The books — and the doctors and midwives — say you must keep feeding when you have a blockage because otherwise the build-up of milk makes things much, much worse.

It's apparently not harmful at all for the baby to feed through mastitis, but for the mother it HURTS LIKE HELL. Imagine a hungry baby sucking on an open wound. It's a bit like that.

Within an hour of feeling that first pain, my fever had kicked in and Jason drove me to the closest medical centre. He stayed with me in the room, holding Coco, and the female doctor asked me some medical-history questions before saying, 'Now, take off your shirt and bra and hop up on the table so I can take a look.'

Much to my surprise, she then pulled the curtain around the table so Jason couldn't see me topless. I'm sure this was simply protocol and possibly I was delirious with fever but this struck me as completely hilarious. I felt like saying, 'See that baby over there? The one in my husband's arms? A few weeks ago, he peered into my vagina and saw her come out of it, okay? And also? Nine months before that, we had sex to make the baby and I'm pretty sure he saw my boobs then.'

Fortunately, we got through the examination without Jason glimpsing any nipples through the protective curtain, the doctor confirmed it was mastitis and we high-tailed it to the chemist to get my antibiotic script filled.

The next forty-eight hours were delightful. Chills. Aches. Nausea. Coco was brought to me to feed in bed. I had to take my antibiotics at least two hours after food and two hours before food. This was impossible to achieve because I was unable to go more than an hour without eating something. Even though I felt sick, I also felt hungry. In the first few months of breastfeeding I am a starving, ravenous beast. Impossible to sate.

When I recovered, I booked an appointment with a lactation consultant who declared I was expressing too much, and that was stimulating my breasts to make an oversupply. This was blocking the ducts and causing the mastitis. I sighed with relief. 'That's easy to fix.' I pumped less and tamed my obsession with freezing as many bottles of breast milk as possible. You know, just in case.

A month later, it happened again. And again. And again. And then again. By the time Coco was seven months old, I'd had mastitis six times. That's when I realised I had a problem. Well, two problems. The first was the recurring mastitis. I'd had an ultrasound to rule out any structural issues but no one could work out why it kept happening. My other problem was that I wasn't ready to give up breastfeeding.

It had been such a beautiful experience with Luca and I was longing to replicate it with Coco. It took me forever to realise that Coco and my breasts never really got along. Supply didn't seem to be the problem — she was gaining weight and growing well. It was that I wanted her to lie peacefully at my breast and gaze up at me lovingly while she fed before dozing off in my arms. Not a big ask, is it really?

But that never happened. It was more like wrestling with a small, angry midget. She fought my nipple, shoved my breast away and squirmed and cried. Peaceful, loving and soothing it was not. Bonding, no. Jo and Karen had both their babies within a few months of me, and when we were together I'd watched enviously as their babies breastfed calmly and quietly while Coco writhed and fought me. The only way I could keep her relatively calm was to swap her from boob to boob every thirty seconds or so like a football in play. It would be years before I would realise she'd had gastric reflux. All that squirming during feeding was because her little throat was burning. That's why she would never feed long enough to empty my boob. But I didn't know that at the time. It was exhausting, dispiriting and demoralising. And yet I soldiered on like a martyr. I had this image in my head of being someone who had no trouble with breastfeeding and I stubbornly refused to accept that this time around I wasn't that person.

This time around I was a person who was being made miserable by her inability to go more than three weeks without being bedridden for days and filling herself with antibiotics almost constantly.

In my post-hormonal, sleep-deprived haze, persevering seemed like my only option.

'Babe, maybe you should think about giving up breastfeeding,' Jason ventured carefully one day when Coco was about five months old and he was fetching me my ugg boots to wear in bed because I was shaking with cold under a doona and two blankets in the middle of a thirty-degree day.

'No way,' I shot back.

My reasons for refusing to even consider weaning were complicated. It was a combination of emotional nourishment (for me) and physical nourishment (for her). I knew I wasn't ready to let go of that intense bond, that physical dependence. I knew I felt guilty that I was thinking about going back to work and leaving her. And I knew all the facts about the benefits of breastfeeding.

I wasn't judgemental of other women's choices to wean at whatever age for whatever reason, but I was very, very judgemental of myself. I hid behind a lot of the physical reasons for martyring on with breastfeeding, but the greater pull I felt was the emotional one.

Strangely, stupidly, I had breastfeeding blindness which allowed me to ignore the fact it was making me terribly ill and taking a toll on my whole family. Not to mention the glaringly obvious: I was repeatedly subjecting Coco to the antibiotics via my breast milk. Doctors swore it was safe but they admitted that some of the medication was indeed being ingested by her. Why was I being so wilfully ignorant about the fact that this was surely doing more harm to her than any good that could come from the breast milk itself?

When Coco was six months old, I went back to work several days a week, expressing in my office so I didn't have to wean. Within a week, it happened again. This time, bed wasn't an option because I had to go to an important client dinner and sit through eighty-seven or so courses of a degustation banquet with my breast on fire and my fever raging as I popped Panadols and antibiotics between courses. This was getting boring.

Still I refused to entertain the idea of weaning. *Especially* now that I was back at work and feeling terribly disconnected from my baby. Guilt, guilt and guilt. How could I throw formula into the mix?

It finally took Alice, my friend who also happens to be a GP, to smack some sense into me. One day over tea and cake she said to me, 'You know, Mia, you've been on antibiotics for seventy days so far this year and it's only June. It's time to wean.'

Okay, she had a point.

During my two most recent bouts, I'd given Coco formula for ten days while I expressed at every feed and tipped my radioactive milk down the sink. This was a Big Deal for me. Luca had never had formula and I had an irrational fear of it. I didn't judge other women for using formula but I'd drawn a mental line in the sand for myself. I may be a hopeless mother who abandoned my baby to go to work — taunted my internal guilty voice — but at least she was exclusively breastfed!

Alice helped me finally realise it was time to bed my fantasy of feeding Coco for a year. Or even another month. Within days, I started dropping feeds, dealing with my guilt and fighting my fear that letting my milk accumulate would trigger yet more mastitis.

I don't remember the last breastfeed. I don't with Luca either. So often in life, you don't realise you're having a Significant

Moment until it's behind you. What I do remember is this: a week or so after weaning, I looked at my breasts in the mirror and I froze.

My inflated fun bags were now deflated windsocks. I burst into tears. Not because of how they looked so much but because of what they represented. That intense, magical period of being pregnant and breastfeeding was over. Conveniently, the massive amounts of pain, frustration and discomfort that had been my breastfeeding experience this time were forgotten and I just mourned the good stuff. In many ways, the fantasy. And then I got over it and enjoyed not being on antibiotics and not feeling like a failure at every feed. Getting into the mojitos again was pretty good too.

GOODBYE
MAGAZINES,
HELLO
PUNISHMENT

SMS to all my girlfriends from me:

'Looking for a nanny. Three days. Help? M x'

I'd known it in my heart for a while. I was finished with magazines. By the time it registered as a conscious thought and I began to say it out loud to Jason and my closest girlfriends, Coco was a few months old.

The past couple of years as Editor-in-Chief of *Cosmo*, *Cleo* and *Dolly* had been good and bad in equal measure. I'd liked reducing the number of staff who reported directly to me from twenty-five to five. I was adamant from the start that each of the editors be responsible for their own staff. This was crucial for their authority and for my sanity. I helped out with any major staff issues they ran into, but the day-to-day dramas of seventy women? I'd rather eat bark.

I loved nurturing my editors, guiding them through the editing process and passing on all the wisdom I'd accumulated from working with great editors myself and making my own mistakes.

I also liked having a job that was easy for me to do so I could focus my energy on falling pregnant. Had this not been my top priority during this time, I would have left ACP much sooner. The boredom that had caused me to step down as editor of *Cosmo* was still lingering.

If anything, it was exacerbated by producing three to four magazines every month. Triple the sealed sections was enough to do anyone's head in. In theory, I left to go on maternity leave for six months. In reality, I knew as I waddled out the door a few weeks before having Coco that I was leaving the building for the last time.

Nothing had happened in the months after giving birth to change my mind. My love affair with magazines was winding up. I still loved them, but I wasn't IN LOVE with them any more. They no longer made my heart race. I had a new media crush: the internet. It appealed to my impatience, my need for speed. How could magazines for young women possibly hope to compete as entertainment or sources of information when they were published monthly? It may as well be annually. We were all measuring our lives in increments of hours and minutes and text messages, not months. Mags just felt frustratingly slow.

There were other challenges, too, which seemed to me insurmountable. How could any kind of sex content stay relevant — let alone titillating — when with two clicks you could be looking at a knicker-free Britney Spears or reading unlimited amounts of salacious and educational material? For free. *Cosmo* and *Cleo* couldn't hope to compete and I felt that a circulation dive was inevitable.

I wanted out. I wanted something different. And then came a job offer from Channel Nine.

Channel Nine was the sister company to ACP, and since I was still under contract, going there was one of my few work options if I wanted to quit magazines. I was also extremely keen for a change. I'd done my time in a cosy, oestrogen-soaked working environment; perhaps working among men would be easier. Sleep deprived and full of antibiotics, it seemed like a good idea at the time.

Was I ready to leave Coco? No. Not full time. But I also knew that I wanted to work. I wouldn't be happy full time at home either. That hadn't changed. I negotiated working a day or two from home and started to put out feelers for a nanny.

There's massive luxury in having someone look after your child in your own home, I know. It eliminates the scramble to and from childcare and all the stresses inherent in dressing and feeding and coercing and cajoling and bribing your child to get out the door. Not to mention the planning all of that requires. It's no wonder working mothers are frazzled before they've even begun their day jobs.

Having someone come into your home to look after your child eases that load considerably. You can walk out the door while your kids are still in their pyjamas, playing with their breakfast in that way they invariably do when you're in a mad rush. You can still go to work when they're sick. There are a hundred wonderful things about having a nanny, and, mindful that I'm extremely fortunate to be able to afford this type of childcare, I've always appreciated every one of them.

It seems pampered and churlish to complain of any downside, but, like every compromise you make as a working mother, it exists. Of course there's the cost, which is, for a lot of people, prohibitive. But you also pay in other more subtle ways. It's a very intimate thing having someone come and work inside your house — inside your family. They don't just have the keys to the front door but also the keys to your life and a window into your privacy.

It's a lot like starting a new relationship, because that's exactly what it is. A nanny sees everything that goes on in your family, at all hours. They see you when you're tired, stressed, vulnerable and when you have your guard down — which is often. They hear you on the phone. They see close up how you interact with your children and your partner and it's not always pretty.

I'd only ever had one proper nanny — Anna the lingerie model — and I was daunted by the idea of hiring another one.

In the process of hiring a nanny, you usually meet them once for an interview. And then, after checking some references from people you've never met, you have to decide. It's a lot like going on one date — a short date, say, for a coffee — and then deciding to move in together. The stakes are that high, as is the potential to make a bad call.

When it's good, having a nanny is a blessing. When it's bad, it's a disaster. It's not dissimilar to having an emotional bomb explode inside your home, but with an added layer of guilt and self-recrimination. The betrayal is absolute.

You can't beat a personal referral when it comes to hiring a babysitter or a nanny, someone connected to someone you know. But this time around, when I put the word out among friends that I was looking, I didn't have any luck.

Reluctantly, nervously, I called an agency, and they said they'd send a couple of girls over for interviews.

The first one I met was Francesca. I warmed to her immediately. She was youngish, about twenty-three. Nice, open, friendly face. Big smile. We walked around the block with Coco. I sussed her out. She'd worked in childcare centres and for a few families privately. Her last job had ended after a year when the family moved overseas. I called her references. They were glowing.

I arranged for Francesca to do a trial day the following week. It went well. Coco seemed to like her as much as a six-month-old can take a view on these things.

I offered Fran the job with a huge sense of relief and without interviewing anyone else. Huge mistake. Gigantic.

THE SLEEP WHISPERER

'Um, hi there, it's Mia Freedman calling. I got your number from Karen and I wanted to see if you were available to come and help me teach my daughter to sleep. It's quite urgent . . . because, well, I'm losing my mind ... so ... um, could you give me a call as soon as possible?'

Before I started work, I had to get some bloody sleep. I was exhausted.

For the first few weeks after Coco had come home, I'd run on a heady mix of hormones and adrenaline, with a generous splash of gratitude that my longed-for baby had arrived safely.

Night feeds were almost a novelty. I felt womanly and invincible, filled with love for my little girl and the world. I willingly slept on a crappy mattress on the floor of her room so that Jason could sleep undisturbed in our bed. I was so grateful to him for helping create this beautiful creature, it was the least I could do. I was a happy martyr. And hey, since I was breastfeeding and he didn't have breasts, what was the point of him getting up at 2 am? Let alone three, four and 5 am.

But after more than a month of waking up to eight times every night to feed and soothe Coco back to sleep, I began to lose my sense of humour. The novelty had worn off, replaced by an overwhelming fatigue that was systematically crushing the life out of me.

Most mornings I couldn't recall what had transpired the night before. I was always certain it had been a train wreck but the details were hazy. Did she wake at 1.15 for a feed, 2.25 for the dummy, another feed at 3.10 and then dummy again at 3.40? Or was it 1.50 for a feed, 3.20 for the dummy and a feed again at 4.15 and dummy at 4.35? Or was that the night before? Or maybe last week? What's my name again? And who is that scary-looking person in the mirror?

Despair is the evil twin of sleep deprivation. Despair that your baby will never sleep more than a few hours in a row. Despair that you'll never feel human again. Despair that nobody will ever understand how pitifully exhausted you are.

At 3 am, no one can hear you scream. That's how it feels when you're up in the middle of the night with a baby who doesn't sleep. I could hear Coco screaming clearly enough. Several times each night. But my own screams? My screams of exhaustion, despair, frustration and loneliness? They were silent, confined to the inside of my head.

Eventually, the despair makes way for a kind of acceptance, where you become institutionalised in your fatigue. You give up. You surrender the fantasy of having a baby who will ever sleep through the night. That's for other people. The mere thought of unbroken sleep feels as likely as winning Lotto. And as much in your control.

It's easier to just stick in the dummy or the bottle or the boob or bring your baby into your bed — whatever it takes to get them, and you, back to sleep quickly. After months of broken sleep, the quick fix will win over the hard yards of a proper solution every time. You're just too exhausted to find a way out of your exhaustion.

I'd made this mistake before, with Luca. Jason and I attempted controlled crying half-heartedly a few times but I refused to persevere because I was worried it might damage our baby psychologically. So we waved the white flag and surrendered to the child who doesn't sleep through the night. In hindsight, this was such false emotional economy. Luca didn't sleep properly until he was four and it caused huge stress in our relationship that first year, which was hard enough because Jason was sick. We vowed we'd do it differently next time.

I should note at this point that dads also do it tough, although not nearly as tough as mums, who usually bear the brunt of night waking, especially if they're breastfeeding. After a long night walking the floor with a crying baby, it's funny how hearing your husband say 'I'm tired' when he wakes at 7 am makes you want to pick up a heavy object and harm him with it.

Every morning, I needed an enormous dose of cheerleading and validation along the lines of: 'You are amazing! You are a hero! You are incredible! I don't know how you do it!' Frequently, even this was not enough to prevent the resentment from building inside me.

I often felt I deserved nothing less than a ticker-tape parade every morning to celebrate my heroism in getting through yet another night. Or possibly a commemorative stamp could be issued with a picture of me wearing a halo and some medals.

Invariably, if your baby doesn't sleep, every other baby you know, and many you don't, will have begun sleeping through the night from two weeks of age. This will make you feel fantastic. 'People lie,' an early childhood nurse once reassured me when I asked in desperation why I had the only non-sleeping baby in Australia. 'Some people's definition of sleeping through the night is 11 pm to 4 am. Don't listen to them.'

Jo's and Karen's babies were both genuinely sleeping well and I never once resented them for that. Okay, maybe once. But they were still the first people I'd want to unload to, the only ones who could empathise enough. Sometimes, they went through rough patches with their babies too.

After particularly bad nights, when one of us would be in the depths of despair, emergency food supplies would be silently left at the front door. Muffins, strawberries, a barbecued chook. Meal preparation is one of the first domestic casualties of sleep deprivation and new motherhood. This food was a godsend. So was the friendship.

It was from Karen that I first heard about The Sleep Whisperer. Her name was Elizabeth and she had magic powers to make babies sleep through the night. Or so it seemed. Karen had used her a few years earlier with her first baby and she'd also worked miracles for other mums we knew. I've since learned there are women like Elizabeth working all over Australia and their phone numbers are passed urgently between desperate new mothers who haven't slept in months, sometimes years.

My first conversation with Elizabeth was when Coco was four months old. At that stage, she was waking up to eight times a night for feeds and to have her dummy plugged back in. I was beside myself. The feeling of dread began every evening as the sun went down and the inevitability of yet another appalling night hit. I felt trapped, helpless, hopeless.

Over the phone, Elizabeth was a fountain of empathy. Even her voice was soothing. But she was adamant that she wouldn't do a 'sleep program', as she called it, before a baby was six months old. Her belief was that younger babies couldn't really learn to sleep through the night and it was not good for them emotionally. As disappointed as I was that my parole had been revoked for two more months, this made me trust Elizabeth even more. The last thing I wanted was to damage my daughter. I just wanted to SLEEP.

Still, I may have lied about Coco's age just a wee bit so Elizabeth would book me in earlier. Which she did, at five and a half months. The day before she was due to arrive, she texted me. 'Just checking you still want me to come for the sleep program tomorrow night.' I texted back so fast I nearly broke my thumbs. 'YES! YES! YES!'

The next morning, she called to talk me through what she would be doing. 'Tonight I'll be there at 6 pm so I can meet Coco before we get started. That first night can be pretty intense, so be prepared for that.'

Gulp.

'On the other nights, I'll come at 10 pm, and each morning I'll leave at 6 am. Before I go, I'll leave you a report detailing how she went. You can read it when you wake up. I usually crack it in three nights but I'll pencil in a couple more, just in case.'

That evening, after her bath, I dressed Coco in her PJs with a mix of apprehension and hope. It felt like taking your baby for immunisations. You know it's for their greater good but your heart is still heavy with guilt and fear for the pain your baby will have to experience.

I liked Elizabeth immediately. With three small boys of her own and a kind yet no-nonsense attitude, she arrived in tracksuit pants and ugg boots, dressed for the wintry night ahead. Straight away, she busied herself in Coco's room as Jason and I sat nervously watching. She modified the bedding, removed the mobile from the cot — 'beds are for sleeping not entertainment' — and made sure the room temperature was correct. She was very sweet with Coco and patiently answered my endless angsty questions.

All sleep 'crutches' were to be banished, including dummies, music, bottles, rocking and patting. And boobs.

The key to success, Elizabeth told us, was that we had to trust her and not crack under the pressure of our baby's cries. Elizabeth believed that by teaching Coco to put herself to sleep, we were giving her a valuable lifelong gift. This was certainly much more palatable to me than the idea I was doing it for my own selfish benefit. Lifelong gift? Sold.

And then it was time. I kissed my innocently smiling daughter goodnight with the sense that I was sending her into battle. And after twenty minutes of screaming, the first report from the frontline was not good. 'Your daughter has one of the more extreme dummy addictions I've ever seen,' Elizabeth announced gravely.

Super. Almost six months old and battling her first addiction. Does that make me her dealer? I first gave her a dummy at four weeks. Bad mother? It was the only thing that would shut her up. I was the one who had encouraged her descent down the slippery slope from casual dummy user to hardcore addict. The instant comfort (hers) and the quiet peace (mine) the dummy brought to our lives was sublime. Soon, the mere act of buying dummies would cheer me up, calm me. They'd replaced shoes as the object of my retail therapy. But on this night, I struggled to recall why I'd bought that first one as Coco's dummy-less cries began to split my head in two.

Through the crying, Elizabeth would go in at various intervals and kindly whisper, 'Shhhh, Coco. Time for sleep.' Then she'd re-tuck the sheets firmly and leave without picking her up or giving her a bottle. Often she wouldn't actually leave but simply hide in the darkness and observe, making sure Coco didn't get into any serious difficulty.

Jason and I retreated nervously to the lounge room with a bottle of wine and turned the TV up loud. Thirty-five minutes after Coco had been put to bed, the first hurdle was cleared. Asleep! High five! But while Elizabeth was pleased, she warned us that Coco hadn't really learned anything, she was simply exhausted. The night wakes would be tougher, she cautioned.

At 10.30 pm, we went to bed ourselves. We were nervous but relieved that Coco was in the capable hands of a professional and that we didn't have to make any judgement calls. As promised, the middle of the night was worse. Almost two hours of screaming. With complete faith in Elizabeth, I was reasonably calm but still tortured. I didn't cry and I didn't interfere. Lifelong gift. Lifelong gift.

As Elizabeth had suggested at the beginning of the night, I stayed in bed, switched on the TV and distracted myself with 'True Hollywood Stories: The Cast of American Pie'. As I watched Tara Reid's tragic journey from starlet to punchline, Jason made sleepy protests at the sound of the TV, so I hit him on the head with a pillow.

Finally, all was quiet. The next thing I remember was hearing Elizabeth letting herself out at 6 am, followed forty-five minutes later by Coco waking up for the day. When I picked her up, I half expected to see betrayal in her eyes, as if to say, 'So where the hell were you last night, bitch?' But her face was as open and as delighted to see me as ever. She appeared undamaged. Lifelong gift.

Night two was better. Sticking carefully to Elizabeth's instructions, I put Coco down in her cot myself at 6.30 pm, prop-free, and after some low-level crying she was asleep in under ten minutes. Could this be the beginning of a new life for us? One with sleep in it?

Elizabeth arrived at 10 pm and we had a cup of tea together. As we chatted, I realised that she truly loved her work. The lifelong-gift stuff wasn't a platitude; she resolutely believed that every baby deserved to learn how to put themself to sleep, and every family deserved the knock-on benefits.

Coco's second night with Elizabeth was a vast improvement on the first. Forty minutes of crying at 2 am but not nearly the intensity of the night before. What was most encouraging was that she woke briefly again at 4 am and put herself back to sleep within a couple of minutes.

Night three she slept through. For the first time in six months, I didn't leave my bed from 10 pm to 6.30 am. It felt like a miracle. Coco was definitely happier during the day. And me? I was doing wild victory laps around my house.

Elizabeth, deciding we were now able to cope without her, left us strict instructions. It was vital that Coco had her proper naps during the day so as not to become over-tired — a classic obstruction to sleep. Dummies were now a distant memory and we weren't to use them ever again, day or night. Most importantly, we must remember this: now that Coco had endured an undeniably tough few nights, it wasn't fair to her if we undid everything she'd learned with 'just one bottle' or 'just one cuddle'. Hold firm. Be strong.

And we were. I texted Elizabeth daily for the first week or two with many, many questions and she gave me strength, encouragement and advice. Don't waver. Don't be discouraged if she slips back a little and begins waking occasionally. Have faith that she'll get herself back to sleep eventually. Stick to the rules. Listen and interpret. Comfort and leave. If she gets sick, all bets are off. But when she's well again, it's back to the rules.

For the first few weeks after Elizabeth's visits, every morning felt like a miracle. Like Christmas. But slowly, imperceptibly, the unimaginable happened: I began to take my sleep for granted again. I went to bed without dread and with the expectation of a full night's sleep. And I got it.

CATAPULTED OUT OF MY COMFORT ZONE

On day two of my new job at Channel Nine, I decided I wanted to quit. I knew with absolute certainty I'd made a terrible mistake. My appointment had not been well received. Outside the network, many people were curious. What exactly would I be doing? Inside the network, many were cynical and disparaging. What *exactly* would I be *doing*? I was too young, too inexperienced and too female. Three strikes.

My job title was broad and ambiguous: Creative Services Director, and my purpose was to inject some female perspective into the network's male-dominated management team. I understood some of the hostility towards me — most of it was expressed covertly, of course, but I could see what was going on.

The network had gone through several CEOs in the previous eighteen months and each one had imposed his own strong ideas and made his own appointments. By the time I moved into my dark, poky office, some of the people who'd weathered the seemingly endless management storms were battle weary to say the least.

It's virtually impossible for an outsider to fully appreciate the stresses inherent in commercial television. I certainly didn't before I arrived. And at Channel Nine, that stress was to the power of a hundred. The media klieg lights shone blindingly on Nine, much as they always have. Much of it is tied up in the mythology of the Packer family.

While Kerry Packer was alive, there had been some grudging respect and fear that kept media coverage from getting too nasty. But after he died, it was suddenly gloves off and game on. There was certainly a lot for the media to write about. How inspired of me to choose to go to Channel Nine at this particular point.

And then there are the opinions. Everyone who owns a TV thinks this entitles them to be a critic. Before working at Nine, I was guilty of this myself. I'd often lobbed unsolicited opinions on some of the Nine executives I met at Publishing and Broadcasting Limited (PBL) conferences when the disparate worlds of magazines, TV, online and casinos would come together under one roof over a weekend to talk business, establish working relationships and identify cross-platform synergies. Everyone wanted more 'synergies'. Even if no one knew exactly what they were.

As soon as my appointment was announced, I was bombarded with 'constructive criticism' about Nine. This was a new experience. In all the years I'd worked in magazines, people rarely ventured an opinion about what went in them. Apart from the obvious debates about magazines containing too much sex or too many skinny models, no one really thought to nit-pick over the content. Perhaps the fact you have to pay for a magazine means a benevolent audience is self-selected.

But with TV? Oh man. When something is freely available, people have a LOT to say. And ninety-eight per cent of it is negative. From the moment anyone found out I worked at Nine, I'd find myself subjected to a long and detailed list of complaints.

These invariably included criticisms about which programs were on, which weren't on and should be, why programs were on at the wrong time or hosted by the wrong person. Then there was my personal favourite: Why Does [insert name of presenter here] Wear Such Shocking Clothes And That Hair Of Hers Is A Bloody Disgrace.

Cab drivers, waiters, relatives, former magazine colleagues, friends, strangers — no one was ever short of an opinion or twenty about Channel Nine and no one was ever shy about expressing them to me. At length.

I believe this is called karma. Payback for all the times I'd voiced similar complaints to friends and colleagues who worked at Nine. Now? It was my turn.

Given that I had no power to do anything about any of it and given that commercial TV networks are generally run for the masses, not an individual who wants to watch 'The Sopranos' at 7.30 pm on a Sunday night, it became frustrating and exhausting almost immediately. We're not in Kansas any more, Toto.

And I could see how for those who had worked in TV for years and who'd had to listen to an endless daily barrage of unsolicited opinion and criticism … well, I could see how that would do your head in. No wonder nobody was interested in hearing what I had to say.

Rumours of a partial sale of PBL, the Packer-controlled company whose media assets included Nine and ACP magazines, didn't help. Frenzied gossip circulated, inside and outside the network. Everything was on hold as lawyers and accountants crunched the numbers and due diligence began. To say the atmosphere at Nine during this period was intense is a bit like saying the equator is kinda warm.

There were virtually no women on the executive team. My arrival had doubled the quota, in fact. The other woman was the head of drama, and while she was warm and welcoming, drama is a separate department and our paths rarely crossed.

The fact that I had two kids at home separated me further from my male colleagues. And it's safe to say that no one else in management was breastfeeding. Twice a day, I'd have to pull the shades in my tiny glass office and whip out my breast pump before stashing breast milk in the boardroom fridge among the beer, wine and soft drinks.

I also had to dash out the door at quarter to six so I could make it home by six-thirty to breastfeed Coco before she went to bed. This was awkward. No one else left before … well, I didn't know when they left because I'd already gone. Apart from all the offices being glass, turning the executive floor into a fishbowl, the walk from my office to the lift was a long one. I'm not the first mother to have to do the Afternoon Walk of Shame — dashing out the door to begin the day's second shift at home — and I won't be the last.

Maybe no one cared. Maybe no one noticed. Certainly nothing was ever said to me. Everyone appeared kind and understanding. But every day as I bolted for the lift, I felt horribly conspicuous. Invariably, I'd bump into someone along the way and, with my handbag over my shoulder and my jacket on, there was only one possible place I could be going. The fact that I'd log on at home and keep working for a few hours after I'd put the kids to bed was irrelevant because it was invisible. I feared that leaving work before my colleagues was, in their eyes, akin to wearing a sandwich board screaming, 'I don't care about my job as much as you do and I'm a big fat slacker. Have a good night!' I'd grow tense even thinking about it as 6 pm approached.

Eventually, I came up with a pathetic strategy. At lunchtime, I'd go and put my handbag and jacket in my car and stash my keys in the glove box. Then, at half-past five, I'd casually saunter to the lift while pretending to talk into my mobile as if I was on my way to a meeting in another part of the building. 'Talking' on the phone ensured no one would engage me in conversation or ask where I was going. When I hit the car park, I'd furtively sneak into my car and drive off very fast, praying no one had seen me leave.

What a degrading, ridiculous waste of energy. And it's not like there was a great pay-off once I got home an hour later. Jo and Karen had returned to work at around the same time as me, and sometimes we'd speak on our mobiles while driving home to see our babies before they went to bed. To debrief, to vent, to bolster each other's spirits in the face of working-mother guilt, doubt, angst and stress. One day, as Jo pulled up in front of her house, she said drily, 'Right, I'm just going inside to spend twenty quality minutes with the children.'

And what an enriching twenty minutes they were. Not. The shift in gears between work and home was impossible for me to execute smoothly. Often, it was more like the grinding clunk that you hear when learner drivers struggle to master a manual gearstick.

At work, I had to be so well defended, so bullet-proof, so … alpha. That didn't cut it at home where my children needed a softer, slower, more nurturing energy. Like many women, I had bits of both in my character, but switching from one mode to other and back again several times a day gave me emotional whiplash. Even then, the results weren't always successful. My wise father gave me some excellent advice. 'When you get to work, take a moment in the car park to close your eyes and take a few deep breaths. Leave home behind and put yourself into work mode. Then do the same in reverse when you get home.'

Problem was, by the time I screeched into the car park every morning, I was usually running late and didn't have a moment to take any breaths because I was already hyperventilating. By the time I got home, same thing. I was so desperate to see my baby — the hunger for her was physical — and spend time with Luca, I couldn't bear to waste even a second. I was usually halfway out of the car before I'd even turned off the engine.

The result of all this was that I always felt inadequate. At work, I felt like a useless mother. At home, I felt hopeless at my job. And when I was making the transition from one to the other, I felt panicked, stressed, anxious and a failure at everything.

Are we having fun yet?

In the morning, the fact I arrived at work by quarter past eight was unremarkable — except to me. After over a decade spent clocking on after 9 am because magazines never start early, it was another shock to my system to have to have my shit together to bolt out the door every day at 7.30 in the morning. But this earned me no cred because by the time I arrived all my male colleagues were already there.

Not only were the long hours seemingly standard, but the entire focus of every day in TV is at 8.30 am, when the previous day's ratings are released.

I quickly learned that this is the big head-fuck of TV. In any other job, you might have one performance review per year. This will be conducted privately and discreetly with just you and your boss in attendance. But in television, you have a performance review every day at 8.30 am, seven days a week.

And this daily review of your performance? It's conducted publicly. If a decision you've made or a program you're involved in isn't doing so well, the happy news of your failure is broadcast to the entire industry every morning at 8.30. The media can then share this information with the world while your colleagues are free to sympathise or gloat over your plight. Invariably, gloat. Even if they work at the same network. Schadenfreude makes the TV world go round.

After fifteen years snuggled securely in the same building, working on the same magazines, with many of the same supportive people, I'd come via the milky bubble of maternity leave into a new industry and a new working environment with new colleagues. The fact that they were all highly competitive men was a big change.

When I first started at Nine, every media interview I did wanted to focus on how I dealt with the 'blokiness factor'. It was too early for me to have a sense of that so I joked my way around the question by pointing out that, on the upside, there were no queues for the women's toilets, but, on the downside, there was far less chocolate available.

In truth, I found the gender change refreshing — at first. Men were upfront. They said what they thought and they were direct. Mostly. I didn't mind a bit of blokiness. It made a change from the unrelenting girliness of my previous work life. But I quickly came to miss the female energy. I'm very much a girl's girl. Sporting analogies (which, bizarrely, I began to use without even really understanding what they meant) are not my first language. I missed empathy and nurturing.

Another thing that was different was the press attention I was receiving. As an editor and a newspaper columnist, I'd had a fairly public profile for most of my career. But even though the media sometimes wrote about me and regularly called me for social commentary on various news stories, the coverage had almost always been positive or neutral. I'm not sure if it was the Nine factor or that I'd dared to stick my neck beyond the safe world of women's magazines, but suddenly I was a target and everything written about me was negative. Some of it was cruel, much of it was bitchy. And I hadn't even done anything yet.

One week there was something printed in a gossip column about an email I'd sent to a colleague. Another time, something about where my car was parked. This was no doubt riveting to absolutely nobody. I was baffled as to what my name was doing in newspapers whose readers didn't know or care who the hell I was, let alone where my car was parked. Surely the general public was far more interested in the antics of actual celebrities like Bec Hewitt and Megan Gale than some D-list media person like me. But it continued and I didn't have a clue how to handle it. It seemed churlish and childish to respond to the things that were written so I didn't. But they stung. Not to mention making me paranoid since there were grains of truth in the items that could only have come from inside the network.

So there I was, a few months in, reeling. I was boxing at shadows, watching my back, trying to win over my colleagues, unsure about what exactly I was meant to be doing, and feeling sickeningly guilty about taking so much toxicity with me home to my family.

Thank God for Fran, our nanny. With work so stressful, I felt incredibly lucky that she had become part of the family. As we sat down to the delicious meals that Fran cooked on the days she came, Jason and I would marvel at how our home lives had improved. For me, with the extra help it felt like I had a wife. A proper one. One far better at cooking than me. It didn't erase my guilt about leaving Coco so I could work, but it reduced it somewhat because Coco seemed happy.

If only I'd known then how much more stressful things were about to become.

FROM SEQUINS TO SUITS

SMS to Jo from me:

'In fitting room. Buying grey jacket and black skirt. RIP fashion.'

A couple of weeks before I started at Nine, I went shopping for Clothes To Wear In My New Life. I was still breastfeeding and hadn't really bought new clothes for months. For me, this was strange. More than strange, it was alarming. Because since I was, oh, about six, if you'd asked me to list my hobbies, 'Shopping For Clothes' would be close to the top. Okay, the top.

Where had my urge to splurge gone?

It appears I'd left it at the hospital with the placenta and my pelvic-floor muscles. Because apart from losing interest in news, popular culture and my ambition, another thing I misplaced after giving birth was my interest in fashion. Poof. Gone. Buh-bye.

It didn't help that escorting me home from the maternity ward like Beyonce's bodyguards were two enormous bosoms strapped to my chest. I'm not used to carrying around gigantic jugs and when nature sends them my way post-partum, I tend to grapple with them awkwardly

Perhaps this is what it feels like after you've had a boob job — like someone else's breasts have been shoved under your skin. By the time my milk comes in, I've gone from a small pre-pregnancy B cup to a D or DD, which is astonishing to me and baffling to my wardrobe. While breastfeeding, my bosoms can accurately be described as 'cumbersome'.

When you're used to having small boobs, big ones are a trip.

I think they look perfectly lovely on other women — but on me? I find them intimidating. They seem to mock everything I try to put them in. There seem to be only two fashion options: mumsy or sexy. And sexy is the last thing I feel when my boobs are big. They may look sexy on other women, but on my body I associate big hooters with fertility and lactation.

If I could have written my clothes a letter when I started at Nine, it would have gone something like this:

Dear Wardrobe,
I think I'm going to have to break up with you. I'm sorry. It's not you, it's me. I've changed. Thanks for the memories. And the sequins. Missing you already.
Love,
Mia xxx

After years of working with some of Australia's most fashion-forward young things, I'd moved to an environment where I was surrounded entirely by men in suits. This played havoc with my fashion headspace.

In my old working life, my staff became nervous if I ever turned up to work wearing black or anything resembling a suit. Even jackets made them fret. Was someone important coming in for a meeting? Was I going to see the big (male) bosses? Might the world be about to end?

The word 'corporate' rarely featured in my fashion vocabulary while I was at ACP. Every day was a riot of colour, layering, sparkles and clashing prints. Denim was a constant and impractical evening shoes were standard. There were no rules.

I was a walking canvas for my own artistic expression and I dressed to impress and entertain, both my team and myself. And they impressed and entertained me right back. I enjoyed the daily fashion banter. It wasn't unusual for me to interrupt a meeting to comment on how great a colleague's cleavage looked and inquire as to whether she'd found a new bra. 'Talk me through your outfit,' was not an unusual form of greeting in the corridors of ACP.

While there was certainly an element of one-upmanship, it was never about labels; more about looks. Whether your outfit came from Supré or Scanlan & Theodore was immaterial; in fact, there was more kudos to be gained from bagging a bargain. How you put it together and how right-now it looked was key.

And then I moved to television. Suddenly I was in a corporate environment where fashion had no currency. No one cared about the new sass & bide jeans or that Willow had done a diffusion line for Portmans. No one asked where I got my shoes. No one referred to clothes at all. Ever. They were just … clothes.

This should have been a crushing disappointment because I've always enjoyed the creativity involved in getting dressed for work. But surprisingly, it was a massive relief. Relief to be off the fancy dress treadmill. Relief that my outfits no longer had to be clever or tricky or of-the-moment. Relief that my clothes were now background noise, not the main event. Relief that not only would no one notice if I wore the same outfit twice in a week, the care factor would be zero if I wore the same outfit every day for a year.

However, this seismic shift from fashion forward to fashion background was not without challenges. Neutral clothes, corporate clothes, clothes that say take-me-seriously? Well, they don't just fall onto your back. You have to find them and buy them and put them together.

A quick inventory of my wardrobe before I started my new job revealed the following: I owned far too many silly shoes, far too many floaty tops and far too much denim for my new life. Fortunately, the copious quantities of sequined and sparkly clothes I possessed had been shoved in a cupboard some months before. Sparkly does not work when you are pregnant or breastfeeding.

Also useless when you're working with men? Anything with an empire line because they think you're pregnant and that makes them nervous and confused. At work and for going out, men just don't understand it when we do fashion irony. White shoes, leggings, dresses over pants, high-waisted jeans, bubble skirts, skivvies under dresses, pinafores, jumpsuits … we think 'fun, amusing and clever', they think, 'Did she get dressed in the dark?'

Back in my wardrobe, after shifting everything denim to one side for weekends, I carefully extracted anything worky. This included a few wrap dresses, a couple of pairs of pants, some tops and no suits because I didn't own any. That would have to change, wouldn't it?

Next problem: what do you wear under a jacket anyway? I have many wafty tops that suddenly seemed unsuitable. Cleavage is not corporate. Neither are visible nipples.

My first sensible purchase was a black skirt. It was unremarkable. I couldn't remember the last time I'd bought a black skirt. I've always gone for the pretty over the practical. The special over the staple. Next, I bought two knitted tops. I've never understood knits. Why wear wool when you can wear sequins? But at last I understood they're what you wear under jackets. So I bought a jacket too. None of this shopping was remotely enjoyable. It felt a lot like buying pens before you go back to school after the summer holidays. Necessary yet slightly depressing.

After more than a decade and a half of working among women who dressed like cast members of Cirque du Soleil and adopting that style myself (fashion forward meets fancy dress) it was a brutal shock to find myself in a sea of suits. I had fashion whiplash.

Even so, I'd never worked in a proper grown-up office before. So at first it was a novelty to dress boringly, a bit like dressing up to play the part of an accountant in a movie about someone else's life. Also, on the plus side, I discovered it took far less time to get ready in the morning when you didn't have to decide whether the multi-strand necklace with gold golf-balls hanging from it worked with the mesh hoodie, cargo pants and fluorescent pink slingbacks or whether in fact the sequined orange skinny scarf would look better as a belt or a headband.

There was another thing I hadn't realised: women bond over clothes. It can be a handy common language when we're trying to forge a new connection. Complimenting another woman on something she's wearing is an invitation for her to tell you a brief story about where it came from and thus open up her life to you a little bit.

Without this default entry point into my new male colleagues' lives, I struggled. Then I discovered that blokes do actually appreciate being asked about their ties. Every tie has an anecdote that gives you a glimpse into the wearer's life. I never really spoke tie before, but I learned fast.

Not for one moment during my time at Nine did anyone tell me what to wear. Nobody ever commented on it. However, I was so paranoid about giving my critics ammunition that I didn't want to draw attention to the more out-there, frivolous, female aspects of me. I was already a fish out of water. Why draw attention to my gills?

THE SECRET IN THE GLOVE BOX

Voicemail to nanny agency from me:

'Hello, it's Mia Freedman calling. I need to speak with someone urgently about a problem with my nanny. Can you please call me back ASAP? Because I'm freaking out. Thanks. Bye.'

'I think my nanny is stealing my clothes,' I blurted to a friend I bumped into at a restaurant. She was not a particularly close friend but I'd been sitting at dinner with Jason feeling utterly anguished and talking about it solidly since we'd arrived.

Over the past twenty-four hours since the realisation hit, Jason and I had exhausted all angles and were now going around in small circles. I needed a fresh perspective.

Here's how it began.

One morning, a couple of weeks after I started at Nine, I went looking for a skirt. It was a grey pencil skirt that had come from a friend who did PR for Portmans. She'd asked me to be a Portmans brand ambassador which just involved wearing some free Portmans clothes. Easy. Except, in fact, this is extremely difficult when you are thirty-four. Most of the things she sent —

shorts, clingy dresses, see-through tops — were inappropriate for my new, jarringly conservative work environment.

I can't remember ever having worn a pencil skirt in my life and it probably would never have occurred to me to buy one, but suddenly this Portmans freebie was a key piece in my wardrobe. It was perfect. And it was missing. Bugger.

I was alert but not alarmed. Losing clothes was not new to me. I had form. To say I can be a little vague about my material possessions is a kind way of putting it. The truth is I'm utterly hopeless.

One of my favourite things to do when I have a rare spare hour on the weekend is to edit my wardrobe. I'm forever making piles of clothes to send to the alterationist, the dry-cleaner, to give away, to sell or to stash in a cupboard belonging to someone else in my house. Everyone in the family has parts of their wardrobes occupied by my clothes, squatting stubbornly and expanding into every available space. Occasionally, during an edit, these piles get mixed up and clothes meant for the dry-cleaner or storage end up at Vinnies. This is very bad. I am very careless.

So I didn't panic when the skirt went missing. A teeny tiny voice in my head whispered, 'Hmmmm, timing is interesting. Fran comes, skirt goes.' But I smothered the little voice with loud logic. 'Why on earth would anyone want to steal a Portmans skirt?' I reasoned to myself. Surely if you were a thief let loose in my cupboard, you'd go for the labels, wouldn't you? And then the labels began to disappear. A few weeks later, while getting ready to go out, I went looking for a sass & bide denim jacket. Gone. Annoying, puzzling, but still no cause for a total freak-out.

I didn't want my nanny to be a thief. I wanted to put my fingers in my ears and loudly sing 'Baa Baa Black Sheep' to drown out the sound of the mounting anecdotal evidence. And so I did. And my clothes continued to disappear. More sass &

bide, jeans this time. A Collette Dinnigan top. A Joseph leather jacket. But also, confusingly, a dress from Bondi markets. A Sportsgirl pair of sandals.

And still, I pushed it to the back of my mind. Perhaps they were all together in a pile somewhere! I also reminded myself how generous I was with Fran. I always gave her clothes and beauty products and magazines because I was forever being sent stuff and I wanted to share it.

I was also genuinely fond of her. She had become like the little sister I never had, one of the traps and, occasionally, benefits of having a young nanny. It's a bit like having another child. When Jamie Oliver came to town and did a series of live shows, I bought her a $150 ticket, knowing how much she loved cooking. I also gave her the afternoon off to go see him and asked my aunt to look after Coco that day as I was at work. Later, my aunt would tell me that when she arrived, Fran had been locked in the bathroom in tears after having a fight with her boyfriend on the phone. At the time, my aunt hadn't thought much of it. But after Fran was gone and we began to unravel what had gone on when I wasn't around, it would be yet another sign that my trusted nanny was a mess. But was she a thief?

One day, when Fran had been with us about six months, I decided to have a baby seat fitted in her car so she could occasionally take Coco out to a playground or to the library. I had Fran follow me in her car to the baby shop where we had someone install a car seat. Afterwards, I went inside to pay while she waited by her car. 'Put this receipt in your glove box so you have proof that the seat was installed by a registered provider,' the salesman told me, handing me an official-looking bit of paper.

I walked outside and as Fran was being shown how best to remove the car seat, I opened the front passenger door and flipped open the glove box to put the receipt inside. Stuffed into that very small space was a denim jacket that looked familiar. Instantly, reflexively, I closed the glove box again. Part of me wanted to delete what I'd just seen and never think about it again.

But in that instant I knew if I didn't look properly, I'd always wonder and by then it would be too late. So I opened the glove box again and pulled out the jacket. 'Oh,' I said in surprise that was part an act, part genuine. I could sense Fran behind me now, but I couldn't bear to turn around and look into her face. Later, I'd regret this.

'Isn't this mine?' I said, trying to keep my voice steady. She replied instantly.

'Yeah it is, I meant to give it back to you. I found it out the front.'

I was overcome, but the strongest sensation I had was to get away from her. I couldn't think straight. I needed to be alone, regroup. I wanted to vomit.

'Right, I'll see you back at the house,' I said over my shoulder, holding my jacket as I walked quickly to my car with Coco and drove away.

I could hardly breathe. So I did what I always do in times of extreme confusion. I called Jo to debrief.

'I found my jacket stuffed in Fran's glove box, and oh my God I think she's stealing from me, and she said she found it out the front and was going to give it back to me, but that's so weird and I couldn't look at her face, and oh my God what am I going to do, and I think I might throw up and I'm totally freaked out and what do I say to her when I get home and — '

'Oh fuck,' said Jo. 'This is bad'.

'Oh, it's soooooo bad,' I wailed melodramatically. 'Soooo baaaaaaad.'

'Look, let's run through this logically. Could she have found the jacket out the front like she said?'

'Well, yes, I suppose if I was carrying it somewhere and I dropped it then it could have been somewhere other than in my closet.'

'Okay, so that's possible.'

'Except I haven't worn this jacket in ages. At least a year.'

'Oh. Fuck.'

'Yes, fuck. What am I going to do?'

'You have to ask her more about where and when she found it. Watch her face this time when she's speaking.'

'Right, yes, good idea. I'll do that and I'll call you back. Stand by.'

My hands were shaking on the steering wheel. This wasn't about the clothes. This was about the possibility that I'd employed a thief. That the person I was entrusting with my most vulnerable and helpless possession, my baby daughter, had the kind of morality that would allow her to come into my home, accept my generosity and steal from me blindly. And then look me in the eye and lie about it.

When I got home, Fran was already in the kitchen preparing Coco's dinner. She seemed normal, cheerful even. This threw me because if I'd been stealing and had just been caught, I would be a mess.

'So Fran, where did you say you found that jacket?' I asked casually, unstacking the dishwasher so I had something to do with my hands while keeping a close eye on her face.

'It was out in the garden near your car,' she replied calmly. Her face revealed nothing. She met my gaze.

'I was going home one day last week and I meant to give it back to you. I'm so sorry about that.'

'Oh well, thanks for picking it up,' I said because I didn't know what else to say and I needed more time to think.

I went into my room and called Jo.

'All right, let's go through this logically,' she said in a no-nonsense way that calmed me down. For a brief moment. 'What kind of access does she have to your wardrobe?'

'Total access. To get to the bathroom where she gives Coco a bath, she has to walk past my wardrobe and you know there are no doors on the cupboards — everything is open.'

'And she's at your place a lot by herself?'

'Yes, most of the time. We're at work and it's just her and Coco.'

'Okay, back to the jacket for a sec. Is it possible she, say, got cold one day and needed to take Coco out for a walk and so she, say, borrowed the jacket without asking and forgot to return it?'

'It definitely smells like her so, yes, she's worn it. But, but ...'

I was struggling to put my finger on something that was niggling. It came to me suddenly.

'It's not like it was just flung casually on the front seat. That would have been more believable. It was the way it was stuffed into a tiny ball in the glove box. That's what screamed "guilty" to me. It was so ... furtive.

'She wasn't expecting that we'd go get the car seat installed today so when I told her to follow me in her car, she must have panicked and tried to hide it.'

'It's all pointing towards her nicking it, isn't it?'

'Oh nooooo,' I wailed. 'It can't! She can't be a thief! What am I going to do? What about today? Should I send her home now?'

'No. Let her finish the day normally. Don't tip her off at this stage until you're ready to confront her. And don't worry about Coco. She loves Coco. She may be a thief but she would never mistreat Coco.'

That night, after Fran left, I did a full inventory of my clothes, looking in every cupboard for the things I knew were missing to absolutely rule out that I'd stashed a pile of clothes somewhere and forgotten about them. No luck.

Instead, I discovered a whole lot of other items that were gone. All things I hadn't looked for until now because I hadn't worn them for a while.

Every missing thing matched her taste. It all made perfect, sickening sense. Jason was home by now and watching TV in the lounge room. I wandered in in a daze.

'More stuff's missing. It's her. There's no question.'

'Oh shit.'

I slept quite well that night. I've never been a tosser and turner, even at times of extreme stress. But when I woke up the next morning, my mind began to gallop down that dark road called 'I'm Fucking Freaking Out Here'. On the way, there were a million 'what ifs' to consider.

What if Fran wasn't who she said she was? If she was a thief, why not a liar? Why not a psycho? Why not a serial killer? She had keys to our house. She knew the alarm code. What if? What if? What if?

Options ran through my head — and my mouth — as Jason and I discussed it endlessly. Should we get a nanny cam installed in my dressing room so we had proof? That would take too long. Should we call the police? No, I didn't want to inflame the situation. If she was a thief, I just wanted her away from our family. Should we hire a private investigator to photograph her wearing my clothes on the weekend as proof? Too slow and too expensive and also possibly too ridiculous. This wasn't 'CSI'.

I decided to call the agency Fran had come from. It was a Saturday but the owner called me back almost immediately.

'I got your message and I've just come in to look at Fran's file. This was the first job we've placed her in so we haven't known her much longer than you, but we did do a thorough background check and her references all stacked up. And you don't have to worry about her not being who she says she is because we checked licences and birth certificates and all that.'

I told her exactly what had happened and my hope that somehow it might be explained by some scenario I hadn't considered.

'Probably not, no,' she said sadly. 'Even if she didn't do it — and you may never know if she did because thieves tend to be very good liars — the trust has broken down so much that she has to go.'

Fantastic.

'Now I'm going to call back all her references and ask some more pointed questions about whether they ever noticed anything going missing. I'll call you back.'

The news was interesting. 'The woman at the day-care centre where she worked was adamant there was no way Fran would ever take anything. But when I rang the last family she worked for, the mother said that a few things had gone missing but at the time she'd assumed it was the cleaner who left around the same time as Fran, so she'd never talked to her about it.'

The evidence was piling up. Next, I called my own cleaner, who worked at our place each Wednesday when Fran looked after Coco.

'Um, hi Josie, sorry to call you on the weekend but, well, I'm having a few problems with Fran and I just wanted to ask you about how you think she's going. Have you noticed anything you think I should know about?'

Our lovely cleaner, who had been with us for years, confessed that she did indeed have a few concerns, but they weren't huge things and she hadn't wanted to get Fran in trouble.

'You know, she never takes Coco out of the house. I always say, "Why don't you take her for a walk or to the park?" but she always says, "Nah, I'm too tired," and just stays home. She's always very, very tired and sometimes she sleeps on the couch when Coco has her nap. And she never feeds her good food. She always takes your money and goes to the café and feeds her muffins. And she's always in front of the television with Coco.'

The nausea was rising again. Why the hell had I never thought to ask Josie before about what she saw? Why hadn't it occurred to me to check up on Fran? Maybe because I desperately wanted to believe it was all fine and that she was doing a terrific job. Ostrich syndrome.

Straight away I made arrangements for Coco to be looked after the following week by her grandparents and my aunt. I knew I wasn't going to let Fran come near Coco again.

It was vital to me that she had no warning of what was about to happen. I didn't want to give her the chance to copy my house key, but also, I wanted to look at her face when I brought up the subject, in the hope that I would know the truth by her reaction. I was devastated on so many levels, but bizarrely, I was devastated for her. Devastated that she'd stuffed up the best job she ever had and that she'd never see Coco again and would instantly be cut out of our family. I felt for her totally, even though I should have just been angry and betrayed. I was those things too. What a mess.

Tuesday afternoon came and I'd arranged for Coco to be with Jason's mother. I didn't even want Fran in the house so I was waiting on the front lawn playing ball with the dog when she arrived. Not expecting me, she was surprised but recovered quickly.

'Coco isn't home from her nanna's yet and I'm working from home this arvo,' I said, a knot of anxiety in my stomach.

'So, Fran, look, I know about you borrowing my clothes …' I'd decided to say 'borrowing' instead of 'stealing' so that the more gentle word might lull her into a confession. It was important to me to know for sure that she'd done it and that I was doing the right thing by sacking her.

She looked blankly at me, her face impassive. 'What do you mean?'

My voice was disappointed but not angry. 'There's a large amount of my stuff missing. Clothes and shoes. There was the jacket in your glove box the other day. I know you've been borrowing my things without asking …'

She scrunched her face a little as if she was having trouble understanding me but she was very calm. Disconcertingly so.

'What do you mean, Mia? I never borrowed anything of yours. My goodness. I told you I found the jacket outside. What's missing? Tell me and maybe I can help work out what happened to it.'

I listed some of the things and she looked puzzled, as if she was genuinely wondering where they might be. 'Goodness, Mia, this is awful,' she said without much emotion. 'I promise that it has nothing to do with me though. Maybe it was Josie.'

'Fran, that's utterly ridiculous. Josie has been with us for years. Look, I'd really like to believe it wasn't you but the trust has just broken down too much and you're going to have to find another job.'

'Oh, okay, I understand,' she said vaguely. 'But really, I don't know what happened to your stuff.'

I wanted her gone. Her utter lack of emotion was throwing me. 'I need you to give me the key back and I need to get Coco's seat from your car,' I said not unkindly, getting to my feet and walking her out to the street.

In the end, her departure was hugely anti-climactic.

'Fran, I'm sorry it had to end this way.'

'Yes, I've enjoyed working for your family.'

And then she was gone. It was only later that I realised. She hadn't even mentioned Coco's name …

The adrenaline left me like the air out of a balloon. The knot in my stomach unravelled. I jumped on the phone to debrief Jason. Then my mum. Then Jo. Then Jason's mum. I needed to talk it through to make sense of it. With each person, I started by asking a question.

'If you were accused of stealing from your employer who then sacked you because of it and you were innocent, how would you react?' I genuinely wanted to know because out of all the scenarios I'd played through in my head, Fran's utter passivity had been a wild card.

Each person I asked replied in the same way. 'I'd get angry and I'd protest my innocence and I'd probably cry.' But mostly they said they'd be angry at the injustice of a false accusation.

There had been not a skerrick of anger in Fran's response. Just mild denial and a passive acceptance that she was to be fired for something she supposedly hadn't done. She'd been dry-eyed. I felt justified.

And as for how much I'd feared for her reaction at never seeing Coco again? The baby she'd grown so close to these past few months? Coco who?

Even if I hadn't elicited the confession I'd hoped for, it was plainly obvious that she was guilty.

As I picked my shredded trust and confidence out of the bin and began the process of finding a new nanny, I still didn't have closure. Or my clothes.

A week after I sacked Fran, I called her mobile number on the pretence of checking up on her.

'Hi Fran, it's Mia. I was just ringing to find out how you're going and to say that we would pay you a fortnight's wage.'

It was 11 am but she sounded groggy, like she'd just woken up. 'Oh, yeah, hi. Well, thanks for that.' Her tone was vague and devoid of much emotion. I tried to make a bit of small talk to glean information.

'So, have you been looking for another job yet?'

'No, I'm really tired and I think I'm going to have a break for a while.'

'Right, okay, well I just wanted to wish you well and again, I'm sorry for how it all ended.'

Jesus, soon I'd be offering to write her a reference and buy her a new car.

Ten minutes after I hung up the phone, my mobile beeped with a text.

From: Fran
Mia, I am sorry for what I did. I don't know why I did it but I know you didn't deserve it. I will try to get some help. Thank you for being so nice. Fran

Bingo. I sat with it a while before I replied.

To: Fran
I'm glad you were honest. Thank you for that. I'd like you to send all my clothes back next week. Just bag them up and drop them over the fence. Thanks.

When they finally arrived, there were eighteen separate items. Nothing had been washed or dry-cleaned, and they were roughly folded and shoved into shopping bags.

She never did get that reference.

WHEN A HOLIDAY ISN'T A HOLIDAY

Voicemail to Jo from me:

'Hi babe, is your holiday going well? Mine not so much. Why does everything fall apart when we go away? Last night was a doozy. Coco kept waking herself up in that fucking noisy nylon travel cot and on about the fourth time, I was staggering to her room with my eyes half closed and I overshot the door and fell down the stairs. It's lucky I was half asleep because my muscles were clearly relaxed and I didn't break anything, although I do have some attractive bruises, which look quite fetching on the beach. Jason heard the noise and came running and didn't know who to comfort first: sobbing baby in cot or sobbing wife on floor. The drama then woke Luca, who wanted a detailed explanation of the situation and how it had all actually occurred. Then Harry decided it was a great thing that all the humans were up and about and why not capitalise on this unexpected treat by running to fetch his ball in the hope someone might throw it for him. Good times. Can I go back to work yet? I need a rest. Love you. Bye.'

The phrase 'Holidays with kids' is an oxymoron. And I'm an actual moron because I always forget this and am surprised when I come home exhausted. So I'd really appreciate it if someone could invent an alternate word for 'holiday' that doesn't imply rest and relaxation. Because then, parents everywhere would have a more accurate way to describe their 'holidays' to their friends and workmates.

Our Christmas holidays to the North Coast after I'd been working at Channel Nine for a few months were not very relaxing. After I'd left Jo the voicemail about my fall down the stairs, she texted me back: 'Don't call it a holiday, call it "moving-the-baby-to-a-different-location".' Truer words never texted.

If you're a working parent, holidays are a great reminder of the difference between spending quality and quantity time with your kids. Kids need both. Quantity is harder.

Without the buffer of childcare, grandparents or even the occasional babysitter, it can be gobsmacking to discover how much hard work full-time parenting is. On the odd occasion I'd make it into the playground at Luca's school of a morning, or when I dashed, late and lumbering in my high heels, into the school hall for a concert or some such thing, other mums would sometimes shake their heads and say to me 'I don't know how you do it'. But back when I worked in magazines, work was the easy part of my life. I had staff, a nice office, an assistant. I was never as knackered as after our annual Christmas holiday. Entertaining children 24/7 is harder than the toughest day at work.

This is the part where stay-at-home mums (and dads) get to high-five themselves while wearing a T-shirt emblazoned with: 'TOLD YOU SO, SUCKERS!' Stay-at-home parents? I endorse your smugness and I salute your T-shirts. I've always thought it's far easier to spend your day at work where no one demands you share your food, drink and toilet time or fractures your concentration span into a million teeny tiny pieces. Full-time at-home parents are legends. Where is their ticker-tape parade?

But a lack of match fitness isn't the only holiday challenge. It's also the lack of props. Homes with kids contain mountains of stuff. Toys, DVDs, play areas, childproof cupboards, computer games, ergonomic change tables, cots, car seats, high chairs, no-more-tears shampoo, bikes, PlayStations, piles of assorted plastic crap, snacks and on and on. You start accumulating this stuff while pregnant and it never stops. Until you go on holiday when you're suddenly cut loose from your stuff mountain and are forced to fend for yourself.

I'm sure there are resourceful parents who embrace the opportunity to fashion a makeshift high chair out of a dog-eared yellow pages and three rubber bands. But not me. Nope. I like my stuff. I neeeeed my stuff.

And I've never needed it more than on this particular holiday. After two weeks trapped indoors with two bored children while so much rain fell on the North Coast, I became demented and began texting friends 'PLEASE SEND ARK'.

To keep my spirits up and my perspective in check, I'd regularly remind myself how lucky I was even to be on holidays. How lucky I was to have happy, healthy children I adore. How lucky I was not to be camping. Or homeless. When all of this lost its cheering power, I dug deeper, trying to summon gratitude for having limbs, oxygen and the ability to blink.

Eventually, around day ten, when the rain became so torrential it was falling horizontally, I said goodbye to my gratitude and my sense of humour. Then I threw such a spectacular tantrum, Jason threatened me with timeout and Coco looked at me with new respect.

Even when the sun is out, family holidays can leave me in need of a stiff drink and a long lie-down. Or, in the case of ten consecutive rainy days, a straitjacket.

I first suspected my Mother Of The Year crown was slipping when Coco pointed to a sleeping Wiggle on the DVD and asked me for the hundredth time 'What's wrong with Jeff?' and I snapped 'Jeff's dead, okay?!'

I'm not proud of this, but in my defence I was very, very tired. This was because by this stage, after the falling-down-the-stairs episode, Coco was now sleeping in her small nylon travel cot next to our bed, waking herself and us every hour as she thrashed about noisily. Are we having fun yet, people?

Well, we're certainly not having sleep. For those without kids, holidays are an all-you-can-eat buffet of sleeping opportunities. Afternoon naps, morning sleep-ins, snoozing on the beach, early nights ... it's all about filling up the sleep tank until it's overflowing.

Fortunately, once I had kids, I stopped wanting to sleep. What really got my juices going after I became a mother was working out how little sleep I needed to maintain basic brain function and then halving it. You will never sleep less — or worse — than when on holidays with your kids.

Jo, in her infinite wisdom (both her children are brilliant sleepers) always packs blackout fabric and a staple gun, which she uses on the kids' bedroom windows wherever they're staying. I used to laugh at her. Until I found myself texting her at 5 am for advice on how I could improvise with alfoil and some sticky tape. Who's laughing now?

One of the best things about holidays is long leisurely dinners. And cocktails at sunset. I find children — especially if they're small and tired — integrate seamlessly into these activities.

My digestion is always enhanced by a wriggling toddler on my lap, trying to hurl the pepper grinder across the table while shoving fistfuls of sea salt into her mouth. Another drink anyone? Oh no, I'll just inject a daiquiri directly into a vein, thanks.

As long as you don't want to actually spend time with your partner, it is possible to get a break. This is called divide and conquer. It requires complex negotiations about who's had more time to themselves and quickly deteriorates into recriminations. 'You got to SLEEP IN this morning while I took the kids to the beach.' 'Yeah but you went shopping in town BY YOURSELF yesterday.' 'Going to the supermarket to buy nappies is hardly me-time and the baby was asleep when I was out so THAT DOESN'T BLOODY COUNT.'

Despite the challenges, there is something wonderfully bonding about all that quantity time in a confined space. And it helps that I'm a goldfish. How else to explain the decision we made on this holiday.

Byron Bay is a good place to make decisions. There's something very grounding, a little bit magic about it. Life slows down when you get to Byron. Because I am a goldfish, I always forget this for the first twenty-four hours after I arrive and find myself constantly impatient with the service and the way people drive. It takes me at least a day to remember I came to Byron Bay *because* everything is slower. And then I slip into the groove and slow down too.

After a few days, I begin pissing off all the new arrivals from Sydney, Brisbane and Melbourne who are antsy that I'm chatting about dolphins with the dreadlocked guy at the counter and putting an extra forty-five seconds between them and their skinny latte.

Lots of people come back from a holiday in Byron Bay with new resolve to change their lives. Often, this includes a plan to move to Byron Bay. And usually, within a week or two, this plan slowly fades into a grey box marked 'Seemed Like A Good Idea At The Time'. Byron time.

For me, the decision I made up at Byron over my Christmas holidays, while radical, was not fanciful. But it certainly was life changing.

I knew TV wasn't my thing. My stress levels were out of control and the medium just didn't suit me. I wanted out. Jason had been planning to sell his business for some time. He wanted out too.

So we made the decision to extricate ourselves from our jobs by midyear and go overseas with the kids for a few months. We'd never travelled with them before and we wanted an adventure.

Full of Byron optimism, at the time I didn't realise that the following six months would be the most tumultuous and emotional period in my professional life.

TV: JUST NOT THAT INTO ME

SMS text to me from Wendy:

*'Don't look at what's been written in the paper today, my darling.
Just don't. xx.'*

So I had this idea for a show. Actually, that's a total lie. It wasn't my idea at all; it was Barbara Walters' idea. She's the iconic American broadcaster who first thought of having an unscripted daytime show with a bunch of women talking about life. She cast herself and four others, plonked everyone around a table and launched 'The View' in the mid 1990s. The women spoke freely about news, current affairs, pop culture and their personal lives and it was like nothing else on TV at the time.

It's sometimes said there are no new ideas in magazines or TV, just recycled ones. If a TV show or a magazine is successful overseas, an Australian version is inevitably launched here. Occasionally, something out-of-the-box comes along, but most of the media we consume is a variation on something that preceded it.

I was flailing around at Nine in the climate of uncertainty that had settled over the network, as rumours we would be sold appeared true. I didn't have much to do and I was enormously frustrated.

So the idea of launching a daytime show like 'The View' for an Australian female audience was hugely appealing. First, it would give me a focus for my energy. A specific project to drive. Something to do. Second, I felt passionately that daytime TV wasn't providing interesting local content to all the women at home with babies and kids, to baby boomers who had retired but who definitely weren't the bridge-playing knitters of a generation ago, and to part-time workers and students. Why was there nothing on TV during the day that catered to this audience of smart, time-poor women? Something that gave them a quick hit of news, social issues and gossip in an hour every day? Pilots had been made by other networks, including Nine, but none had made it to air. Naïvely, I thought I could be the one to do it. How hard could it be?

I believed the key to getting this show right was the casting. I wanted women who had lots of complicated notches on their life belts. Women who had lived and loved and suffered and triumphed and would be prepared to be honest about it all on TV. Not because I wanted to make a sensationalist show but because I was sick of the polished images of women in the media and I wanted something more real — something women at home could relate to emotionally.

Once we'd settled on four hosts — Mary Moody, Lisa Oldfield, Zoë Sheridan and Libbi Gorr — we brought them together for a screen test and they gelled straight away. Once I'd had the cast signed off by my bosses, the next key appointment was the executive producer. This was the day-to-day manager of the show and I knew I needed someone very experienced. At the suggestion of one of my colleagues, we signed up Tara Smithson, who was the most tenacious, hard-working person I've ever met and from whom I was to learn so much.

The next couple of months were a whirlwind of organisation. From set design to staffing the production team, meetings about lighting and PR and marketing and sponsorship and budgets. It was exhilarating to be so busy. I was working closely and intensely with a small team, mostly women and a few men. All of them were passionate and excited about what we were doing.

I can pinpoint the day the first nail was hammered into the coffin of 'The Catch-Up' and it was my fault entirely. It was weeks before the first show even went to air. While we were in development and casting, I'd heard repeated rumours that Seven were planning their own daytime show to rival 'The Catch-Up' and I was worried they'd beat us to air, gobbling up scarce ad dollars and forcing us to shelve our plans. Contract negotiations with the hosts were dragging on because it was January and everyone was on holidays.

I was impatient and anxious, and I wanted to plant our flag in the daytime turf before anyone else did. In hindsight, I'm not sure if this was a legitimate concern, an impulsive response to an imagined threat or just plain ol' paranoia. Maybe all three.

The ideal and obvious thing would have been to send out a press release announcing the show with a glossy group shot of the cast. But we were still fine-tuning contracts and the hosts weren't yet available to be photographed. The media section of *The Australian* had been keen to do an interview with me when I started at Nine but I'd demurred because I didn't really have anything to say. Now I did. But I was wary. So I made a request to the journalist who wanted a photo to go with the story. 'If you need a photo, I don't want it to be a solo one.' As an alternative, I suggested a group shot with three of the women who were working with me behind the scenes on the show: the casting director, the ad sales manager and the executive producer.

'Sure,' she replied.

I organised for all four of us to get spruced up before the shoot in the hair and make-up department, and when the photographer arrived, he obligingly shot the four of us together. After the others had left, he casually asked, 'Mia, can I just get one of you by yourself so we have it for the files?'

This was a tricky question and I wavered. My brain said, 'Say no. You don't want them to have any solo shots that they could possibly use for this story.' But my ego said, 'Why not? You've had your hair and make-up done and you're wearing a nice frock and the file shots they have of you are crap. Wouldn't it be nice if they had a decent photo to use for anything they write in the future? Wouldn't it? Huh? Huh?'

Ego won. Bloody, bloody ego.

The day the story was published, I woke at 5.30 am to read it online. At first glance, it seemed okay. It wasn't a puff piece — there was valid criticism about my having no TV experience and the show sounding like a rip-off of 'The View', but I was expecting that. It was true. There was no picture, but often photos weren't published online.

I was working from home that day and it was late in the morning by the time I made it to the newsagent. Oh fuck. On the front page of the paper — I hadn't even got to the media section yet — was a horrible photo of me, taken from below. My arms were crossed in front of me. I was all chins and a terrible 'power' pose. What a dumb cliché. I knew it had been a mistake when the photographer had suggested I should fold my arms while he crouched on the floor with his camera pointed up at me. But I was in polite, compliant mode and didn't want to come across like a diva so I agreed. Fool? That would be me.

I quickly paid for the paper, dashed to the car and rummaged for the media section inside. Fuck, fuck, fuck. My picture was huge and it took up most of the front page of the section. I was wearing a red dress and was sitting on a chair in an empty TV studio. My legs were crossed and you could see halfway up my skirt. I was smiling widely and looking decidedly horsey, as if my teeth might leap out of my mouth and into the face of the reader at any moment. Hello rising nausea.

I knew instantly that this was going to be trouble. I was devastated that they hadn't used the photo of the four of us and not just because I passionately felt those women deserved public recognition. Part of my sick feeling was because I knew there'd be people inside and outside Channel Nine who would be resentful that I was receiving this kind of attention. I was totally unproven in TV, I wasn't on-air talent and 'The Catch-Up' wasn't even a prime-time show. Why the hell should I be on the front page? And they were right. That would be the first nail then.

In another body blow to a show that hadn't even launched yet, it had been decided that the network needed to change the predominantly fifty-plus daytime audience to a younger one. The lowest hanging fruit on the tree was the long-running American soap 'The Young and the Restless', whose audience was older — therefore less attractive to advertisers — than any other daytime show on the network. The economic reasons for axing 'Y&R' were sound, but the PR consequences were an absolute nightmare.

The show's loyal audience, some of whom had been following the soapie for decades, certainly weren't going to go quietly into the sunset. They were livid.

They didn't have to look far for a target for their fury because the show that was replacing 'Y&R' was 'The Catch-Up'. So before it even began there was a large, established group of pissed-off viewers who wanted 'The Catch-Up' to die a fast and agonising death as punishment for replacing their beloved soap. Their outrage received mass media coverage.

For me, the highlight of this pre-launch media attack came when a particularly savage piece ran in the paper. It slammed the idea of the show and criticised me personally. Increasingly touchy and exasperated, I'd been fuming about this story all morning and was returning from the canteen with a sandwich when I found myself face to face in the lift with the journalist who had written it. What are the chances of that? He'd been invited to the station with other TV critics to preview a new program and was no doubt thrilled to be stuck in a confined space with someone he'd dissed in his column.

It was instantly and horribly awkward but I couldn't help blurting out, 'Thanks for your delightful story this morning.' To which he replied, 'Well, it's what I think and it's all true.' We ended up in a heated slanging match in the middle of the executive floor, which lasted at least fifteen minutes and only ended because someone from Nine publicity came and discreetly ushered him into the screening room while trying not to glare at me.

News of our dust-up quickly circulated around the network and the media. Ding-ding! Next round. I was beginning to feel a little punch-drunk, and we hadn't even gone to air yet.

The day 'The Catch-Up' premiered, I was nervous but exhilarated. I was way out of my depth but in one sense I was back in my element, working with a small group of passionate people striving to produce something we all believed in. It wasn't unlike magazines but had infinitely more adrenaline and pressure. Oh, and infinitely more people gunning for it to fail.

Day one's ratings came in and they were great. One of my colleagues had come up with the idea of launching on Oscars day so we could cross to the red carpet and do the first televised look at the frocks. This worked a treat. The show's ratings were well above what 'Y&R's had been and the demographic was significantly younger.

The next day, the audience dropped massively and I was gutted. Welcome to the roller coaster, I was told by my empathetic colleagues who rode it regularly. Fasten your seatbelt and grab a vomit bag. You'll need it.

It didn't take long. Within days, I began to absolutely dread 8.30 am. Ratings o'clock. I'd never experienced stress and nervous anticipation like it. The numbers that pinged onto my screen at 8.30 dictated the mood of my day and my view of the show. When the numbers were good, I was happy with what we were doing. When they were bad, I wanted to change everything. 'Go easy and take some deep breaths,' I was cautioned by the more experienced executives who knew what they were talking about. 'The daytime sample is very small — only a couple of thousand people — so you have to expect wild fluctuations. We won't really know anything for weeks until things settle down and some patterns emerge.'

This was welcome advice. But still, I began waking at 3 am, obsessing about what the numbers would be. I was chewing my cuticles until they bled. I began to lose weight.

'The Catch-Up' quickly became a lightning rod for media attention and punched well above its weight in press coverage. It was all overwhelmingly negative. Other Nine executives were as gobsmacked by the avalanche of attention as I was. There was daily coverage in all the major metropolitan papers. Double-page features in the Sunday papers. Endless amounts of talkback-radio snarking.

This was unheard of for a non-prime-time show and even prime-time shows would struggle to garner as much media attention and hold it for so long. But it wasn't the kind of attention we wanted. It was all poisonous. The media absolutely hated 'The Catch-Up' and were united in their desire to help kick it to death.

Perhaps it was because the hosts were unlike any other women on TV in their spontaneity and honesty and willingness to expose their flaws and discuss their lives. We'd deliberately chosen candid, interesting and opinionated women with big life experiences and divergent world views. No pre-packaged, glossy sound bites from this lot.

I'm not sure if it was nerves or naïvety or competitiveness or the kind of TV Tourette syndrome I had once suffered from, but in those first few weeks, the on-screen confessions didn't stop. Each one was more sensational than the last. Lisa said she'd been a drug addict. Zoë talked about one-night stands. Mary discussed her affairs and mentioned that after her mother died, they'd had her open coffin on the kitchen table. Libbi showed the birth photos from her caesarean. Individually, they were brave, moving moments. Together, it was a little … overwhelming.

The media could barely keep up with the revelations and neither could viewers. Then, Pauline Hanson released her autobiography in which she claimed she'd had an affair with David Oldfield — before he married Lisa. David denied it live on our show but then went on 'Today Tonight' and failed a lie-detector test.

'Shameless publicity stunts,' sneered many journalists, accusing us of planting these sensational revelations to boost ratings. But in reality, the combination of the show's unscripted format, the fact we were live and that our hosts were all so fast and open meant that we couldn't avoid controversy, let alone control it. Stuff just came out. We never knew what they'd say. It was exciting and terrifying. Sitting in the control room as we went to air live without a delay button, there were many, many days when the executive producer and I would look at each other, mouths gaping, after one of the co-hosts revealed something we hadn't expected. Probably an expression not dissimilar to the one on Steve Liebmann's face that morning on 'Today' when I'd asked him about sperm falling into underpants. Ah, live TV.

Apart from the surprise revelations, the media was extremely interested in the relationship between the four women. In truth? Sometimes it was rocky. Given that we had deliberately chosen women with vastly different political and social views, you wouldn't expect it to be a total laugh-riot love-fest and it wasn't. Did they clash? Sure they did. On air and off air. But we never tried to make any secret of that. They had interesting and articulate debates on the show about everything from abortion to immigration, gun control and politics.

Ultimately, it was an intense experience and friendships formed, some closer than others.

Meanwhile, rumours and press reports portrayed the cast as a pack of backstabbing bitches who hated each other. When interviewed about the alleged catfights on the set, I joked, 'They sometimes disagree but they all love each other and they even play with each other's hair.'

When the hell will I learn to play it straight in print interviews? When this comment was printed in the context of a story about the show being a disaster, my throwaway line about hair came across as moronic. Some things just don't translate and you'd think I'd have learned that by now. But I'm always nervous talking to newspapers because my natural inclination towards humour, irony and piss-taking is a car crash when you read it in black and white

We all had a lot of laughs together, but with all the negative coverage, it was proving very difficult to shake the stench of failure. Even though the ratings were still up and down, it was painfully clear that the show hadn't been an instant hit. Everyone's morale was starting to lurch, including mine. One day I remember picking up a newspaper to read that since my embarrassing quote about the hosts of 'The Catch-Up' playing with each other's hair had been published, I'd been 'gagged' from speaking to the press. That day was perhaps my skin's thinnest moment. I fled my fishbowl office and went into the bathroom to cry, wondering for the hundredth time if I'd truly fucked my career by moving to TV. One good thing about working in a male-dominated environment? There's nobody to hear you cry in the female toilets.

I became a bit paralysed at this point. I wanted desperately to turn things around and salvage the show but I didn't know what exactly to do. Repeatedly, I asked for advice. Repeatedly, I was told the show was okay, and that sometimes there's just no explanation for why something isn't kicking. Ratings in Melbourne and Sydney were passable, but in Perth, Adelaide and Brisbane they were dire.

I'd decided I wanted to leave Nine well before 'The Catch-Up' started, but I'd been determined to launch the show and stabilise it first. Now the day-to-day running of the show was in the skilled hands of the production team, and apart from providing moral support and leadership, I just didn't know what else to do.

Quietly, behind the scenes, I began to talk to management about my exit.

Since nothing about Channel Nine at that time was ever quiet, rumours of my resignation quickly began appearing in the papers. I stayed silent.

As 'The Catch-Up' prepared to celebrate one hundred episodes, a timeslot change a few weeks earlier was showing encouraging signs of building the audience. In the coveted twenty-five to fifty-four-year-old demographic, the show was beginning to regularly win its timeslot in several cities. Its future was far from guaranteed and sponsors were shaky but things looked tentatively hopeful.

Against that backdrop, I finalised my departure not just from Channel Nine but from ACP as well. I'd been consulting for some of the magazines as part of my contract but it was getting harder and harder to maintain my interest and they deserved more attention than I was willing to give them. It was time, after more than fifteen years with PBL, to say goodbye to the only company I'd worked for in my adult life. Itching to close the chapter of my brief and unimpressive TV career, we finally agreed on a departure date and I helped draft the press release that would go out that same day. There was no reason to stick around. I'd been ready to go for months. TV just wasn't that into me and the feeling was mutual.

But it wasn't over yet. I knew there would be intense media interest in my exit because it was Channel Nine and because I was a woman and because I'd not even lasted a year in TV. On the day of my departure I met with an experienced PR friend for breakfast to receive some detailed instructions on how to handle the inevitable media fallout. I was nervous and skittish and wanted to hide under my bed. She gave me strength and advice. And with my Rescue Remedy in my jacket pocket, I headed in to work.

On what was to be my last day at Channel Nine, as I prepared to tell my colleagues and the cast and crew of 'The Catch-Up' that I was leaving, I received a voicemail message. It was one of the Nine sales reps. 'I just wanted to say I heard about "The Catch-Up" being axed and I'm sorry.'

'Are those rumours about "The Catch-Up" being axed going around again?' I called across the corridor to a colleague. Her expression changed. 'They're not rumours. It's being axed today.'

The blood rushed from my head and I felt disoriented. My meeting with the cast and crew after the show to tell them I was leaving the network had suddenly changed. Now I'd be announcing that the show had been axed and they were all out of a job.

The hosts took it well. They were immediately concerned for the younger members of the production staff who had given up jobs elsewhere to join the team.

While I was talking to the cast and crew, the press releases about my departure and the show's axing were landing almost simultaneously, making my exit a far more dramatic and newsworthy story. My phone exploded.

As everyone dispersed to attend to the sudden wreckage of their careers and finances, I hugged various people and headed quickly to my car. I may have left skid marks in the car park in my haste to get the hell out of there.

I was free.

AFTER NINE

I expected to feel huge relief when I left Channel Nine but it wasn't so simple. There was definitely relief there, yes. But the anxiety I'd lived with for almost a year stuck around like a toxic hangover.

My mind and body were taking their sweet damn time to catch up to my changed reality. After being on the defensive against hostility — real and imagined — for so long, I was stuck in a fight-or-flight response. Prickly with adrenaline but nothing to run from any more.

The twenty-four hours after my departure was announced were mental. Having just learned that 'The Catch-Up' had been axed and that I had to tell the team, I was reeling and sought refuge in the only place at the network I felt safe — my car. From there, I quickly called my PR friend and filled her in. While we were on the phone, I got word via text that a newspaper was sending a photographer to Nine to try to get photos of me and

'The Catch-Up' hosts — hoping for a weepy group hug no doubt. 'Get out of there,' she instructed.

At home, I went straight to Coco, who was playing happily with her wonderful new nanny, the polar opposite of Nanny Klepto. Kissing my little girl, I immediately remembered what was important in my life. I quickly changed into my trackies, closed my bedroom door and sat cross-legged on my bed with my laptop, landline, Blackberry and mobile laid out in front of me.

With the caution of a bomb-disposal expert approaching an unexploded device, I turned on my phone and watched it implode. Twenty-seven messages. Thirty-four missed calls. Right.

Among all the media inquiries were concerned messages from friends, family and a few former colleagues asking if I was okay and sending their love.

One newspaper asked if I would agree to sit in a café so they could take a 'surprise' paparazzi photo from across the street. 'It won't look posed or anything,' they said. No. Another reporter said, 'I'm sorry but I have to ask this, can we send a photographer to your house to take a photo of you with your children?' Sure thing, I'll just put the kettle on for you now; how do you take your tea? No.

Agreeing to a photo would have meant the story would run bigger and earlier in the news section of the paper which was the last thing I wanted. I just wanted to crawl under a rock and make it all go away. As it was, the next day it ran anyway. They all made do with file pictures. Damn those file pictures.

Under strict tutelage from my PR guru, I kept all conversations brief and tried to remain diplomatic, discreet and neutral. 'After fifteen years with PBL, I just felt it was time to move on,' I said. 'I really enjoyed my time in TV even though it was brief and I wish everyone at Nine all the very best.' I knew the mere whiff of scandal or bitterness would make the story bigger and keep it running longer.

Still, journalists knew that no one left Nine without controversy. Did I know 'The Catch-Up' was going to be axed? Uh no, it was a surprise to me. Had the blokiness of Nine driven me away? Um, no, I made some great friends there. Is it impossible for a woman to succeed in commercial television? I hope not; it just wasn't the right place for me.

Finally, after four hours of returning calls, I emerged from my bedroom, utterly drained. My parents came over to look after the kids and Jason and I headed to the pub to meet half a dozen close friends for champagne and pizza. I'd survived with my reputation massively dented (as is the fate of virtually every Channel Nine ex-employee) but my sanity intact. Mostly.

In many ways, the hardest bit was still to come.

For more than fifteen years, my identity had been inextricably linked to what I did. I had a title. A business card. And, for the past ten years, an assistant. Staff. A nice office. A car spot. An infrastructure that supplied me with magazines and newspapers. Couriers. IT support. A helpdesk. I had someone to buy my lunch, open my mail, screen my calls, RSVP to my invitations and make me tea, although I usually did this myself. I'm very particular about my tea.

This all sounds terribly princessy because it was. I'd become used to the trappings of my job and they were lovely. I would miss them. But all that was nothing compared to the mental adjustment I now had to make.

Who was I if I didn't have an impressive title and work at a big media company? Deborah Thomas's words came back to me yet again. 'It's not about you; it's about your job. Don't confuse the two.'

And so it was. Once again, with my perceived influence gone, I found myself dropped from invitation lists overnight. Fortunately, after more than a decade of being obliged to attend work functions, staying home was a gift and a blessing rather than a loss.

As petulant as it sounds, however, even though I went to virtually nothing I was invited to unless I absolutely had to, I still liked being invited. The instant evaporation of invitations to parties, movie premieres, watch launches, lipstick lunches, bar openings and various other red-carpet nonsense was slightly bittersweet. There was mostly relief that I no longer had to feel guilty about saying no 99.9 per cent of the time. There was also a splash of disappointment that the choice to say no was no longer mine. All of this was silly window dressing compared to the far more overwhelming anxiety: what now?

I stuck around at home and spent time with the kids, although I was not in the least bit present. My mind was a million miles away, wondering whether going to Nine had been the biggest mistake of my life. I spent every day convinced that I'd totally fucked my career.

Looking for distraction and perspective, I began to think about going overseas for a long break, just as we'd promised ourselves at the beginning of the year. It was time to start making plans.

Except I couldn't. To my extreme bewilderment, I couldn't do anything. With nothing to actually do each day, I was confounded by my inability to accomplish the simplest task. If I had one thing to achieve in a day — say, going to the bank to deposit a cheque, or buying a barbecued chicken for dinner — I'd manage not to do it. Not because I was lazy or busy. I didn't know why it was, actually. I just knew that I was flat and incredibly anxious at the same time.

After years of managing multi-million-dollar budgets and dozens of staff and a thousand appointments and meetings and emails every day, the fact I couldn't get my head straight enough to buy a chicken was frustrating. And distressing.

What the hell was wrong with me? I didn't recognise myself in the mirror — I hadn't for months. I was extremely thin, my eyes were sunken into my pinched face and there was no light in them. I felt hollow and I looked grey.

Finally realising I couldn't untangle my state of mind by myself, I went to see my therapist. She looked at me and she listened and after half an hour she said, 'I think you are quite seriously depressed and you're also suffering from anxiety.'

It was a shock to hear those words because they sounded so serious. But it was also a comfort. Apparently, an inability to complete even the simplest task is a classic symptom of depression. Hence the chook. I didn't feel quite ready to go on anti-depressants because we were about to go overseas and I was hopeful our trip would be the circuit-breaker I needed. I had no previous history of depression so it seemed what I was going through was situational rather than chemical. That's what my therapist thought and I hoped she was right.

Our plans for the holiday had begun to take shape, despite my inability to make anything resembling a decision. Once he understood I was depressed, not just hopeless, Jason stepped in to pick up the slack.

The trip was amazing, despite my fears. I've never been a natural traveller. Perhaps that's why on every holiday I've ever taken, I've come home early. Or tried to. In the first few days after arriving anywhere from Noosa to Positano, it is not unusual to find me perched on my hotel bed on the phone to Qantas, planning an early escape. Flexible fares are my friend.

This is particularly fun for those travelling with me. They are always — understandably — baffled and frustrated by my inability to kick back and enjoy myself. I even tried to come home early from my honeymoon although, in my defence, I did have food poisoning. As with so many of my odd quirks, Jason has learned to live with my eccentric holiday aversion and doesn't take it personally.

I've given a lot of thought to my travelling aversion and I've come up with two key reasons for it. The first is my fear of flying, which I'm finally getting a handle on. But there is another major obstacle between me and happy holidays: routine and my love of it.

For many years until recently, I've enjoyed being a goat on a goat track. I ate the same thing for breakfast. I drank the same number of cups of tea made in the same way. I did the same exercise for the same amount of time. I put on the same amount of make-up using the same products. I surfed the same websites. I dined at the same restaurants with the same friends and I ordered the same thing. I got the same spicy chicken noodles from the same Thai takeaway. Part control freak, part borderline OCD.

And thus my problem: routine and travel are not compatible. They are sworn enemies, in fact. The specific purpose of travel is to blow up your daily grind. To embrace the mystery meat of life with a large order of spontaneity on the side. And my problem is that I've always struggled with spontaneity.

But somehow, embarking on this trip in such a scrambled headspace where I barely knew which way was up freed me to embrace a proper holiday — and its inherent spontaneity — for the first time since I was a kid.

We made a conscious decision to cut off from home and I went cold turkey from the internet. No news from Australia. No email. No gossip. For two months, as we travelled through Europe, we had virtually no contact with home and absolutely no idea what was going on in the news.

After the past year of extreme work pressure for both Jason and me, it was an intense but exhilarating re-entry into the lives of our children — and each other. The saturation method you might call it. We were together as a family 24/7 and everyone benefited. It was magic.

Before we'd left, I'd hoped that by the end of the two months, I'd be able to look in the mirror and recognise the person staring back. That the life would eventually come back into my eyes. It took around two weeks. Being physically away from Australia gave me invaluable perspective about what a tiny place the media industry was and ultimately, how inconsequential. More importantly, I realised what an insignificant part of it I was. I wasn't going to let myself be defined by my CV.

In my head I'd become so obsessed with what everyone thought and said and wrote about me and that was a recipe for insecurity, paranoia, anxiety and depression. Tick, tick, tick, tick.

As I wrestled with the idea that I was not defined by my job and contemplated Relevance Deficiency Syndrome, I thought again of Helen Gurley Brown. In one of the many interviews she gave as she prepared to end her thirty-one-year tenure at the top of US *Cosmo*, she was disarmingly candid about her fears. 'I'm worried about not being as popular,' she told a journalist. 'People seek me out to dine with me and talk to me because my publication is important. Now all that will be gone …'

I'd heard her say the same thing one night to a table of editors at one of our conferences around the same time. When we insisted it was *her* they wanted to dine with, not just her job, she wasn't convinced. 'Oh, I don't think so,' she said sadly in her small, breathy voice. 'I'm not anybody special. I won't be asked to so many of those things.'

I thought that was unspeakably sad. To be such an icon and yet so insecure about your work. To peg your identity and self-esteem so completely to your job. To define yourself so utterly by your business card.

I was determined not to fall into that abyss. I'd forge a different path.

When we returned home, I felt reborn. I needed to look as different as I felt inside, so I went and had all my hair lopped off. Always cathartic. Time for phase three of my life and my career.

ROLE OF A LIFETIME

Voicemail to Jason from me:

'Um, babe, call me.'

And then I was pregnant again. It had been a few months now since I'd left Channel Nine and I was settling into a brand-new, post-management phase.

I soon discovered I was a nicer mother, wife and person away from the stress of a full-time office job. I also remembered that being a domestic goddess was not my thing. The feminist in me knows I shouldn't define myself by my husband and my children. But some deeply ingrained belief — possibly gleaned from watching too many episodes of 'The Brady Bunch' — whispers that being a mother should be enough. But it's not enough. Not for me. To be the best mother I can be, I need to feed myself in other ways too.

For me, this means working. But after so many years in senior management, I knew I wanted something different.

The higher I'd risen up the corporate ladder, I realised, the further I'd distanced myself from my true love: hands-on creativity. And communicating directly to an audience.

So I resisted the temptation to jump straight into another high-pressure, high-paying, high-profile media job. My ego really wanted to but my head and my heart weren't keen. This wasn't so hard because once I'd left Nine the phone didn't ring nearly as much as I expected it to. Whenever it did, though, I said no.

I wanted a break from the treadmill, from staff, from stress, from the exhausting politics of management and office life. Fortunately, I still had my newspaper column, something I'd hung onto through my time in magazines and TV. During those years, it was always my favourite thing, a way to be creative and express myself without layers and politics. Just me and my laptop.

So despite having a massively reduced income after leaving PBL, I still had an income. And since I'd stopped shopping and was wearing jeans and T-shirts every day, my expenditure was also drastically less.

Before I left Nine, I'd decided I wanted to start my own website. Magazines no longer floated my boat but I was still a pop-culture junkie. Now, instead of mags and TV, I gorged on the internet. As a consumer, I was moving from old media to new media. So why not as a content provider too? Like my column, the idea of having a direct channel to communicate with an audience was hugely appealing. I registered a domain name, found someone to design my site and began writing every day. And mamamia.com.au was launched.

The word 'launched' sounds far more exciting than what actually happened, which was that I didn't know quite what to say. So it was stilted at first. Eventually, I found my groove: a mix of opinion, news, body image, fashion and motherhood. It was whatever I felt like writing about and exactly like producing my own magazine every single day, with no barrier between me and my audience — which started slowly and then, as I became more comfortable, began to build.

I started writing occasional freelance features for magazines like the *Australian Women's Weekly*, *Madison* and *The Good Weekend*. I took on some consulting work for media companies. I did some radio. Wrote for the newspaper. Said yes to corporate speaking work. Started writing this book. And then, unexpectedly, two lines on the stick.

I was shocked. Happily so. It had been so difficult to fall pregnant with Coco, I'd assumed my fertility was compromised. Apparently it wasn't.

I was elated by this pregnancy. It felt right. And somehow it took away the angst I'd felt about this new stage of my career — which had now become a new stage in my life. I'd found some perspective about my time at Nine, as difficult as it had been. My fifteen cosy years cosseted at ACP had been the other extreme. Did I really wish I'd just stayed put and churned out another few dozen sealed sections? Absolutely not. Sometimes, experiencing what you don't want helps you work out what you do want. And it also helped me define what was important to me in my career and in my life as a wife and a mother. Suddenly, working from home, for myself, being creative and spending more time with my family was exactly what I wanted to do.

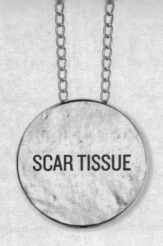

SCAR TISSUE

I was pregnant and I felt guilty. Guilty that it had been so easy, an accident. Guilty that with three children, I would have almost an embarrassment of riches at a time when so many friends were confronting huge challenges around babies, and pregnancy and fertility.

Like the beautiful women they were, they all wished me well and wished me love. I knew from experience though, that when it's not working for you, there's nothing quite like the quick jab to the chest you feel when someone in your world becomes pregnant.

'Goodness, this one was a surprise,' I'd say, almost apologetically. 'Oh I'm so happy for you,' they'd reply and mean it and yet still I'd hear something so subtle under their voice that you only recognise it if you've ever heard it in your own.

One friend had just had a miscarriage at fourteen weeks after her fourth round of IVF. Two others were at different stages of grief, having each lost a baby in the past few years, one from SIDS, another from a genetic condition.

Another was awaiting the results of a CVS test after being told at her twelve-week scan that her baby was at high risk for Down syndrome. Then there's the friend who was waiting to find out if her second round of IVF was successful. She'd already decided that if it wasn't, she wouldn't try again. This was it. Her final roll of the dice at forty-one.

Another woman I know was desperate to do IVF at age thirty-eight after trying for ten years, but she couldn't afford it. She was unable to comprehend that her chance to be a mother had come down to a balance sheet.

At the same time, I had three friends who were grieving in different ways for the mothers they never had a chance to be. They'd always wanted children and would have been extraordinary parents but they just didn't find the right partner in time.

Other friends had scar tissue buried even deeper. One friend had two children but came from a big family and didn't yet feel she was 'done'. Neither did her husband. After having a son and a daughter in quick succession, she fell pregnant again only to miscarry at ten weeks. Six months later, the same thing happened at fifteen weeks. A year later, yet again, at thirteen weeks. Another year later, at six weeks. Her grief was absolute, and despite the well-meaning platitudes of 'Well, aren't you lucky you've got two already?' — yes, thank you, she knew that — she carried the intense sadness of the four children she didn't have. The four babies she lost. Her kids were teenagers now and her window was closed. Her grief wasn't acute any more but occasionally it bubbled to the surface on the anniversary of her miscarriages or when holding someone else's freshly baked newborn.

Then there's the friend who fell pregnant soon after meeting her now husband. They were just about to go backpacking together. Commitment and marriage would be years into their future. They were young and there was no real indication the relationship would last. They were just having fun. So she had an abortion. Her partner picked her up from the clinic and she cried in his arms. I'm not sure what he thought. He didn't speak about it much with her although she told me afterwards his relief seemed palpable. She was relieved too in a way because she knew a baby at this point in their relationship would be too much pressure for it to bear. But her small sense of relief was intermingled with grief and a much stronger sense of loss.

Years later, when she and her partner had their first son, all her complex, unresolved feelings about the termination rushed to the surface. Her grieving process began afresh. As did her questioning of herself. 'That baby would have been our son's brother or sister,' she mused sadly to me during one conversation about it. I nodded, trying hard not to solve, just to listen. Soon, she began doing that thing women are so good at, arguing with herself. 'But then maybe if I hadn't had the termination and we'd had a baby so early in our relationship, the pressure would have broken us up and this baby would never have been born.' I nodded again. There are no right answers in a 'What if' conversation about babies.

Equally heartbreaking, I knew half a dozen women who had watched helplessly from the sidelines as their reproductive windows slowly shut. These were not 'oops-I-forgot-to-have-a-baby' career-woman clichés. I've never met one of those, never even heard about a real one. Women don't 'forget' to have babies.

But there are some women, women who always presumed they would become mothers, women who would have been incredible at it but who tragically miss their chance. Damn that biological clock and its inability to always synchronise with the myriad factors required to make a baby. Factors like a stable financial situation. A committed and supportive relationship. Medical problems. A partner who always thought he wanted children but then suddenly wasn't so sure. A partner who desperately wants children but discovers he's infertile. A hundred big and little things that divert you from the course of motherhood before it becomes a dead end and choice is no longer part of the equation.

Against this landscape of hopes and dreams and sadness and determination by so many women in my world, I felt particularly privileged to be pregnant again.

AND THEN WE WERE FIVE

SMS to Lisa Wilkinson from me:

'Have to cancel lunch. Sorry. Appear to be giving birth instead. M x'

Of all the days for Jason to be doing canteen duty at Luca's school, the day I go into labour is not the best one. It is ten days before my due date and mild contractions have begun early in the morning. I'm not even certain this is 'it'. That's why I assure Jason it is fine to go to school and report to the canteen as planned.

Shortly after he leaves, while timing my contractions, which are still pretty mild, I have a shower and pack my hospital bag. Given this is the third time around, I am surprisingly clueless about what to put in it. Or perhaps I just care less. The other times I consulted lists in books and from other mothers. I bought special new pyjamas for a treat and tops that buttoned down the front for easy boob access. I packed my toiletries carefully and diligently, weeks in advance.

This time I am slacker. More laissez faire. I chuck in some PJs, tops, trackies, newborn nappies, wipes, wraps, camera, phone, and a U-shaped pillow I can no longer sleep without. And Rescue Remedy.

Then I call Jason. 'Come home,' I grunt. He's been at the canteen less than an hour and has made several sandwiches. His reason for leaving so soon is was fairly impressive as far as excuses go. He receives a round of applause from his fellow tuckshop volunteers as he bolts towards his car.

It's all very civilised doing this during daylight. Our nanny arrives to look after Coco and they wave us off. We are so calm that the midwife I speak to when I call the hospital to say we are coming in tries to dissuade me — I don't sound like I am in enough pain to have advanced very far into labour. But I'm not having a bar of it. I know what's happening.

I quite like this third-time thing. Everyone assumes I know what I am doing. I feel mildly accomplished. An old hand. Still nervous though, which is why I want to get to the hospital. I feel safer there, surrounded by doctors and midwives and machines and monitors. And drugs. I need to be near the drugs.

It is a different hospital from last time and I immediately feel more comfortable. My name is already written up on the whiteboard and I've been allocated a room. An actual room. Not a car park or a public toilet. My delivery room has an en suite bathroom and even a TV. This is good. Very good.

'Hi, I'm Kat,' says the midwife. She is young and English and chatty. I am still okay with chatty. Just. The contractions are getting stronger but I'm not at barnyard-animal stage yet. Kat examines me and I am hopeful.

But I'm only one and a half centimetres dilated. Even though I've been having contractions for a few hours. On the upside, Kat doesn't for a moment try to send me home. Still, I decide it can't hurt to tell her about Amy, just in case. She listens patiently, pretending to care. I am used to this reaction when I tell the Amy story. It does not deter me. Finally, I am finished.

She feigns sympathy. 'Goodness Mia, that sounds dreadful. Anyway, why don't you get comfortable? Maybe run a bath. That usually helps with the pain.'

'When can she have an epidural?' asks Jason.

'Any time,' says beautiful, lovely Kat, whom I already adore. 'You may want to get things a little more established first because the epidural may slow things down. But ultimately it's up to you.'

I look at the bath sceptically but decide to climb in anyway. The heat and the floating help. I haven't felt weightless in a long time and the novelty distracts me until things kick up a notch and the barnyard animals take up residence in my vocal cords. Jason had popped down to the car to get my bags and returns munching cheerfully on some banana bread. He follows the animal noises into the bathroom and offers me some.

'Nooooooooooooooooooo,' I mooo. He wanders back into the room, makes a few phone calls and turns on the TV. The Beijing Olympics are on. I can feel myself going into the next stage where I become disconnected from him and my surroundings and journey far away to The Land Of Excruciating Pain.

When I'm having a contraction, I am quite lucid. Every five minutes though, I lose the power of speech and disappear into the abyss. Jason comes in every so often to see how I am going and to say helpful things like, 'I should take a movie of you now so I can show it to you next time you say you want to have another baby.' My contraction subsides and I splash him crossly.

What to do? I want an epidural but I am scared it will slow things down. I am also scared that without an epidural, the pain will trigger the fear in my brain from last time and I'll slow things down myself. I choose pain relief.

We'd arrived at the hospital at 10.30 and it is now noon. 'Uuugghh,' I grunt to Jason, who translates to Kat. 'She'd like that epidural now, please.'

'No problem, I'll get the anaesthetist.'

'How long will that take?' I ask, fearful of her answer.

'Oh, just a few minutes, I'll prepare everything right now.'

And it is that simple. As promised, minutes later, he arrives, jabs me in the back and my ability to chat returns. The next few hours are extremely pleasant.

There is some confusion about whether my waters have broken or not and Kat and another midwife have a good rummage around, trying to establish that fact. The verdict is 'yes, probably'. Jolly good. Then there is a bit of concern as to whether there is some meconium in the fluid. The verdict is 'probably not'.

I am calm through all this because apart from being pain-free, I am hooked up to a foetal heart-rate monitor. Nothing makes me happier in the world than being hooked up to machines for reassurance purposes. While Jason watches the Olympics, I watch the two graphs with my contractions and my baby's heart rate. Oh happy, happy day.

As Kat mentioned, the epidural has slowed my contractions right down. In phone contact with my doctor, he suggests to Kat that we kick them along with some drug or other. Totally fine by me.

A couple of hours after the epidural went in, Kat examines me again so she can update Dr Stephen, who is trying to juggle my delivery with a caesar he has to do on the other side of the city. We are all stunned by what she has discovered. 'Oh, goodness, the baby is right here,' she exclaims. 'Hold on a sec!'

Jason summons our parents and the kids to the hospital. It is 3 pm. We've been at the hospital for less than five hours. A few minutes later, Dr Stephen walks in and we're good to go. I feel no pain. 'Push now,' he instructs and I do.

One more push and the baby's head is out. It lets out a little cry. I look down and register that it is rather extraordinary to have a crying head protruding from my vagina.

'No need to push any more. Just let the contractions push the baby out,' says Dr Stephen. And they do.

And that is how, with two pushes, our second son came into the world. Remy. Named by his big brother.

SMOKY EYE

Voicemail to the nurse at my local Early Childhood Centre from me:

'Um, I'm really worried. My baby doesn't cry. Why doesn't he cry? What's wrong with him? Could someone please call me as soon as possible?'

I am nothing if not hypocritical. When I am committed to a particular way of doing something, I will become convinced that anyone doing it differently is an idiot. Until I too choose to do it differently at which point everyone doing it the original way is an idiot.

And so it is with routine. Luca, as a baby, had no routine. Not because Jason and I deliberately made that decision, but merely as a default position. We were clueless. So our baby fell asleep wherever he lay during the day: in his bouncer, the car, on a rug, in our arms. He fed whenever he wanted to. Slept, woke, whatever. It suited us. And him.

A few years later when Jo had her first baby, she was very strict. She had a book called *The Contented Baby* and she followed its detailed daily-routine instructions with precision. I mocked her openly. 'How can you be bothered with all that? Why don't you just chill out and let him fall asleep in the car while you're driving or the pram or wherever. He'll get used to it and it means you can leave the house.'

Jo shook her head. She was resolute. 'It works for me and he's happy.' I rolled my eyes.

Until I had Coco. Suddenly, the only rolling my eyes were doing was out of my head with exhaustion and despair. She was an intense baby. At first, I went with it, applying the same go-with-the-flow strategy I'd used with Luca. I knew no other way. But with Coco, there was no flow to go with. She was restless and cried a lot. She wasn't even happy while she was feeding. So one day when she was about six weeks and I was feeling desperate, Jo quietly dropped over her dog-eared copy of *The Contented Baby*. 'It can't hurt to try,' she said.

I gave it a whirl. And it worked. Well, it seemed to. The carrot it dangled in the way of a promise was that if you applied the magic rigid schedule and followed it precisely, your baby would only wake up for one feed during the night. And that was a pretty damn sexy carrot.

Immediately, Coco fell into step. I took a little longer to adapt.

The schedule broke the day into ten-minute bite-sized chunks. I was so tired that I kept losing the book, which was a disaster because I could never remember what Coco was meant to be doing. So I stuck little post-it note reminders all over the house like someone with Alzheimer's. But Coco wouldn't follow them. It seemed she couldn't read and this was most inconvenient. She was always awake when she was meant to be asleep. Jo was my mentor. I sent her a lot of texts like:

*The book says 'put the drowsy baby in the cot'. But I don't
HAVE a drowsy baby. I have a screaming baby and THE*

FUCKING BOOK DOESN'T MENTION WHAT TO
DO WITH ONE OF THOSE.

Coco was constantly napping when she was meant to be playing on the mat. Falling asleep on the boob when she was meant to be feeding. Crying when she was meant to be sleeping.

The book was grave about the dire consequences of such transgressions. 'Do NOT let the baby sleep longer than fifteen minutes or she will not go down properly at night,' it warned. 'MAKE SURE the baby does not fall asleep before 2 pm. OR YOU WILL NEVER SLEEP AGAIN IN YOUR LIFE, NOT EVEN FOR ONE HOUR.' Or something like that.

It all made me increasingly anxious, but with Jo's encouragement and the dangling carrot payoff of only one night-time feed, we persevered. For a little while, apart from my anxiety, it did seem to work. During this brief phase, I decided anyone *not* doing *The Contented Baby* was an idiot. It all went to hell at about four months when Coco literally spat the dummy and told the book to fuck off. I don't blame her. That's when we developed a splendid new routine where Coco woke me up at every hour throughout the night so I could stick her dummy back in. Those were good times. We stuck with that until she was nearly six months old and the Sleep Whisperer arrived and in three nights had her sleeping from 7 pm to 7 am and gave me back my life, thank you God.

After the chaos that was Coco, with Remy I went back to basics. No routine. Go with the flow again. Instinctively, it felt right. I had a primal need to keep him close and he was so easygoing that a routine didn't seem necessary. He spent those first few weeks literally curled up on my chest. He never cried. He. Never. Cried.

And so, in the absence of anything to be anxious about, I created something. 'I'm worried about my baby,' I blurted down the phone to the nurse at the Early Childhood Centre.

'What seems to be the problem?'

'He doesn't cry.'

'Right. He doesn't cry. And that's a problem because …?'

'Well, *why* doesn't he cry? Is there something wrong with him?'

'Is this your first baby?'

'No, my third.'

'Ah. That's why then. You're intuiting his needs without even realising it. You're giving him what he wants before he has the *chance* to cry.'

I consider this for a moment. 'Wait, do you mean … I'm a good mother?'

'Yes! I do!'

I pause. Briefly. 'No, that can't be it. There must be something wrong with him …

Could she have been right? Could it be right that I have a clue? The thought is a revolutionary one. I've spent my entire mothering life feeling guilty and apologetic for my failings. Indeed, I'd created my own internal list of maternal shortcomings. My Crap List. But now I wondered could I actually have learned a thing or two along the way with Luca and Coco? Did I have something to feel smug about — another entry to add to my Smug List of noble parenting achievements? Should I be high-fiving myself at long last? Or was Remy simply a chilled baby?

I believe every mother has a Smug List and a Crap List. On these lists are all the things you feel certain you've done absolutely right and absolutely wrong as a parent.

On your Smug List go the mothering acts of which you are most proud. All the things you feel are worthy of a medal. Pat-yourself-on-the-back things. These things will often have been achieved at considerable personal sacrifice — the more you sacrifice, the smugger you can be.

You keep your Smug List in a small corner of your brain (in my case, I only need a small corner because it is a very small list) and refer to it when you're feeling like a particularly bad mother and need to reassure yourself that you're not. Well, not always.

Every mother also has a Crap List. I need more mental storage for this list because it is long and bubble-wrapped in guilt. On your Crap List go all your mothering failings. Print it out and set it aside to give to your child's therapist later in life.

In a perfect world, these lists would cancel each other out and we'd all just walk around Getting On With It instead of judging each other and ourselves. But then we would be called 'men'.

For what it's worth, here is my Smug List:

1. I breastfed Luca for thirteen months.
2. I only spent two nights apart from Coco (not in a row — extra smug points) until she was almost two and a half. I have spent a total of five nights apart from her in her life.
3. I breastfed Coco until she was eight months old despite having mastitis seven times.
4. None of my kids have TVs in their rooms. Yet.
5. Luca has beautiful manners and is a great cook. Coco is very kind. Remy smiles a lot.

I told you it was a short list. I'm actually not even sure if that third point should be on the Smug List or the Crap List because it can't have been good for Coco to have ingested all those second-hand antibiotics. For the sake of fairness, I will put it on both lists. And before you assume that I am saying breast is better than bottle, I'm not. I don't judge any woman who uses formula (other than myself). I'm just grasping at straws because my list is so pathetically short. And I am still tossing up whether I can attribute Remy's Zen-like calmness to my superb mothering skills.

In the spirit of full disclosure, here is my Crap List. It continues to grow at an alarming rate, but this is an excerpt at the time of publication.

1. In the space of six months while I was at Nine, I forgot to pick Luca up from after-school care on two separate occasions. (Disclaimer: he was in the care of responsible adults and untraumatised both times, gulp).

2. I sometimes feed my children cereal for dinner. Hey, Weetbix with banana and milk covers most food groups. Maybe this should go on my Smug List.

3. I dislike playing any kind of children's games, including cars, tea parties, puzzles, blocks, hide and seek, dress-ups, craft and singing nursery rhymes.

4. I breastfed Coco through seven bouts of mastitis and seventy days worth of antibiotics.

5. I eat my children's Easter eggs and birthday party lolly bags when they are asleep.

6. I constantly steal — I mean borrow — birthday money from Luca's wallet to pay the cleaner or the Thai takeaway man because I've forgotten to go to the bank. His wallet is full of hastily scrawled notes saying: 'IOU $50. Love Mummy xx.'

7. I always try to choose the book with the least number of words when it's time for bedtime stories. I hide the books I can't bear to read One More Time.

8. I hate playgrounds and will do virtually anything to avoid taking my children to them.

9. I think my kids look better with a slight tan. I call it 'a bit of colour'. Others would call it 'sun damage'.
10. I've managed to convince my daughter that eating tuna or baked beans directly out of a can is a 'special treat'.
11. I bite my nails and hence my two eldest children bite theirs too. Frequently, I must remove my own fingers from my mouth in order to bark at them, 'Stop biting your nails!'
12. Sometimes, at the end of the day, Coco calls me by our nanny's name.
13. My husband is a better parent than I am. He'll do the hard yards of discipline and boundaries when I'm more likely to say, 'I know! Let's eat biscuits!'
14. My children don't have specific amounts of time they're allowed to watch TV. They 'self-regulate'.
15. I have discovered that it is possible to read aloud to your child while thinking about other things. I do this frequently.
16. I often listen to FM music stations that play songs with inappropriate lyrics while my children are in the car. Sometimes I sing along.

I wish more women would disclose their Crap Lists. I love hearing them because they always make me feel better. Far better than reading yet another interview with a celebrity who insists she only feeds her child organic meals and that they've never tasted sugar or white flour, they've never had antibiotics and they were breastfed until they were three. Naturally, her body just 'bounced back' within hours of the birth and her baby has slept through the night since coming home from hospital.

When I read these kinds of stories, I am overcome by the uncontrollable urge to poke said mother in the eye with my pinky finger. If we could all be more truthful and less competitive about mothering, the world would be a happier and less guilty place.

Still, we all need our own Smug List in which to seek some solace sometimes, a Smug List to neutralise the recriminations our Crap Lists hurl at us. There's certainly no danger of us becoming over-confident. As soon as our children are old enough to talk, they begin to pass judgement.

Before I had kids, I had no idea how brutally honest they could be. Now I know; I've learned through experience. Kids can get away with saying things to you no one else can. Like the time after dinner when I bent down to give Coco a goodnight kiss. 'Ooooh, yuck! You stink!' she shrieked and began retching. Coco has a sensitive gag reflex and an acute sense of smell, a combination that was particularly challenging when it was time for a nappy change. Or, it seems, kissing Mummy after she's eaten pasta with garlic in it.

A few nights later, heavily pregnant with Remy, I was on my way out to launch my friend Zoë's book. To feel a little less frump-like and to celebrate getting out of my trackies, I'd gone to the hairdresser and issued her with the following instructions: 'I want my hair to look kind of wavy and messy and sexy.' She'd obliged, and I was quite pleased with the result.

Or so I thought. 'Oh my God, what happened to your hair?' were Luca's first words when he came home from soccer training to find me ready to go out.

'It's *meant* to look this way!' I protested. 'I went to the hairdresser! It cost money!'

If someone else had dissed my hair, I might have been annoyed ... But somehow, when it's your child, they manage to dismantle your defences, and defensiveness, and inspire a totally different reaction. I looked in the mirror and saw myself through Luca's eyes, and laughed.

'Also, your skirt is too short,' he added, now plainly on a roll. I was wearing one of my favourite Ginger & Smart frocks, kind of a loose shirt-dress that I wore a lot before I was pregnant. As one of the few things I owned that could still fit over my stomach, it was my only option.

Admittedly, my bump made it a bit shorter than usual but it was still longer than mid-thigh. But the combination of winter and pregnancy meant that no one had seen my bare legs in months, so that probably contributed to his alarm.

He wasn't finished. 'And your eye make-up is all smudgy.'

'That's the look I'm going for,' I explained patiently. 'It's called A SMOKY EYE.'

'Oh.' Pause. 'It just looks like you made a mistake.'

'Thanks, darling, I'm feeling great now! Ready to hide under the doona!'

'Sorry,' he said with a slightly contrite pat of my arm.

I laughed, and pretended to hit him.

Because they call it how they see it, without tact or diplomacy the words of our children can penetrate. And not just about fashion.

I remember one time, when I was still an editor, I was sitting on the couch with a huge pile of magazines, catching up on reading. Luca was asking me something and I wasn't really listening. I was concentrating on the latest Kate Moss shenanigans. He repeated himself and I finally looked up and vaguely said, 'What, darling?'

He looked at me and said, 'Sometimes it seems like you love magazines more than you love me.'

Ouch. Arrow to the heart.

Of course it wasn't true and deep down he knew it wasn't true (please let him know it wasn't true), but in that moment, when he was trying to communicate with me and I was far away and distracted, it was one hundred per cent true FOR HIM.

And the simple, honest way in which he was able to express himself made me reassess the amount of time I was spending on work when I got home.

Sometimes the truth hurts, other times it's just funny. But when it's delivered by your children, it's a short-cut past all your defences. And that's a good thing. Children are the greatest arbiters of the truth, and the best moderators of every parent's internal Crap List and Smug List. It is the achievement of my life to be the mother of three such direct and entirely unique people, and I'm forever grateful for their ability to cut through all the noise and remind me of what's important. And it's not a smoky eye.

EPILOGUE

I'm standing on the set of 'Today', trying not to vomit. Eighteen years after I first sat down opposite Lisa Wilkinson for an interview, I'm about to do it again. Except today it will be live on national television.

The last time I was here at Channel Nine, I was painfully thin, horribly anxious and deeply miserable. Two years later, I am neither thin nor miserable. In fact, I'm all post-baby curves and extremely happy. But I am anxious. So. Very. Anxious.

Trying to hold it together, I focus on Lisa's warm, smiling face to keep me calm. She waves when she sees me across the studio and comes over during a commercial break to give me a hug. Lisa knows how nervous I am, how reluctant I've been to venture back here after my brief, humiliating fling with TV.

I've come to be interviewed about body image after recently being appointed chair of the federal government's National Body Image Advisory Group. It's ironic then that I am wearing fat-sucking undies. It's been several years since I've been on TV and almost that long since I've had to wear proper pants.

Working from home, combined with pregnancy and its aftermath, has been a welcome get-out-of-fashion-jail-free card and I've been letting it all hang out. Quite literally. However, I've recently been introduced to the concept of fat-sucking undies by friends and mamamia.com.au readers, who all, it seems, swear by them. I thought they were just for nannas and Bridget Jones. Who knew?

Certainly, my impressive post-baby muffin can do with all the help it can get. Tired of tucking my stomach into my jeans LIKE A SHIRT, I bolted to Kmart and picked up some of those magic knickers, and today I'm using my first media foray as the body image group's chair to take them for a spin. A bundle of contradictions? Oh yes.

I stifle a yawn. My day began early. Or did my night finish late? In fact, I think the two just collided at ungodly o'clock when The Middle of the Night somehow became The Crack of Dawn.

Coco had woken for some ridiculous reason at one-thirty, three and then again at 4 am. Something about it being 'too dark' and 'grasshoppers'. At the third wake, I lost it. 'I'm not getting up again,' I hissed to Jason with that rising feeling of panic I get when my allotted window for sleep is closing fast. 'I can't stand it! We're doing controlled crying!' If that's even possible with a three-year-old.

When the whingeing started up again ten minutes later, I angrily huffed out of bed, marched into her room and shout-whispered, 'Coco! Go back to sleep! This is ridiculous! It's night-time!' before marching back into our room and stubbing my toe on Remy's cot, waking him up. Again.

I'd already breastfed him at 2 am and, to be fair, Jason had got up for Coco the first two times. Hello, delirium. Nights weren't usually this bad. Ever since the Sleep Whisperer came and worked her magic when Coco was nearly six months old, she'd been a terrific sleeper. But there were aberrations very occasionally and this night was one of them. Why not torture

Mummy in the hours before she has to go on TV for the first time in two years, huh? HUH?

I was coping with Remy's night feeds because he usually went straight back to sleep afterwards and I knew the Sleep Whisperer would be coming to fix him too in a few weeks, but four times awake in one night with both kids had pushed me over the edge and into shouty-shrew territory. I was not match fit.

As I rubbed my toe and swore like an angry pirate, Jason mumbled, 'I think it's called controlled crying because the adults are meant to be in control.'

Instantly, my exasperation evaporated and I smiled in the dark. As always, Jason had managed to gently hold up a mirror when my head was flying off, enabling me to see the humour in the situation while making a salient point. My God I love that man.

Back at 'Today', the audio guy attaches my microphone and hurries me to the interview chair. Suddenly my throat goes dry. 'Water! Help!' I gasp as the floor manager counts down the five seconds before we go live. This has never happened to me before. Must be all that Rescue Remedy I needed so I could drive back through the network gates without having a panic attack. Someone thrusts a glass in my hand and I take a quick gulp, spilling it down my top.

The next few minutes pass in a fuzzy and slightly soggy blur. It's surreal sitting here discussing body image with Lisa but it also feels entirely natural and surprisingly comfortable. Towards the end of the interview, she asks the curly question: 'What would you say to those who claim it's people like you and me — having worked in women's magazines — who have contributed to the problem of poor body image in the first place?'

I take a breath. I'm not nervous any more. 'I think that's a really fair point. Women's magazines have to take responsibility for the images they publish and the effect they can have on all women, but particularly on young people. I like to think I did a lot of things right when I was an editor but I'm the first to admit I also did a lot of things wrong, things like retouching. I'm not proud of that. Magazines have taken a strong leadership role in the past and helped change attitudes towards smoking and sun-baking so we know it IS possible.

'Lisa, I really hope more editors will start to take a similarly responsible approach about how they portray women. We need more diversity. Of size, of age and of skin colour. And not just from magazines but from all media.'

And then it's over. Another quick hug from Lisa and a few former colleagues and I'm back in my car driving out of the Channel Nine gates. No skid marks this time. I've actually enjoyed myself and slain a few of my demons at the same time. Who cares if I wasn't cut out to be a TV executive? Not me; not any more. At least now I have conclusive proof that I don't want to play with the high-flying big boys. There are no hard feelings. The fit was just completely wrong. But if I hadn't learned this the hard way, I'd have never found the courage to press eject on my own high-flying career. I would have stayed resolutely on my managerial goat-track and I might never have discovered how happy I am on a much, much smaller scale. Working for myself, creatively, on my own terms.

I dash back home to finish writing my Sunday column and to post on my website for the first of half a dozen times today. In the car on the way, my phone beeps with a text message. '*It's a girl! Rosie. Born at 6.35 am. We are over the moon …*' My eyes briefly prickle with tears as they always do when I hear news of a baby being born to someone I love. Like so many others, this girlfriend had been through some very dark times over the past few years while trying to fall pregnant. We'd had many conversations about it. She'd shed so many tears. I pull into the driveway at home but before I go inside, I take a moment to text my reply. '*Oh what beautiful news! You know all those endless years when you were desperate to be pregnant? When you were heartbroken and couldn't understand why it was taking so long? This is why. You were waiting for Rosie. Only you didn't know that until today.*'

That's how I feel about Coco. Each of my children is special and extraordinary and different to me. Luca and I will always be incredibly connected because he was my first and only child for eight years. Our intense bond is something I find hard to explain or even understand sometimes, but I'm grateful for it. Coco is the reason I endured the deep pain and grief of losing the baby girl Jason and I never got to meet. Not for a moment did it ever occur to me that the soul of our lost baby returned in Coco. Oh no. Coco is utterly individual and has a very different energy to the one I feel around the baby who died. But still, Coco healed many deep wounds. Hers was the only birth at which I shed a tear — for all that went before she arrived and with an enormous sense of relief that she'd finally turned up. It has all been for a reason. For my beautiful girl. And Remy? He's just sunshine. Pure and uncomplicated. My gorgeous littlest guy.

My head and my heart are full of all these thoughts and emotions as I walk back into the house and the warm, manic energy of my family. Luca is about to leave for school and he wants to know if he can cook dinner tonight. I pretend to think about it for a moment before I agree. He's chuffed. My big boy wants to be a chef and he takes it very seriously. His specialties are *linguine vongole* and chocolate self-saucing pudding. Since his mother's specialties are tuna-out-of-a-can and cereal-for-dinner, this is a most welcome development.

Surrounded by kids and chaos already, I say a silent thank you to the universe that I'm fortunate enough to work from home and able to dip in and out with the kids during the day instead of just those twenty 'quality' minutes I used to snatch with them each evening when I was an executive. I can't imagine going back to that life. It seems as if it belonged to someone else. Someone far better dressed and far more stressed than I want to be. Sure, it would be nice to still have her exec salary, but, on balance, the other stuff just isn't worth it. Not for me. Not right now.

I quickly breastfeed Remy while distractedly trying to answer seventeen questions from my inquisitive daughter about life, the universe and Dora the Explorer. My mind is elsewhere and I try hard to wrestle it back. I'm already thinking about what I want to write today. Being present and appreciating the moment is still something I struggle with.

So is anxiety. From time to time I still return to my therapist when I feel like I need some help, when I feel overwhelmed or confused about something. I'm far better now at asking for help in all aspects of my life — emotional and practical. From our families, from my girlfriends and from Jason. It doesn't quite come naturally yet and the words often stick in my throat, but the benefits of asking are manifold and the alternative sucks. I understand now that I just can't do it alone. Sometimes even just saying 'I'm not coping' makes coping a little bit easier.

I hand over Remy to our beloved nanny, Mel, and he gives a delighted squeal. With Mel officially in charge of the kids for the day so I can write, I quickly scrub off my TV make-up, scrape my hair into a ponytail and emancipate my muffin from my fat-sucking underwear. Ah, sweet relief. I change into jeans, a T-shirt and sneakers and head to my desk with a giant cup of tea, the first of a hundred for the day. I begin writing my column, I post on my website, I trawl the internet for information and inspiration.

At lunchtime, I walk up the road to my local café, and while I wait for my sandwich to be toasted, I glance over at the pile of magazines. I feel mildly curious but mostly ambivalent. Once, I'd have descended on them hungrily. Now, I've become one of those people who absentmindedly flick through magazines in cafés, at supermarket checkouts and at the hairdresser. I will always have a great affection for magazines and enormous respect for the people who produce them. Mags were my first media love and I feel that kind of slightly wistful nostalgia you have when you think about past boyfriends

Many of my friends remain there. One of them, Bron, is getting married next weekend and Jason and I are looking forward to her wedding. In an uncanny echo of my relationship with Lisa, I first met Bron when I was editing *Cosmo* and she applied for the role of my PA. We clicked the moment she walked into my office and while I gave her the job almost instantly, I knew she was made for far bigger and better things. Over the next few years I promoted her to beauty editor and then editor of *Dolly*. With every promotion, she out-performed my highest expectations. A year or so after I left ACP, she was appointed editor of *Cosmo* and her first day on the job was … my birthday. In the cycle of mentoring and friendship I learned from Lisa and Pat, Bron is one of many women I was proud and lucky to nurture while I worked in magazines and one of only a handful to become a close friend as well.

I pay for my lunch and quickly walk back home to finish my column before deadline with the radio on and the sounds of Coco and Remy playing in the background.

As a woman and a Libra, I still struggle to find the elusive balance between work and family, socialising and solitude, writing about life and participating in it, and the million other things competing for my time and attention, inside and outside my head.

I am reminded once again of those people who spin plates on sticks. Women's lives are a lot like that I think — spinning plates. Just when you think all the plates are stable, one wobbles and then suddenly four are teetering as another two crash to the ground. Occasionally, like today, I have brief flashes of contentment when I feel like all my plates are spinning at once. I know it's fleeting, this sense of balance. It's a day-by-day and sometimes moment-by-moment proposition. But on this day? At this moment? The plates are spinning and I smile.

THANKS

If writing a memoir is somewhat like having a baby (and it is — long gestation period, discomfort, confusion, weight gain, loss of inhibitions, indignity, joy and the desire for pain medication), there are so many people who helped me deliver this book and to whom I am so grateful.

Firstly, to Paula, Wendy and Kirsten, for listening to me vent, telling me when I'm being ridiculous, reading countless early drafts, making tea and soothing noises and being the most incredibly generous, patient, supportive, wise and inspirational women I know.

To my parents who have given me nothing but support and love and understanding, even during the times in my life when I've been a complete pain in the bum. Also to Lynn, Nita, John, Rod, Les, Joy, Mick and Beryl with love. And Marian. I couldn't have done any of this without you.

To Julian, for being the finest double godfather in the land. And to Nobby, Pete and Mike for your invaluable male perspectives.

To my cherished girlfriends Justine, Nikoll, Bron, Zoe, Maria, Amanda, Tessa, Sophia, Jackie, Sophie, Nicky, Lisa, Louise, Emma, Leila, Natalie, Vanessa, Sarah, Sonia, Tania and Nicole for your ongoing support and friendship. Our conversations colour every chapter of this book.

To Lisa Wilkinson and Pat Ingram, the best bosses and mentors I could have hoped for. To my agent, Tara, at Curtis Brown, who has calmly talked me out of the trees when necessary and is the most unflappable woman I know.

To Shona and Mel at HarperCollins, who have always had faith in me and understood what this book was going to be, even before I did. To my editor, Jo, for your kindness, patience and huge smarts. It's not easy editing a former editor. You've taught me so much. And to Jane, publicity guru, for your inherent understanding and guidance when I've wanted to hide under my bed.

To all the readers of mamamia.com.au, who give me so much encouragement and read what I write every day.

On the home-front, enormous thanks to Melissa for enabling me to write this book knowing that my children are so well loved and cared for. And Gabby, you too.

To my three beautiful muses, Luca, Coco and Remy, for putting up with a mother who is so often writing inside her head and for giving me more joy and laughter than I thought possible. And finally, to Jason … one word … love.

ABOUT MIA

Mia Freedman became editor of Australian *Cosmopolitan* at the age of twenty-four — the youngest-ever person to edit the magazine in the world. She went on to become Editor-in-Chief of *Cosmopolitan*, *Cleo* and *Dolly*. She is a much sought-after commentator on television and radio, and currently writes a popular column for the *Sun-Herald* and the *Sunday Age*. She also has her own website and blog at mamamia.com.au

Mia lives in Sydney with her husband, three children, dog and two ducks.

MORE MIA

If you're keen to contact Mia, discuss her book and read more of her writing, head to mamamia.com.au

There, she writes every day about body image, motherhood, celebrities, relationships, fashion and pop culture and continues her quest to reassure women that whatever they're feeling, they're not alone.